A CHRISTIAN ANSWER

TO

JEWISH POLEMICS

A Thesis Presented to
the Faculty of
Simon Greenleaf School of Law,
now part of Trinity International University

by
Royle D. Johnson

𝔅
Bedrock Publishing
Arlington, Washington

Library of Congress Cataloging-in-Publication Data
A Christian Answer to Jewish Polemics / Royle D. Johnson.
Includes bibliographical references and Index.
Ruth Lascelle, Chief Editor; Duane Bagaas, Editor; Wuffy Evans, Associate Editor.
1. Jewish Polemics. 2. Christian Apologetics. 3. Origin, Uniqueness and Divisions within Judaism. 4. Judaism's Rejection of Jesus. 5. Rabbinic Writings, Messianic Prophecies, and Expectations. 6. Anti-Semitism. 7. New Testament Contradictions. 8. Atonement for Sin. 9. Pagan Origins of Christian Doctrines.

Library of Congress Catalog Card Number: 98-71213
ISBN 0-9654519-5-X

Cover design by Bedrock Publishing

Printed in the United States of America
by
Gorham Printing
Rochester, Washington

A CHRISTIAN ANSWER

TO

JEWISH POLEMICS

*This thesis is
dedicated to
my wonderful wife Bogusia, whose
encouragement and help made
this presentation possible.*

*I would also like to dedicate
this work to the memory of
my parents, Pastor Roy and Viola Johnson,
who faithfully loved and served
the Lord Jesus Christ and His Church
in over 40 years of Gospel Ministry.*

053198

EXPLANATION

We are pleased to have prepared this fine work for your education, information and reading enjoyment.

This originally was "a thesis presented to the Faculty of the Simon Greenleaf School of Law in partial fulfillment of the requirements for the Degree Master of Arts" by Royle D. Johnson in March, 1985.

On every hand, we have attempted to retain the original flavor of the thesis. Adjustments to text were made sparingly.

The one absolute original piece of work we carried over was the Approval Page.

—Bedrock Publishing
Arlington, Washington, 1998

All Scriptures quoted are from the
King James Version of the Bible
unless otherwise noted.

AUTHOR'S PREFACE

As a young person growing up in a Christian home, I often entertained questions about my faith in Jesus Christ. Sometimes I would find the answers rather easily, and at other times the answers came much more slowly. However, I learned that persistent evaluation and inquiry would always lead to a deeper and stronger commitment to Jesus and His Gospel. The Christian message of the Lord Jesus Christ is a clear proclamation based in truth, and truth always welcomes questions. The great part about truth is that it also provides answers—solid, concrete, lasting answers.

It is my desire that this book will provide answers to the inquiring reader, both Jew and Gentile, and point to the One who is the Way, the Truth and the Life—our Messiah, Jesus Christ.

FOREWORD

I was so pleased when Royle Johnson, the son of my esteemed pastor Roy Johnson, entered Seattle Bible College (graduating in 1980) where I was one of the instructors. Little did I dream that our paths would meet again many years later.

Upon graduation from *Simon Greenleaf School of Law*, Royle offered as his thesis "A Christian Answer to Jewish Polemics." His mother knew I would be interested, since I am Jewish, and brought the thesis to me for review.

When I read Royle's work, I was amazed at his tremendous amount of research, careful analysis, consideration and sensitive approach to the subject of the thesis. I found the arguments to be tactful and correct in every detail. Since I was experienced in Judaism and knew of the Hebrew terms before I became a believer in Jesus as my Messiah, I found this material very scholarly. I strongly recommend it to the dedicated student of Hebrew-Christian studies.

When Royle's mother returned for my evaluation, I said that I was very much impressed–so much so that I thought this thesis should be published as a book to be placed in every Bible school and public library! I advised her to give Royle my suggestion. However, nothing was done until 1997 when my daughter, (Wuffy Evans), son, (Duane Bagaas) and I had been operating as Bedrock Publishing. I contacted Royle concerning his work and the rest is history. It is with great pleasure we have taken this thesis, *A Christian Answer to Jewish Polemics,* and published it in book form. We have spent many hours editing, formatting and adding an index to this important work. Suffice it to say, those hours were delightful and a learning experience beyond our expectations!

—Ruth Specter Lascelle,
Bedrock Publishing
Arlington, Washington, 1998

Table of Contents

Charts and Lists

APPROVAL

A CHRISTIAN ANSWER TO JEWISH POLEMICS

A Thesis
Presented to
the faculty of
Simon Greenleaf School of Law

In Partial Fulfillment
of the Requirements for the Degree
Master of Arts in Christian Apologetics

by
Royle D. Johnson

March, 1985

Approved by _Charles L. Manske, Chairman_

Approved by _Robert Meyer_

Approved by _William Philip Wesley_

Date _April 26, 1985_

CHAPTER 1
Introduction to Jewish Polemics and Christian Apologetics

he goals of this thesis are to set forth and explain the basic arguments upon which Jewish polemics against the Christian faith have traditionally rested. This will be concluded in each case by a Christian apologetic in which the truthfulness and uniqueness of the Christian message will be defended. It is the intent of this thesis to represent the views of Judaism fairly and honestly, evidenced by a spirit of respect for the Jewish people and their faith.

Definitions

It would be proper to begin this examination of Jewish polemics and Christian apologetics by defining *terms*. Some definitions of "polemics" are listed as follows:

> An aggressive attack on or the refutation of the opinions or principles of another.[1]

> The art and practice of argumentation, controversy, debate. Polemics, from a Greek word meaning hostile or opposed, especially applies to arguments in church circles to refute errors of belief.[2]

Polemics put simply, is the art or practice of disputation. In this particular case of study, polemics is applied to those arguments and issues that are directed from Jewish sources toward the Christian faith, attempting to undermine and if possible destroy the foundation upon which faith in Jesus as Lord and Messiah rests. The challenge of Jewish polemics against Christianity has traditionally been met, starting with the apostolic Church and on through history to the present. The branch of Christian theology that involves itself in this most important aspect of the Gospel proclamation is called *Christian Apologetics*. A definition of "apologetics" is as follows:

> 1) Systematic argumentative tactics or discourse in defense (as of a doctrine, a historical character, or particular actions). 2) That branch of theology devoted to the defense of a religious faith and addressed primarily to criticism originating from outside the religious faith, esp.: such as, defense of the Christian faith.[3]

Christian apologetics simply defined is the defense of the Gospel in all areas against the refuting attacks of its opponents.

Jewish Polemics

From *The Jewish Encyclopedia* this interesting description on the background of Jewish polemics is stated:

The first works wholly devoted to the refutation of Christianity appeared in the second half of the twelfth century in Spain, the pre-eminently fertile source of anti-Jewish writings, between the sixth and fifteenth century. They were the outgrowth of the restless aggressiveness of the Christian clergy, who taking advantage of the eruption of fanaticism marking the period of the Crusades, planned the wholesale conversion of the Jews through the medium of polemical works written by converts from Judaism. These converts, instead of confining themselves to the usual arguments drawn from the Old Testament, claimed to demonstrate from the Haggadah (part of the Mishnah) that Jesus was the Messiah ... To arm themselves against these attacks, learned Spanish Jews began to compose manuals of polemics. About a quarter of a century after the composition of Judah ha-Levi's famous apologetical work, *The Cuzari*, in which Judaism was defended against the attacks of Christians, Karaites and philosophers, Jacob ben Reuben wrote the *Sefer Milhamot Adonai*. This is divided into twelve chapters and contains, besides refutations of the Christian arguments drawn from the Old Testament, a thorough criticism of the Gospels and the Acts of the Apostles, in which he points out many contradictions.[4]

From this description of Jewish polemics it can be seen that the development of Jewish arguments against the Christian faith did not find their present force until the 12th Century. Polemics were most definitely a part of the Jewish response to the Christian Church long before this, but not to a degree that would bring about the survival of a large amount of polemical literature.

In the 13th Century, the number of Jewish polemical works increased.

Regular treatises in defense of Judaism against the attacks of Christianity began to appear in southern France. The most important of these were: the *Sefer ha-Berit* of Joseph Kimchi; the *Mahazik ha-Emunah* of Mordecai ben Josiphiah. *The Milhemet Mizwah* of Meir ben Simon of Narbonne; and three works by Isaac ben Nathan—a refutation of ... Samuel of Morocco ... ; *Tokahat Mat'eh* against Geronimo de Santa Fe,' and *Mibzai Yizhak,* a general attack upon Christianity.[5]

Examples of two especially interesting polemic works are The *Nizzahon Vetus* and the *Hizzuk Emunah*. Concerning The *Nizzahon Vetus* the following information is provided:

The *Nizzahon Vetus*, or *Old Book of Polemics*, is a striking example of Jewish disputation in its most aggressive mode. ... Refutations of christological exegesis, attacks on the rationality of Christian doctrine, a critique of the Gospels and Church ritual, denunciations of Christian morality, all of these and more are presented in an exceptionally vigorous style.[6]

Nizzahon Vetus ... and some other Jewish polemics, cite a series of verses which, they say, are aimed directly at Christianity. Several of these constitute clever responses to Christian assertions, (e.g. the copper serpent does indeed represent Jesus and that is why Moses was commanded to hang it). One polemicist, in fact, cited such a verse immediately after a Christian question asking how the Torah could have omitted all reference to Jesus. Thus, the Bible explicitly warned against trusting in man (Jeremiah 17:5: Psalm 146:3). It told Jews to punish a man who would claim to have a mother, but not a father (Deuteronomy 13:7); and it spoke of the humbling of anyone who pretended to be divine (Isaiah 2:11). Such citations were hardly central to Jewish polemics, but they represent an effort by Jews to turn the tables on their opponents by finding "christological" verses of their own.[7]

Regarding the Hizzuk Emunah, The Jewish Encyclopedia states:

> The Jewish work which more than any other aroused the antagonism of Christian writers was the *Hizzuk Emunah* of the Karaite, Isaac Troki, which was written in Poland, and translated into Latin, German, Spanish and English. It occupies two volumes and is subdivided into ninety-nine chapters. The book begins by demonstrating that Jesus was not the Messiah predicted by the Prophets. 'This' says the author, 'is evident 1) from his pedigree, 2) from his acts, 3) from the period in which he lived, and 4) from the fact that during his existence, the promises that related to the advent of the expected Messiah *were not fulfilled.*'[8]

In later chapters, the arguments of these two Jewish sources will be presented. These two works are fairly representative of the general objections directed toward the Christian faith.

Daniel J. Lasker gives some input regarding the methodology and tactical approach used by Jewish polemicists:

> In combating the doctrines of Christianity, Jewish polemicists employed a variety of types of argumentations to strengthen their own beliefs. These arguments may be divided into three distinct categories:
>
> 1) exegetical arguments (*min-ha-ketuvim*) 2) historical arguments (*min-ha-mezi'ut*) 3) rational arguments (*min-ha-sek-hel*).[9]

The Jewish polemicists also used the New Testament in their work. Mr. Lasker states:

> The Jews ... referred to the New Testament as '*aven gillayon*' (falsehood of blank paper) or '*avon gillayon*' (sinfulness of blank paper), making a play on the Greek '*evangelion*,'...[10]

He goes on to say:

> In their use of the New Testament for controversial purposes, the Jewish polemicists followed two general methods. The first was to denigrate New Testament stories. The second was to demonstrate that latter-day Christianity, with which they were familiar, was unfaithful to its own sacred writings and hence had no validity even for the Christian, let alone the Jew.[11]

These very types of arguments were raised by many Jewish polemicists during the 12th through 17th Century. Men such as Joseph Kimchi, Jacob ben Reuben, Meir of Narbonne, Joseph Official (Yosef Ha-Meganne) and his father Nathan, Moses of Salerno, Mordecai of Avignon, Nahmanides, Jacob of Venice, Solomon de' Rossi, the anonymous author of Nizzahon Vetus, Isaac Troki and others were central figures in Jewish polemics during these years.

In later years, other men produced Jewish objections to Christianity: Moses Mendelssohn (1729-1786), Joseph Salvader (1796-1873), Solomon Steinheim (1789-1866), Samuel Hirsch (1815-1889), Elijah Benamozegh (1823-1900), Hermann Cohen (1842-1918). Those of more recent date, such as Isaac Mayer Wise (1819-1900), Leo Baeck (1873-1956), and Martin Buber (1878-1965), are important figures in the shaping of the Jewish view and response to Christianity. Each of these men were, of course, influenced by the time periods in which they lived. Their attitudes and approach toward Christianity vary greatly, some of them being very harsh and outspoken while others tended to be peaceful and scholastic in nature.

The present-day polemicists have each been influenced by these men already listed. Depending upon which division of Judaism they originate from (this will be examined in the next chapter), their polemics will all basically represent the arguments formulated by those dating prior to them. Men such as Gerald Sigal, Samuel Levine, Norman Mirsky, Ben Zion Bokser, and others represent a rather hard-hitting approach toward the Christian faith. Others such as Leo Trepp, Samuel Sandmel, Jacob Agus, and Pinchas Lapide take a scholastic type of attack in their methodology, yet the issues against the Christian faith still remain. A somewhat famous name in Jewish polemics is Hugh J. Schonfield, author of *The Passover Plot, The Jesus Party,* and *After the Cross.*

Four primary Jewish sources will be appealed to in this thesis. They are: *Hizzuk Emunah* by Isaac Troki, *You Take Jesus, I'll Take God* by Samuel Levine, *The Nizzahon Vetus* by an anonymous author and *The Jew and the Christian Missionary* by Gerald Sigal. These four polemic works provide an overall picture of the Jewish argumentation against the Christian faith. Isaac Troki (1533-1594), author of *Hizzuk Emunah,* was a Karaite Jew. He made the standard appeal of his arguments from the Hebrew Scriptures in which he examined Hebrew Messianic prophecies concerning Jesus and provided objections to their fulfillment in Him. He also dealt with the New Testament, even though he had no education in the Greek language. His work has been considered the most forceful Jewish attack to have ever been written and it still serves today as a foundation for much of the modern Jewish argumentation against the Christian faith. *The Nizzahon Vetus,* written by an anonymous author, is a collection of

Jewish arguments formulated in the Middle Ages. It provides hundreds of Jewish objections to the claims of Christ. Samuel Levine, author of *You Take Jesus, I'll Take God* and Gerald Sigal, author of *The Jew and the Christian Missionary,* provide much of the present-day material upon which popular Jewish argumentation rests. These books can be found in any Jewish book store, and possibly supply the Jewish community with the present-day objections to Jesus with greater success than do the more scholarly approaches. The Jewish material in this thesis will come primarily from these four works, although occasionally other polemic sources will be referred to.

To conclude this short survey of Jewish polemics, it is important to point out that the overwhelming majority of Jewish polemic writing is directed against Christianity. While other belief systems are dealt with, the Christian faith is by far the most popular. For example, in the Twelfth through Sixteenth Century, only a small amount of Jewish polemic material was directed against the Islamic faith.

> On the Jews' part, very little was written against Islam, and besides occasional attacks scattered through the Biblical commentaries of the Rabbinites and Karaites. ... Jewish literature contains but two productions of any extent that are devoted to an attack upon Islam.[12]

From this it can be seen that the chief opponent of Jewish polemics is the Christian faith. This demands that Christians respond to the Jewish challenge.

Christian Apologetics

1. New Testament Origin

The Greek word for *defense* is the word "apologia," (the basic English translation is *apology*). It means to defend or to give an answer or reason in defense of something.[13] It is used eight times in the New Testament (Acts 22:1; Acts 25:16; 1 Corinthians 9:3; 2 Corinthians 7:11; Philippians 1:7,17; 2 Timothy 4:16; 1 Peter 3:15).

> *"But sanctify the Lord God in your hearts: and be ready always to give an answer to every man that asks you a reason of the hope that is in you with meekness and fear"* (1 Peter 3:15).

Christian apologetics finds its origin in the apostolic Church. Throughout the Book of Acts, the apostles defend the Faith and give evidence for the truthfulness of the Gospel. Interestingly enough, the first apologetic appeals were made to the Pharisees, the Rabbinic form of Judaism which represents contemporary Orthodox Judaism today. Church Fathers such as Justin Martyr, Irenaeus, Origen, Tertullian, Augustine and Jerome were all involved in defending the Christian faith and dealing with Jewish arguments. Through the Middle Ages, the Reformation and on into the present time, Christians have been answering the Jewish issues and problems levied against Christianity, defending and giving evidence for belief in Jesus as Lord and Messiah.

2. The Christian Answer to Judaism

The chief source of Jewish argumentation referred to in this thesis, *Hizzuk Emunah* by Isaac Troki, has been answered by a number of Christian scholars. Bradanus Henricus Gebhardi, professor of theology in Greifswald, wrote: *Centum Loca Novi Testamenti, quae R. Isaac Ben Abraham, in suo, Munimine Fidei depravaverat, vindicata*, 1699. Also, Jacobus Gussetius (Gousset), professor of theology in Groningen (Holland), wrote: *sive Jesus Christi Evangeliique Veritas Salutifera, demonstrata in confutatione Libri Chizzouk Emounah, a R. Isaco spripti*, Amstelodami, 1712. Lastly A. Lukyn Williams, a Church of England scholar, authored the book, *Christian Evidences for Jewish People*. Others have dealt with Troki's arguments; however, these three are surely some of the finest Christian apologetic works that have dealt with the objections of *Hizzuk Emunah*. [14]

Presently, there are Messianic Jewish organizations that are providing much input in answering the Jewish arguments. The American Board of Missions to the Jews, Jews for Jesus, Friends of Israel, Ariel Ministries and scores of other fine mission outreaches are involved in Christian apologetics. The need for this type of work is of vital importance when dealing with any form of Jewish evangelism and outreach.

3. Basis of Christian Apologetics

It must be emphasized that based on human persuasion alone, no amount of Christian witness can convince a Jewish non-believer of the truth of the Gospel. If a Jewish person is unwilling to believe, apologetic truth and evidence will not alter his views. Proof takes place in the mind, but it is all dependent upon the attitude of the heart. The prejudiced Jewish person does not need or want proof. His heart is hard, he has already prejudged the Gospel and his mind is made up. The old saying applies here: "a man convinced against his will is of the same opinion still." A situation such as this demands the supernatural work of the Holy Spirit. What then is the purpose and reason for apologetics and the giving of evidence to Jewish people concerning the truthfulness of the Gospel?

First of all, the early Church used evidences in their witnessing (Acts 4:33; 14:15-17; 1 Corinthians 15:1-8; Romans 1:20). They continually appealed to the evidence of the resurrection of Christ, fulfilled prophecy and miracles, and the fact that they were witnesses of the life and ministry of Jesus. They preached the truthfulness of the Gospel by laying down the facts upon which faith in Jesus as

Lord and Savior must rest. Because of this, peoples' lives were changed by the power of the Holy Spirit (Acts 26:9-22; 1 Timothy 1:12-16). God also gave other evidence in the gifts of the Holy Spirit, healings, tongues, prophecy, and supernatural manifestations along with powerful conversion experiences (Acts 26:1-27; 19:1-8, 11-12; 28:8-9). Present-day apologetics is therefore based on this New Testament principle.

Second, the Christian message must be defended because it claims to be absolutely unique. If Christianity stated that it was only one of many spiritual roads to God, then defending it and giving factual evidence for its truthfulness would be futile. But the foundation of the Bible and Christianity is established in such a way that it is either totally true or completely false. Look how unique the Christian faith is. The God of the Bible is claimed to be the only true God (Jeremiah 10:10-12; Isaiah 45:18). Jesus Christ claims to be the *only* way to God (John 14:6; John 8:24; 1 Timothy 2:5). The Bible claims to be the *only* true Word from God to men (Isaiah 8:20). It is not to be added to nor subtracted from (Revelation 22:19). The way of salvation as outlined in the Bible is claimed to be the *only* way (Isaiah 45:21,22; Acts 4:12). The uniqueness and importance of the Gospel message therefore compels the defense of its claims.

Third, because of so much skepticism and unbelief within Judaism, it can be very hard to even receive a hearing of the Gospel unless the removal of doubts, misunderstandings, false ideas of supposed errors and contradictions have been taken care of. Many times in dealing with Jewish people, a foundation for the truthfulness of the Bible and the Christian faith must be given first before the listener can be truly open to hear the Gospel. The areas in which Jewish polemics have attacked the truthfulness of Christianity require an apologetic defense from those who are a part of the Church. Any time a challenge is directed against the Gospel, Christians have the Scriptural injunction to respond (1 Peter 3:15; Philippians 1:7, 17). Those who have been influenced by the skills of these arguments must see the other side and this is the obligation of Christian apologetics.

Fourth, and last, an answer to Judaism is called for because the very Lord Christians serve is the One whom Judaism seeks. Christians share with Judaism the common ground of the Hebrew Scriptures, which point to the coming One, the Messiah. This mutual foundation is an important factor in relating the truthfulness of the Gospel.

Conclusion

In an historical account from the Second Century, *Dialogue With Trypho*, Justin Martyr (AD 150), an early Church Father, dialogues with a Jew named Trypho. He discusses with him concerning the evidence from the Hebrew Scriptures relating to prophetic fulfillment in Jesus as the Messiah. Who Trypho was is not totally certain; however, there is good reason to believe that he may have represented the Jewish belief regarding the Suffering Messiah in the Second Century. In response to Justin Martyr, Trypho states:

> Let these things be as you say, namely that it was foretold Messiah would suffer and is called a stone and after his first advent, in which it had been announced he would suffer, would come in glory and be judge finally of all, and eternal King and Priest. Now show if this man [Jesus] is he of whom these prophecies were made. You have sufficiently proved by means of scriptures previously quoted by you, that it is declared in the scriptures that the Messiah must suffer and come again with glory and receive the eternal Kingdom over all the nations, every Kingdom being made subject to him. Now show us that this man [Jesus] is he.[15]

This is exactly the purpose of the Christian answer to Judaism, to demonstrate from the Scriptures that *Jesus is He* of whom the prophets spoke. This is why a Christian answer to Judaism must be given.

∅ ∂

ENDNOTES — CHAPTER 1

1. *Webster's Third New International Dictionary* (Springfield, Mass: G. and C. Merriam Company Pub., 1981), p. 1,753.

2. C.H. Holman, *A Handbook to Literature* (3d ed.; New York: Odyssey Press, 1936), p. 294.

3. *Webster's Third New International Dictionary,* op. cit., p. 101.

4. *The Jewish Encyclopedia,* Vol. 10 (New York: Funk and Wagnalls Co.), p. 105.

5. *Ibid.,* p. 107.

6. Daniel J. Lasker, *Jewish Philosophical Polemics Against Christianity in the Middle Ages* (New York: KTAV Publishing House Inc., 1977), p. 3.

7. *Ibid,* pp. 12,13.

8. *The Jewish Encyclopedia,* op. cit., p. 108.

9. Lasker, loc. cit.

10. *Ibid.,* p. 4.

11. *Ibid.*

12. *The Jewish Encyclopedia,* op. cit., p. 109.

13. Wilbur Smith, *Therefore Stand* (Grand Rapids: Baker Book House, 1945), p. 481.

14. A. Lukyn Williams, *Christian Evidences for Jewish People, Vol. I* Cambridge: W. Heffer and Sons Limited, 1911), p. XII.

15. Justin Martyr, *Dialogue with Trypho.* 39:7.

CHAPTER 2

Judaism

Origin of Judaism

he origin of Judaism begins with a man named Abraham (2000-1800 BC), who was called by God to leave his home in the *Ur of Chaldees* to go to an area foreign to him, known today as the land of Israel. This land was given to Abraham and his descendants as part of an everlasting covenant (Genesis 12:7; 13:14-18). God promised Abraham that he would become the father of a great nation and through him all the nations of the earth would be blessed.

"And I [the Lord] *will make of thee a great nation, and I will bless thee, and make thy name great; and thou shalt be a blessing" (Genesis 12:2).*

God revealed Himself to Abraham as the only true and living God, and this revelation changed the direction of Abraham's life. The history of Abraham is found in the Book of Genesis in the Hebrew Bible (Protestant Old Testament). Abraham had a son named Isaac, who later had a son named Jacob (also called Israel). Jacob had 12 sons from which the 12 tribes of the nation of Israel were derived. Around 1400 BC, God revealed Himself again to a man named Moses, who was a descendant of Abraham. At this time (1400 BC), the people of Israel were in slavery to the nation of Egypt. God delivered them out of their bondage by tremendous miracles and supernatural wonders under the leadership of Moses.

Through Moses, God revealed to Israel His will, purposes and commandments and on this basis entered into a covenant relationship with Israel. Israel was given the special privilege of being a holy nation unto God.

By the year 1000 BC, the people of Israel were in possession of the land given to Abraham and were firmly established as a great nation under a good king named David. Later David's son, Solomon, built a beautiful Temple in the chief city of Israel, Jerusalem, which was a worship center to the Lord God. However, Israel's history gave way to a long line of corrupt kings, finally being conquered by other stronger nations in the years of 721 BC and 586 BC. A summary of this historical period is found in Nehemiah 9:6-38. This passage relates events beginning with the life of Abraham and extending to the time period of Nehemiah (440 BC).

In the year AD 70, the second Temple was destroyed and the Jews were forced out of their homeland. The history of the Jewish people has continued on to the present, and the faith of the Jew

(Judaism) still holds a vital place in the Jewish community. The Jewish history and faith is probably the most interesting and unique of any sociological historical study. The fact that the Jewish people and their religious faith still exists after years of persecution and dispersion throughout the world, points to the supernatural intervention of God.

Judaism may very well be the oldest of all world religions, depending upon which beginning date is used. Christian scholar Henry J. Heydt affirms:

> Some have wrongly listed the origin of Judaism as beginning with Moses. This would constitute Hinduism an older faith than Judaism. It was Abraham however, who was the progenitor of the Chosen People, and the Jews to this day trace their descent to him. Furthermore, the Hebrew Scriptures go back beyond Abraham to creation itself and trace the descent to Abraham from the very first man. According to its own Scriptures, therefore, Judaism is not only the oldest extant religion, but the oldest of all religions.[1]

The Uniqueness of Judaism

Judaism is a religion that is in a special sense tied to the people of Israel. The history of Israel becomes essentially the history of Judaism.

1. The Scriptures

The history of Israel, the writings of the prophets and the revelations of God given to the people of Israel are recorded in the sacred book of Judaism, the Hebrew Scriptures. In these writings, the history from the first man Adam, until around 400 BC, is accurately stated.

The main thrust of Judaism historically has been to consider these Scriptures as the very Word of God. The Hebrew Bible is divided into three sections:

First—The Law—(*Torah*) which are the first five books written by Moses.
Second—The Prophets—(*Nebiim*).
Third—The Writings—(*Ketubim*).

These books form the revelational foundation upon which much of Judaism rests.

2. The Unity of God

The first and central tenet of Judaism is the "Shema" (Deuteronomy 6:4).

Shema Yisroel Adonay Elohaynu Adonay Echod—Hear O Israel, the Lord our God, the Lord is One.[2]

These are the most important words within the Jewish faith, and they can be heard in the Synagogues during *all* the times of prayer. Ward J. Fellows states:

> These words from Deuteronomy are the most important words in Judaism ... they are on the lips of the faithful many times a day; they are the last words a devout Jew utters in this life.[3]

The Hebrew Scriptures directly declare that the God of Israel is the Only, Eternal, Self-Existent, Creator of the Universe.

"I am the first and the last and beside me there is no God."[4]

I am the Lord and there is none else; there is no God beside me."[5]

For thus saith the Lord that created the heavens; God Himself that formed the earth and made it; He hath established it, He created it not in vain, He formed it to be inhabited: I am the Lord and there is none else."[6]

These two areas—the Hebrew Scriptures with emphasis on the Torah, and the "Shema" or the oneness of God—generally represent the overall uniqueness of Judaism.

The Divisions Within Judaism

Judaism falls into three basic divisions. The *Orthodox* (traditional), the *Reform*, and the *Conservative*. The Reform segment of Judaism is the liberal, rationalistic branch which holds to a modern changeable approach to Judaism. On the other side theologically is the Orthodox which asserts that Judaism is and must always be in total agreement with the unchanging Hebrew Scriptures and Jewish tradition. Conservative Judaism takes the middle road between these two opposing positions, trying to hold to a somewhat Orthodox view, while also endorsing many of the liberal ideas of Reform Judaism as well. Arnold G. Fruchtenbaum states concerning the present divisions of Judaism:

> Modern Judaism is not the same as biblical Judaism, nor is it the 'Father of Christianity.' At best it can be called its brother, and biblical Judaism is the father of both. Of the different types of Judaism, Hebrew Christianity has more in common with Orthodox Judaism than with the other two major forms. In fact, there is more common ground between Hebrew Christianity and Orthodox Judaism than between the latter and Reform Judaism.[7]

1. Reform Judaism

This branch of Judaism found its origin in Germany during the late 1700's and early 1800's. Moses Mendelssohn (1729-1786), who is considered by many to be the "father of Reform Judaism," sought to combine Judaism with the western culture of his day.[8] He taught that rationalism and the use of reason was the basis upon which all truth must rest. As a result, Reform leaders were influenced by the higher critical view of the Scriptures, which blatantly attacked the validity and trustworthiness of the Hebrew Bible. Today some Reform rabbis and leaders totally reject the reliability of the Scriptures and teach that its authority has run its course and that rationalism, as it interprets and over-rides the Scriptures, has taken its place. Even though lip service to the Scriptures is made, this rejection is quite evident. This has led to doubt even the existence of God on the part of certain groups of rabbis.

2. Orthodox Judaism

This segment of Judaism on the other hand, takes a very different view of their faith. The Orthodox Jew believes that the essentials of his faith have not been altered for over 3,000 years, and he refuses to bow to any changes. He accepts the Hebrew Bible as God's revealed will and he will hold to all of the major beliefs of Judaism in the strictest terms. The observance of the Sabbath, the principal times of worship, and all the festivals and holy days are carefully regarded and kept. Strict compliance to the laws and ordinances of Jewish traditionalism found within the Oral Law (Talmud) are rigidly adhered to, such as dietary, burial, marriage, and ethical laws. This can vary among the Orthodox from ultra-extreme, such as *Hasidim* to a more moderate view.

3. Conservative Judaism

This division began in the middle of the 19th Century in both Europe and the United States. It was known then as "Historical Judaism." Men such as Isaac Leeser, and Solomon Schechter led this movement.[9] The attitude of Conservative Judaism is to find a middle representation of Judaism between the Reform and Orthodox divisions, somewhat as Neo-Orthodoxy attempts to find a middle ground between Liberal Christianity and Biblical Orthodox Christianity.

There are also subdivisions that categorize into lesser and greater degrees in this group. These can range from a somewhat traditional Jewish approach to a more liberal viewpoint similar to Reform.

4. Other Groups

Of course, not all Jews fit into these three general groups. Other ideologies and movements such as Reconstructionism, Zionism, and Biblical Messianic Judaism have a place in the Jewish community. There are also, many Jews who have no affiliation with Judaism at all, holding to an atheistic or agnostic world view. Smaller movements inside Judaism can also be found, but space does not permit the investigation of these.

Outline of Judaism

The following is a general outline of Judaism. Because of the varied theological concepts within Judaism, total agreement on each of these categories will not be possible. It must be kept in mind that in areas of the application of the Torah, Talmudic tradition, Kosher laws, ethical principles, Messianic promises, etc. , there will be a wide spectrum of interpretations within each division. Arnold G. Fruchtenbaum, a Messianic Jewish leader, states:

> There is an old axiom that states: Where there are two Jews, there are three opinions. Its truth is borne out in practice, for while there are Jewish leaders, no one can be called the spokesman for the Jews.[10]

So, with this in mind, the following is a general description in an outline form of Judaism.

Judaism:

The word "Judaism" comes from a Latin word "Judaismus," which in turn comes from a Greek word "Ioudaismos," which translated means "the Jews' Religion." The term "Judaism" was first used about 100 BC, and was then referred to as "the Jews' Religion."[11]

Motif of Thought:

"Hear 0 Israel, the Lord our God is One Lord" (Deuteronomy 6:4). YAHWEH (JHVH) is the One eternal God, Creator and Ruler of all. All other beings depend totally on Him and all good flows from Him. Through His laws, as revealed in the Torah, man is able to ascertain His will and purpose for this earth and the world to come.

Beliefs:

Jewish scholar Moses Maimonides (1135-1204) is a very important figure in the history of the Jewish faith. His scholastic influence upon Judaism has indeed been significant and would be comparable to that of Thomas Aquinas and his impact upon the Roman Catholic Church.

Maimonides developed a statement of faith, entitled *The Thirteen Articles of Faith* ["The Thirteen Credos"]. This creed is found in most prayer books used in Jewish Synagogues. Here is a summary of this creed:

1. God is the author and guide of everything that has been and will be created.
2. God is Unity, there is none like unto His Unity and He alone is our God.
3. God is not a body and He has no form whatsoever.
4. God is the first and the last.
5. We must pray to God alone and to no one else.

6. All the words of the prophets are true.
7. Moses is the chief of all prophets whose prophecy is true.
8. The Torah which we possess is the same that was given to Moses.
9. The Torah will never be changed and there will never be any other law of God.
10. God discerns the hearts of all men, knows all their thoughts and deeds.
11. God rewards those who keep His commandments and punishes those who transgress them.
12. Messiah, though He tarry, will come.
13. There will be a resurrection of the dead.[12]

God:

It was Moses Maimonides who stated:

The foundation of all foundations, the pillar supporting all wisdoms, is the recognition of the reality of God.[13]

Judaism teaches that there is one God, who has created all things, and within His creation there is a purpose and a plan. God is not a part of nature, but rather is separate and distinct from His creation ruling over it and sustaining all living things. Because He is a purposeful God, there was a beginning and there will be a consummation. God is Spirit and does not possess a body or physical limitations of any kind. He is Eternal, always existing in the past and in the future. God is the Supreme, Eternal Creator of all, and worship belongs only to Him. To worship creation rather than the Creator is "idolatry."

Man:

Man is of the earth, made of the dust of the ground, but he also contains the divine spark. He is fashioned in the image of God and this means that above everything else, he has been given freedom in life. He has the right to choose either good or evil.

Sin:

There is no such thing as original sin. Adam's fall is not seen as a stain that is given to each person at birth. Instead it is a fault that is continually repeated by man because of human weakness. Every moment of his life man will face the choice between that which is evil and good.

Attitude Toward the Law:

God has revealed His Law in the "Torah," the five books of Moses as found in the Bible. These laws are absolute, unchanging and apply to all men. The Orthodox Jew considers the "Torah" the most sacred object in Jewish worship. Without it, life has no meaning nor value. God has revealed His laws to man with the intention that man will be obedient and thus fulfill God's purpose and plan. The Conservative and Reform movements within Judaism, take a somewhat different application regarding the Torah than the Orthodox. However, the general response within Judaism is to place a strong emphasis upon the foundation teachings of the Torah. In Judaism, the very fact that the Law exists is proof that people are capable of obeying it. Therefore the Law is to be highly loved and respected. When a young Jewish boy first begins his study of the Torah, a small drop of honey is placed on the page to establish that his duty in study is also to be of great joy.

Salvation:
Judaism does not accept the idea of atonement or of salvation through Christ. Every man is responsible for his own salvation. No one serves as a mediator between God and man. Each person as an individual, must stand before God. However, God is not only a righteous terrible Judge, He is also loving, kind and merciful. He knows and understands that human beings are weak and sinful and upon this basis He does pardon and forgive sin. The Hebrew Scriptures clearly teach the atonement of sin by the shedding of blood (Leviticus 17:11). In the pre-Christian period, Judaism practiced this God-given method of atoning for sin (Exodus 29:36; Leviticus 1:1-4; 4:13-36; 9:7; 10:17; Numbers 15:22-28). However, due to the destruction of the Temple and the separation of the Jews from their homeland in AD 70, they have replaced the altar with the Torah.

Judgment:
Orthodox and Conservative Judaism believe in the resurrection of all men, the immortality of the soul, and the judgment of God upon all mankind. God will reward those who will obey His laws and commandments, and He will punish those who transgress them. Reform Judaism has taken a very liberal view toward the area of judgment and resurrection, and some Reform rabbis totally reject these doctrines.

The Messiah:
The future for Judaism revolves around the coming of the Messiah who will be the champion of Israel. The Messiah will be the one who brings peace, justice and righteousness to the world. For Orthodox and Conservative Jews, the Messiah is still to come on the scene. The proof that He has come will be the end of all evil and the establishing of a new era of peace and justice. Reform Judaism does not believe in a personal Messiah, but rather in the coming of a Messianic Age (the Messianic hopes being fulfilled in an age of peace and truth that will eventually take place on the earth).

Worship Patterns:
The Talmud describes worship as *avodah sheh bah-lev*, "the service of the heart."[14] Jewish worship is not a formal, dead type, but

rather is warm and enthusiastic, reflecting personal joy in the Lord. *The Daily prayer:* "Shema," "Hear, O Israel, the Lord our God, the Lord is One."[15]

The Sabbath:

The seventh day: On this day all work must stop. This is carried into very strict terms within some forms of Orthodox Judaism. Worship takes place on this day each week. A Sabbath service will include prayer, reading from the Torah, chants and hymns. Each worshipper must have something on his head at all times. Skull caps, prayer books, prayer shawls and phylacteries (leather strips with boxes containing Scripture verses) are a vital part of traditional forms of Judaism. A *minyan*[16] (a quorum of 10 men) must be present to have worship.

The Principal Times of Worship:

1. Daily Prayer: Three times each day; morning, afternoon and evening.
2. Sabbath Evening and Day.
3. Special Festivals.
4. Day of Atonement.

Festivals and Holy Days:

Each feast has a historical significance for Israel as a nation.

Passover .... Salvation from Egyptian slavery.
Unleavened Bread .... Cleansing of sin (leaven is a symbol of sin).
First Fruits .... Thanksgiving for the first fruits and the harvest to come.
Pentecost .... Thanksgiving for the first harvest.
Trumpets .... Assembly to prepare for the Day of Atonement.
Day of Atonement .... Time of repentance and forgiveness.
Booths .... Harvest celebration and memorial of the Tabernacle in the wilderness.

Synagogue:

Public worship takes place in the synagogue. Every synagogue must have the ark which contains copies of the "Torah." Each synagogue is built facing the east toward Jerusalem.

Rabbi:

The word *rabbi* means "teacher." He is in no sense a mediator between man and God. He rarely leads services. The influence of a rabbi is determined by his ability to keep the respect of layman through his knowledge of the Scriptures. His authority is based on his learning, not his position.

Ethics:

Judaism stresses the love of learning, all based on a knowledge of the Torah, the worship of God and good deeds toward fellow men.

Marriage:
Marriage is a three-way partnership between husband, wife and God. Marriage must always remain inside the faith.

Sacred Writings:
1) The Hebrew Scriptures consist of the Law, the Prophets and the Writings.[17]
2) Talmud: Interpretations and studies of the Old Testament. It is not authoritative, but it is very influential to all groups of Jews.

Groups Found in U.S.A.:

Orthodox Judaism
1. Rabbinical Council of America
   220 Park Ave. South, New York, NY 10003
2. Union of Orthodox Jewish Congregations
3. Women's League for Conservative Judaism

Conservative Judaism
1. Jewish Theological Seminary of America
   3080 Broadway, New York, NY 10027
2. Women's League for Conservative Judaism
3. United Synagogue of America

Reform Judaism
1. Union of American Hebrew Congregations
   838 5th Ave., New York, NY 10021
2. Hebrew Union College [Cincinnati, Ohio]
3. Central Conference of American Rabbis

There are six million Jews in the United States, which is the largest Jewish population in the world. Of these six million Jews, approximately two million align themselves with each of the three branches of Judaism respectively.[18]

HEBREW TERMS

Adonai–Hebrew name meaning "Lord." Adonai is a plural word.

Amidah–Means "standing," a prayer of affirmation and petition, recited three times daily while *standing*.

Averah–"Transgression, sin."

Bar Mitzvah–"Son of Commandment," religious ceremony for boys who at 13 years of age enter the religious life of an adult Jew.

Bat Mitzveh–"Daughter of Commandment," a new ceremony in some modern movements within Judaism. It is a ceremony for Jewish girls at 12 years of age who have completed Jewish study and are now prepared to understand the Jewish heritage.

Beracha–"Blessing, praise, benediction."

Brit Milah–"Covenant of Circumcision," ceremony for all Jewish male infants on the eighth day after birth. Cutting off the foreskin of the male organ. This practice is over 4,000 years old and was given to Abraham by God (Genesis 17:9-14).

Caballah–Jewish mystical tradition and writings.

Chuppah (huppah), "canopy"–Jewish marriage ceremony.

Covenant–The agreement between God and the Jews as received by Moses on Mount Sinai.

Decalogue–The Ten Commandments.

Diaspora–"Dispersion" refers to the dispersing of the Jews from their land in Palestine after the Babylonian exile.

Elohim–Plural name for God.

Gemara–The commentary of the Talmud giving interpretation and elaboration of the oral Law. Two chief collections–the Babylonian and the Palestinian.

Haggada–The non-legal part of the *Mishnah*, it is basically a story or legend. Also used at the Passover Seder "telling" the story of the Exodus.

Halacha–Oral law tradition of Mishnah, dealing with usage and customs.

Hanukkah–"Dedication" festival, commemorating the rededication of the altar in the temple–165 BC.

Hasidim–A Jewish sect; means "pious or godly ones."

Haskalah–Enlightenment movement among Jews in East and Central Europe.

Hatikvah–"*The Hope.*" A song composed in 1878 by Naphtali Herz Imber, dealing with the Jewish desire to return to Zion. It is Israel's national anthem.

Jehovah–Combining form of JHVH and Adonay, name of the Lord God of Israel (Exodus 6:1-3).

JHVH (YHWH)–The Tetragrammaton; four Hebrew letters giving the Holy name of God.

Kabbalah–Tradition, specifically the mystical tradition in Judaism.

Kaddish–A Jewish prayer which speaks of the greatness of God. It is recited in many different types of Jewish ceremonies.

Ketubim (Ketuvim)–"The Writings," devotional and wisdom books of the Hebrew Bible.

Kosher–"Fit, proper": applies to ritually acceptable food in accordance with Jewish practice–dietary laws–Kosher laws.

Meshumad–"To destroy," "a traitor"–applied to Jewish Christians.

Messiah–Fulfillment of God's purposes and promises for Israel, to be completed in a man, ruler, king: (some within Judaism, mainly the Reform, interpret this as a Messianic Age).

Mezuzah–"Doorpost," small box nailed to the door of a Jewish home containing Scripture passages inside on a parchment scroll.

Midrash–A collection of expositions of the Hebrew Scriptures which are basically doctrinal in material matter.

Minyan–"Number" or "Quorum"–to constitute a quorum for public worship. Ten men, 13 years or older, are required.

Mishnah–Hebrew writings dealing with Jewish traditions and expositions of Oral Law. It forms the basis of the Talmud.

Mishpat–"Court" justice that God demands of men–"hate evil, love good, and establish justice" (Amos 5:15).

Mitzvah–"Commitment, obligation"–any act of kindness or support for a deserving cause.

Nebiim (Neviim)–"Prophets," the prophetic books of the Hebrew Bible.

Passover (Pesach)–Commemorates the deliverance of Israel's firstborn from the judgment which God carried out upon the Egyptians during Israel's liberation from Egyptian slavery.

Pentateuch–First five books of the Hebrew Bible.

Purim–"Lots," the feast commemorating victory over Haman.

Rabbi–Jewish teacher and instructor.

Rosh Hashana–"Head of the Year," the Jewish celebration of their New Year's day on Tishri 1.

Shabbat (Sabbath)–"Rest," to cease from work. The seventh day of the week is the Sabbath day.

Seder–"Order" of the Passover meal, with ceremony on first night.

Shavuot–"Weeks" or "Weeks of Weeks"–Pentecost or "Feast of Weeks."

Shema–"Hear," first word of Deuteronomy 6:4–"Hear, O Israel, the Lord our God, the Lord is One."

Shochet–Man trained in Jewish law who slaughters animals in accordance with ritual requirements.

Sukkot–"Booths," the Feast of Booths, Tabernacles.

Synagogue–Greek word for assembly–house of worship for the Jews.

Talmud–Body of civil and canonical Law. First, it was oral, later written.

Tashlich–"Casting off" of sins.

Tefillin–(From the word "tefilla," meaning "prayer.") Phylacteries–inscriptions are made on parchment encased in two small leather cubicles and attached to the arm and head by leather strips.

Tenach–Three sections of the Hebrew Scriptures: Torah, Neviim, Ketuvim—initial letters T-N-K vowelized.

Torah–The Law, fundamental basis of Judaism—first five books of the Hebrew Bible. In a broader scope it refers to the entire domain of Jewish learning as a general discipline.

Yom Kippur–Day of Atonement.

Zohar–Writings of Jewish doctrines concerning the mystical and unknown truths concerning the Universe and God.

Zionism–A movement to obtain a Jewish State and Nation in Palestine [now Israel].

ENDNOTES — CHAPTER 2

1. Henry J. Heydt, *A Comparison of World Religions* (Fort Washington, Penn: Christian Literature Crusade, 1967), p. 11.
2. Ward J. Fellows, *Religion East and West* (New York: Holt, Rinehart and Winston, 1979) p. 291.
3. *Ibid.*, pp. 291,292.
4. Isaiah 44:6b.
5. Isaiah 45:5a.
6. Isaiah 45:18.
7. Arnold G. Fruchtenbaum, *Hebrew Christianity: Its Theology, History and Philosophy* (Washington D.C.: Canon Press, 1974), p. 106.
8. Louis Goldberg, *Our Jewish Friends* (Neptune, New Jersey: Loizeaux Brothers, 1977), p. 21.
9. *Ibid.*, p. 23
10. Fruchtenbaum, *op. cit.*, preface.
11. Heydt, *A Comparison of World Religions, op. cit.*, p. 12.
12. Abraham M. Heller, *The Vocabulary of Jewish Life* (Revised ed.; New York: Hebrew Publishing Company, 1967), pp. 191,192.
13. Howard R. Greenstein, *Judaism—An Eternal Covenant* (Philadelphia: Fortress Press, 1983), p. 3.
14. Fellows, *op. cit.*, p. 297.
15. Deuteronomy 6:4.
16. Henry J. Heydt, *Studies in Jewish Evangelism* (New York: American Board of Missions to the Jews Inc., 1951), p. 185.
17. A comparison between the Hebrew Scriptures and the Protestant and Catholic Old Testament books are as follows. The Hebrew Scriptures consist of 22 books [Josephus considered 22; Jewish count is 24 today]; the Protestant Old Testament—39 books and the Catholic Old Testament—46 books. The Protestant Old Testament contains the same books as the Hebrew Scriptures, the difference being in the division of the books. The Hebrew Scriptures treat Hosea through Malachi as one book entitled, The Twelve. This results in a difference of eleven books between the Hebrew list and the Protestant list. The books of Joshua—Judges—Ruth; 1 and 2 Chronicles; Ezra—Nehemiah; 1 and 2 Kings and 1 and 2 Samuel are each respectively treated as one book. This results in a further reduction of six. The comparison between the Hebrew Scriptures and the Protestant Old Testament would then be: Hebrew Scriptures = 22 books, and Protestant Old Testament = 39 minus 17 or 22 books. The Catholic Old Testament contains 11 Apocryphal books that are not accepted in the Hebrew Canon of Scripture nor the Protestant Old Testament. For further information see Norman L. Geisler and William E. Nix, *A General Introduction to the Bible* (Chicago: Moody Press, 1968), pp. 127-178.
18. Statistics taken from Dr. Charles Manske, professor of World Religions, *Simon Greenleaf School of Law*, Comparative Religions notes, p. 27.

CHAPTER 3

Judaism's Rejection of Jesus

he Jewish "rejection of Jesus" does not imply that all Jewish persons have rejected Jesus of Nazareth as the Messiah. The Christian faith was born within Biblical Judaism and the New Testament teaches that almost all of the members of the early Church were Jewish. All of the writers of the New Testament books were Jewish, with the possible exception of Luke. The history of Messianic Jews, which are Jewish people who have received Jesus as their Messiah and Savior, is indeed a long and impressive one. The following list provides a few names of men who have been outstanding Christians. Many of these Jewish believers were important figures in the history of the Church.

David Baron, Christian writer and missionary.
Paul Cassel, Theologian of the German Reformed Church.
Alfred Edersheim, Scholar and writer.
Solomon Ginsburg, Missionary to Brazil.
Isaac Lichtenstein, Jewish rabbi.
Isidor Lowenthal, Bible translator.
Agustus Neander, Church historian.

This list could continue with thousands of Jewish believers who will never be heard of, but whose faith is as genuine as any Christian of history or the present. Sadly however, the vast majority of Jewish people have historically rejected the message of Jesus.

Tradition Regarding Jesus

Jewish tradition reveals that the caricature of Jesus of Nazareth has been possibly one of the most abused and degraded of any person within all of Jewish history. David Baron, a great Jewish-Christian scholar comments regarding this:

All through the centuries no name has called forth such intense abhorrence among the Jewish people as the name of Jesus ... In the filthy legends about Him in the Talmud, and later productions, the very names by which He is called are blasphemies. The precious name of Yeshua (Jesus-Savior) has been changed into 'Yeshu' made up of initial letters, which mean 'Let His name and His memory be blotted out.' This Holy One who knew no sin, nor was guile found in His mouth, was often styled, 'The Transgressor': There are other filthy designations, such as 'Ben Stada,' or 'Ben Pandera,' which imply blasphemies not only against Him, but against her who is 'blessed among women.' Israel's blind hatred to the Messiah did not stop short of His Person or His virgin mother, but extended also to those of their nation who took upon themselves His reproach and followed Him. ... Not satisfied with classifying them as 'apostates' and 'worse than heathen,' Rabbis at the end of the first century of our era instituted a daily public prayer in the most solemn part of their liturgy that the 'Nazarenes may, together with all apostates, be 'suddenly destroyed,' and 'be blotted out of the book of life.'[1]

There are two forms of Jewish tradition concerning the history of Jesus. The early tradition comes from the Rabbinical writings and the later tradition comes from documents such as the *Tol'doth Yeshu*.

Concerning the early traditional material, both the Talmud and Midrashic literature contain references to the person of Jesus Christ. From this material, the clear rejection of Jesus and His claims is evident. Jewish scholar, Joseph Klausner relates concerning these writings,

> They partake rather of the nature of vituperation and polemic against the founder of a hated party, than objective accounts of historical value.[2]

Most Jewish scholars do agree on this point, that this material is legendary and not genuinely historically valid. But it does give an idea of the early view of Jesus and the general historicity attributed to Him. Jakob Jocz, professor of Jewish studies, summarizes the material found in the Talmud concerning Jesus;

> Jesus, called ha-Notzri, B. Stada or Pandira, was born out of wedlock. His mother was called Miriam, and was a dresser of women's hair. Her husband was Pappus B. Judah and her paramour (illicit lover) Pandira. She is said to have been the descendant of princes and rulers and to have played the harlot with a carpenter. Jesus had been in Egypt and had brought magic thence. He was a magician and deceived and led Israel astray. He caused the multitude to sin. He mocked at the words of the wise and was excommunicated. He was tainted with heresy. He called himself God, also the Son of Man, and said that he would go up to heaven. He made himself live by the name of God. He was tried in Lydda as a deceiver and as a teacher of apostasy. Witnesses were concealed so as to hear his statements and a lamp was lighted over him that his face might be seen. He was executed in Lydda, on the eve of the Passover, which also was the eve of the Sabbath; he was stoned and hung (or crucified). A herald proclaimed, during forty days, that he was to be stoned and invited evidence in his favor, but none was given. He (under the name of Balaam) was put to death by Pinhas the robber (Pontius Pilatus) and at the time was thirty-three years old. He was punished in Gehenna by means of boiling. ... He had five disciples. Under the name Balaam, he was excluded from the world to come.[3]

There are other Rabbinical writings that contain references to Jesus, consistently using different names for Him. Yet all of them present Jesus in a twisted and perverted light.

A second form of Jewish tradition regarding Jesus comes from later sources (Fifth to Sixth Century). An example of this is found in an old Jewish story called the *Tol'doth Yeshu.* Professor Jakob Jocz states:

> The main gist of the story is the assertion that Jesus was an illegitimate child; that he performed miracles by means of sorcery which he learned from the Egyptians; that he had acquired the power of performing miracles by stealing the Ineffable Name from the Temple and sewing it underneath his skin; that he was arrested on the eve of the Passover; that he was hanged on a cabbage stem (the reason given is that Jesus had previously adjured all trees by the Ineffable Name not to receive his body, but he failed to adjure the cabbage stem which does not count as a tree); that his body was removed on the eve of the Sabbath and interred; that the gardener removed his body and cast it into a cesspool.[4]

The story goes on to add,

> His disciples, on being unable later to find the body in the tomb, made it public that Jesus had been raised from the dead. This report, being believed in high quarters, looked like bringing swift punishment on those who had instigated what was now coming to look like the murder of the Lord's Anointed. The Jews were in great distress at this prospect and a fast was declared. Finally, by the good providence of God, the dead body of Jesus was actually found in the very spot where it had been thrown by the gardener. The Jewish authorities ordered its removal, and to expose the deception publicly, they had it [the body of Jesus] dragged through the streets tied to the tail of a horse. The disciples of Jesus fled and ultimately formed themselves into a community with religious rite and ceremonies distinct from those of the rest of the Jews.[5]

The *Tol' doth Yeshu* had a large circulation and acceptance among Jewish people in the Middle Ages. It was used among many Jews as a sort of Christmas story book. The general view of its date of composition is around the Fifth or Sixth Century. This type of material generally represents the view that Judaism has historically taken concerning Jesus Christ in the Middle Ages.

In the 11th and 12th Centuries, the great Jewish scholar, Moses Maimonides verbalized Judaism's view of Jesus. Concerning Jesus of Nazareth, he says:

> Has there ever been a greater stumbling block than this? All the prophets affirmed that the Messiah would redeem Israel, save them, gather their dispersed and confirm the commandments. But he caused Israel to be destroyed by the sword, their remnant to be dispersed and humiliated. He was instrumental in changing the Torah and causing the world to fall into error and to serve another besides God.[6]

The present-day view of Jesus is not unlike that of history past. Samuel Levine, a Jewish educator who specializes in attempting to refute Christian claims concerning Jesus, says in his book, *You Take Jesus, I'll Take God,*

> Since the main prophecies about the Messiah were not fulfilled by Jesus, and only such prophecies as riding on a donkey or getting beaten up were ostensibly fulfilled by him, why should one believe this Jesus was the Messiah? [7]

Examples of quotes like this from other Jewish sources could be enlarged upon; however, this one by Mr. Levine is a particularly good example. Even today there is as clear a refusal to believe the claims of Jesus as there has ever been throughout the history of the Jewish response to Christianity. As stated earlier, this is not the total response to Jesus by the Jewish community; however, it is fairly representative of the general historical perspective of Christ and the Church.

Origin of the Jewish Rejection

Where did this rejection of Jesus start? Jacob Agus argues,

> The faith and career of Paul are generally regarded as marking the tragic break between Judaism and Christianity. While many Jewish scholars maintain that Jesus lived and taught within the ambience of Judaism, they agree that Paul was responsible for the separation of the two faiths and their mutual hostility. [8]

Along with Paul and his teachings, another alleged cause for this rejection and division was the failure of Christians to support the Jewish revolt against Rome. In AD 132-135, the Jews revolted against Roman domination under their leader Bar Kochba. The records of Jewish history clearly affirm that the Christians did join in on this revolt until Bar Kochba was titled the "Jewish Messiah." On this basis, the Christians refused to fight, recognizing that this was a clear rejection of their faith in Jesus of Nazareth as the Messiah of the Scriptures. At this point a definite severing between Hebrew Christians and fellow Jews took place. But neither of these causes are correct in identifying the origin of the separation between the Christian faith and Judaism.

According to the New Testament, the conflict between Jesus and Judaism was based on the extraordinary claims of Jesus. It was not the controversy over the validity and permanence of the Law or another theological, problem of that type, nor was it the claim that Jesus made of being the Messiah. Instead, it was the claim of total and unique authority that Jesus affirmed was His and to this the leadership of Judaism reacted. The following is an example of only a few passages which illustrate this point.

> *"And they were astonished at his doctrine: for his word was with power* [authority]. *And they were all amazed and spake among themselves, saying, What a word is this! for with authority and power he commandeth the unclean spirits, and they come out"* (Luke 4:32, 36).

"And they come again to Jerusalem: and as he was walking in the temple, there come to him the chief priests, and the scribes and the elders, and say unto him, By what authority doest thou these things? And who gave thee this authority to do these things?" (Mark 11:27-28).

"But there were certain scribes sitting there and reasoning in their hearts, Why doth this man thus speak blasphemies? Who can forgive sins but God only?" (Mark 2:6-7).

"Therefore the Jews sought the more to kill him, because he not only had broken the sabbath, but said also that God was his Father, making himself equal to God" (John 5:18).

"Jesus said unto them, Verily, verily, I say unto you, Before Abraham was, I am. Then took they up stones to cast at him ..." (John 8:58).

"The Jews answered him, saying, For a good work we stone thee not; but for blasphemy: and because that thou, being a man, makest thyself God" (John 10:33).

"After two days was the feast of the passover and of the unleavened bread: and the chief priests and the scribes sought how they might take him by craft and put him to death" (Mark 14:1).

From these passages it is obvious that the problems the Jewish leadership had with Jesus started within the origins of the Christian faith.

Why the Rejection of Jesus?

1. Tradition

The authority of Jesus and His claims of ultimate power were totally foreign to the traditions of Judaism. The New Testament provides numerous examples of this. In the Gospel of Mark, a particularly clear one is found.

"Then the Pharisees and the scribes asked him, Why walk not thy disciples according to the tradition of the elders, but eat bread with unwashen hands?

He answered and said unto them, Well hath Esaias prophesied of you hypocrites, as it is written, This people honoreth me with their lips, but their heart is far from me.

Howbeit in vain do they worship me, teaching for doctrines the commandments of men.

For laying aside the commandment of God, ye hold the tradition of men, as the washing of pots and cups: and many other such like things ye do.

And he said unto them, Full well ye reject the commandment of God, that ye may keep your own tradition.

For Moses said, Honor thy father and thy mother; and, Whoso curseth father or mother, let him die the death:

But ye say, If a man shall say to his father or mother, It is Corban, that is to say, a gift, by whatsoever thou mightest be profited by me, he shall be free.

And ye suffer him no more to do ought for his father or his mother,

Making the word of God of none effect through your tradition, which ye have delivered: and many such like things do ye" (Mark 7:5-13)

The statements of Jesus, such as the "I AM's" of the Gospel of John; the right to receive worship; the power to forgive sin; the ability to produce miracles; the pointing to Himself as the means of obtaining eternal life; the superior authority concerning the Law, the Sabbath and the traditions of the elders—all of these qualities and claims were contrary to the Messianic traditions and teachings of the rabbis and scribes.

As was shown in the outline of Judaism, the Jewish faith is immersed in tradition. This tradition and interpretation of the Hebrew Scriptures started with a group of scholars, brought together by Ezra around 450 BC, called the Sopherim. The Sopherim were the religious leaders of this time period and their functions were to translate and explain the Scriptures. Examples from the Hebrew Scriptures regarding these men and their work can be seen in Nehemiah 8:7-8. Their oral interpretation and exegesis of the Scriptures continued until around 180 BC. By this time, the gradual process of oral paraphrasing and interpreting had continued to such a point that almost every book in the Hebrew Scriptures had its own traditional understanding. These oral paraphrases, called Targums, were then committed to writing. Following this Targumim tradition, there came another body of tradition which became known as the Mishnah. These traditions dealt with the legal portions of the Scriptures: explanations, commentaries, interpretations regarding ethical and law-related areas in the Torah. The *Mishnah* (also called the Second Law) was first carried orally, but around AD 200, it was put into written form. Next came the development of the Gemara, which was put together by a group of scholars called the Amoraim (which means interpreters).[9] The Gemara is basically a commentary or explanation of the Mishnah, and was put into writing around AD 500. These two together (the *Mishnah* and the *Gemara*) form the body of material known as the Talmud. Judaism claims that the *Talmud* (Oral Law) and the Torah (Written Law) both originate in Moses. The Talmud is therefore the basis of the traditionalism within Judaism. Jewish scholar, Jacob Neusner explains this:

Judaism is based upon both the written Torah and a second Torah, just as Christianity is based upon the Old Testament and a second New 'Testament' or covenant. Where do we now find this second Torah, this other ... oral revelation? It is found in the Mishnah, a corpus of traditions and laws written down at the end of the second century CE.[10]

He goes on to further explain regarding the main body of the Talmud, the Mishnah:

> The Mishnah is essentially a law code. It is divided into six major parts called Seders or orders, encompassing the vast themes of reality covered by the Oral Torah. These are, first, agricultural law; second, Sabbath and festival laws; third, family laws; fourth, civil and criminal laws; fifth, laws concerning sacrifices ... and finally, laws concerning purities.
>
> ... The Mishnah is the fundamental document of Rabbinic Judaism.[11]

The chart that follows gives an overall survey of this development process.[12] It was *this very tradition* that Jesus referred to in Mark 7:5-13. These interpretations of the Scriptures literally form the core of the faith of Rabbinic Judaism. Therefore, when Jesus made statements and claims that countered the teachings of the Mishnah (later known as the Talmud), He was rejected.

Jewish scholar Trude Weiss-Rosmarin relates the traditional perspective concerning the claims of Jesus. She states,

> None of the prophets in Israel ever taught in his own name and on his own responsibility. The 'I' of Jesus, however, is he himself. He [Jesus] taught on his own authority, frequently in opposition to the authoritative teachings of the rabbis of the time and he stressed his own personal opinions beyond anything that had ever been heard of in Israel ... The traditional and perennial task of the Prophets was to castigate their contemporaries for their sins, but not to forgive sins. Jesus, however, abrogated to himself the power of forgiving sin ... He represents himself as the one who performs the cure, revives the dead or causes the miracle to come about. The Hebrew Bible, too, knows of miracles performed by Prophets. But none of the Prophets ever wrought a miracle on his own authority or represented it to be a sign of his own power and strength.[13]

Jesus' ministry and teaching was most definitely contrary to the traditionalism as represented in the above passage, and on this basis He was considered "a deceiver and a teacher of apostasy."[14]

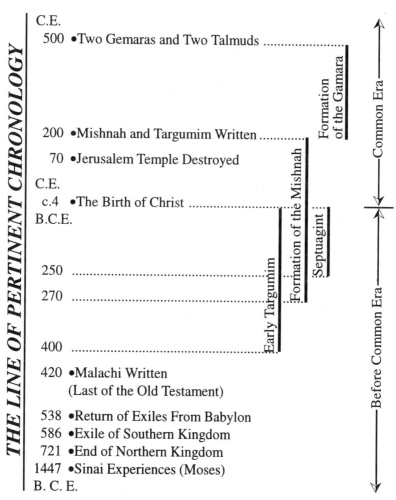

THE LINE OF PERTINENT CHRONOLOGY

C.E.
500 •Two Gemaras and Two Talmuds ....

Formation of the Gamara

Common Era

200 •Mishnah and Targumim Written ....

70 •Jerusalem Temple Destroyed

Formation of the Mishnah

C.E.
c.4 •The Birth of Christ ....

B.C.E.

Early Targumim

Formation of the Mishnah

Septuagint

Before Common Era

250 ....

270 ....

400 ....

420 •Malachi Written
(Last of the Old Testament)

538 •Return of Exiles From Babylon
586 •Exile of Southern Kingdom
721 •End of Northern Kingdom
1447 •Sinai Experiences (Moses)
B. C. E.

When Jesus' position as the Messiah was compared with the traditional Messianic concepts, further conflict developed. The traditional Jewish belief in the time period of Jesus concerning the Messiah was that he (the Messiah) would be a national leader and deliverer. Instead of working miracles relating primarily to human-spiritual need, the Messiah was to produce political-related miracles. The Messiah was not to be the Son of God, but was rather a man, being used of God to establish the kingdom and the nation of Israel. The fact that Israel was under Roman domination during this time period greatly encouraged this type of concept. The desire for peace, security and nationalistic freedom helped to shape the Jewish mind and attitude regarding the Messiah. Jewish rabbi Samuel Umen relates,

In Judaism, the Messiah was expected to serve as God's agent; He would usher in an age of peace, prosperity and spiritual regeneration for Israel and mankind.[15]

Jewish writers Dennis Prager and Joseph Telushkin give some additional input regarding this; They state,

> Judaism does not believe that Jesus was the Messiah because he did not fulfill any messianic prophecies. The major prophecy concerning the messianic days is that 'nation shall not lift up sword against nation nor shall they learn war anymore' (Isaiah 2:1-4; 11:1-10). World peace must accompany the Messiah and should peace not come, the Messiah has obviously not come. It has been obvious for over nineteen hundred years that the messianic days of peace have not arrived, yet Christians still contend that Jesus was the Messiah.[16]

To illustrate this point, a story may help to clarify, taken from the book *Jews and Jewish Christianity*, by David Berger and Michael Wyschogrod. They relate:

> A story is told about a modern rabbi and a Christian missionary ...
>
> One of the great rabbis of the last hundred years, was riding on a train in Russia and overheard a conversation between a Christian missionary and some deeply religious, but uneducated Jews. The Jews had just expressed their confidence in the judgment of the ancient rabbis concerning the Messiah. 'In that case,' asked the Christian 'how can you explain the fact that Rabbi Akiva (one of the greatest Talmudic rabbis) initially thought that Bar Kochba (a Jewish revolutionary of the second century) was the Messiah?' The Jews were taken aback and could find no answer. The rabbi, who had been listening quietly, turned to the Christian and asked, 'How do you know that Bar Kochba wasn't the Messiah?' 'That's obvious,' he replied. 'Bar Kochba was killed without bringing the redemption.'[17]

This story demonstrates the persistency of the argument, that the Messiah is going to bring a national and political deliverance. He is not going to die or fail at this task. However, there is a basic fallacy to this argument because the Hebrew Scriptures not only emphasize that the Messiah will bring world peace and nationalistic supremacy for Israel, but they also affirm that the Messiah is to suffer, die and rise again to bring a spiritual deliverance for mankind. The Scriptures teach that he will be rejected and killed, yet through his death, salvation and forgiveness of sin will be made available to all. Later in this work, the dual aspects of the Messiah, as taught in the Hebrew Scriptures and as viewed by Jewish rabbis prior to the time of Christ will be examined. Both the Suffering Servant and the Reigning Ruler Messianic concepts are present within the Hebrew Scriptures. In Jesus' first coming He satisfied the Suffering Servant prophecies and in His return, He will fulfill that of the Reigning Ruler bringing world peace. The Jewish leadership during Jesus' ministry refused to see this

Scriptural truth and therefore, because of countering the expectations of rabbinical thought, He was refused. This is the strength of Jewish tradition.

2. Human Attitude

The second factor that presented problems within Judaism regarding Jesus was that of the rabbinical attitude regarding man's sin condition. The Jewish concept of God, man's sin, the need of a savior and the methodology of salvation from a sinful state back into a relationship with God, lies on two totally different foundations when compared with the Christian message. Jakob Jocz deals with this issue and he states,

> Thus the differences between the Church and the Synagogue are not mere thought-differences, but real differences between men and men. They reveal a difference of attitude to the complex phenomena of life ... Deeply imbedded within the human soul is the inexorable will of man to work out his own salvation and to remain the master of his own fate. The Christian attitude is essentially the attitude of surrender. Christianity begins with man in crisis; Judaism begins with the assertion of human strength. The real difference between Judaism and Christianity lies in the difference of attitude to God on the part of the individual believer.[18]

The view of sin, man, his need of a savior, atonement for sin, the mercy and justice of God etc., are some of the basic differences between the teaching of Rabbinic Judaism and that of the New Testament. The New Testament teaches that all men are sinners and that salvation, forgiveness of sin, and a relationship with God, comes only through the atoning work of Jesus Christ through His death on the cross. Only by personal faith in Jesus as the resurrected Savior and Lord are men delivered from sin. (John 3:16, 36; 10:9-10; Matthew 26:27-28; Mark 16:16-17; Luke 24:46-47; Romans 3:23; 6:23; 10:1-13). In the traditional concept among the Jewish leadership in Jesus' time period, this was not the basis upon which salvation rested. Rather, salvation was based upon human worthiness, obedience to the moral, ethical and ceremonial laws as found in the Torah and involvement in good works and life service to God. This view is still the core attitude of Judaism. Man and his sinfulness was and is not viewed in Judaism as it is declared throughout the Bible.[19] As discussed earlier, Judaism affirms that man has a free moral choice between good and evil. He still retains the "divine spark" and has freedom in life. He is not bound in sin, but is above any slavery and bondage to a fallen nature. Because man is viewed this way within Judaism there is no need of a mediator or savior. This obviously eliminates any need for the person and work of the Lord Jesus (1 Timothy 2:4-6).

3. Unbelief

Regardless of the basic origins of Judaism's refusal of Jesus as the Messiah, it still all boils down to human unbelief. Jakob Jocz expresses it this way.

To the Christian, the Jewish refusal to see in Jesus of Nazareth the promised Messiah is unbelief; not Jewish unbelief, but human unbelief. For the Jew in retaining his attitude of negation to the Son of Man, becomes part and parcel of an unbelieving world. The Synagogue's no is the human no to the Son of God, who still knocks at the door of the heart of humanity.[20]

The New Testament affirms regarding Jewish unbelief:

"And he did not many mighty works there because of their unbelief" (Matthew 13:58).

"Art thou the Christ? tell us. And he said unto them, If I tell you, ye will not believe" (Luke 22:67).

"Jesus answered them, I told you, and ye believed not: the works that I do in my Father's name, they bear witness of me. But ye believe not ..." (John 10:25-26).

Unbelief has been and will always be a hindrance to the work of God. Because of the hardness of heart, men have refused to believe in God's purposes and plans. In the Hebrew Scriptures many examples of this can be noted.

"Therefore the Lord heard this, and was wroth: so a fire was kindled against Jacob and anger also came up against Israel;

Because they believed not in God and trusted not in his salvation" (Psalm 78:21-22).

"For all this they sinned still and believed not in his wondrous works" (Psalm 78:32).

The rejection of Jesus as Savior and Lord is primarily based on this terrible sin of unbelief and the Jewish situation is no exception. The human mind naturally doubts the miraculous and finds it easier to be skeptical than to simply believe matters that exceed the understanding. The Gospel is a supernatural message and it requires believing and trusting in God's miraculous power. The New Testament provides a solid foundation for faith in Jesus and appeals to facts as the basis for faith. However, child-like faith is necessary to be a follower of Jesus (Matthew 11:25-26; 18:1-4; 21:16). This requirement of faith was a problem for many Jews who heard the message of Jesus and it resulted in their rejection of Him. The Prophet Isaiah said concerning the Messiah and Jewish unbelief,

"Who hath believed our report? and to whom is the arm of the Lord revealed?" (Isaiah 53:1).

The Jewish Problem Today

The problems that Jewish persons have today with receiving Jesus as Messiah include the reasons referred to earlier and also other factors that have added to the Jewish situation since the days of the Lord Jesus and the early Church. Problems such as the persecution of Jews in the name of Christ, the Holocaust, the rationalistic approach to the

Scriptures (Reform Judaism), the history of Messianic failures and a general lack of interest in spiritual things have left much of the Jewish community alienated from the Gospel message. Many Jewish people have lost faith in the God of Israel and have no interest in the teachings of the Scripture. This presents a tremendous challenge for the Christian witness to Jews. Loving the Jewish people and demonstrating the relevancy of the Bible and the power of the Gospel is exactly what is required in order to penetrate beyond these obstacles. This is a period of great opportunity for Jewish evangelism and as Christians become more aware of what is needed to reach and lead Jewish people to Jesus, greater results will occur. In chapter 15, more information concerning Jewish evangelism is provided.

There are two particularly prevalent factors that influence the Jewish view of Jesus today. Many Jewish persons consider the verdict of First Century rabbis to be the final court of appeal and leave off with any further discussion of Jesus. A second source that influences the Jewish refusal of Jesus is the "traitor-complex." Many Jews feel that to become a Christian requires giving up their entire Jewish heritage and history. By becoming a Christian they, in a sense, surrender to the enemy.

Concerning the first problem mentioned here, Jewish polemicist, Samuel Levine says,

> How could we know more about Jesus today, after 1900 years, than the people in his own generation? After all, when it comes to history, the more primary the source the more authoritative it is, and so why accept one whom the Jews rejected? [21]

In general, it was not the Jewish people who rejected Jesus as Messiah but rather it was the Jewish leadership that refused Him. In examining the Book of Acts, it is clear that a large number of the Jewish community believed that Jesus was the Messiah (Acts 2:41; 4:4, 32; 5:14; 6:1, 7; 11:21). The Church was a Jewish movement in its early years and grew and expanded from that basis. It is not correct therefore, to state that the Jewish people rejected Jesus. The facts of that time period deny any such assumption. However, even if it is true that the majority of the Jews did not believe in Jesus, it does not follow that their decision was correct. In Israel's exodus from the Egyptian captivity (1400-1300 BC), there were numerous instances in which the overwhelming majority of the Jewish people rebelled against God's revealed will (Numbers 10-20; Exodus 31-33). The books of the Old Testament that deal with Israel's history relate many instances where the vast majority of the nation was living in rebellion against God and refused the words of the prophets (Joshua through Nehemiah in the Protestant Bible). In no possible way would the majority decision have been the correct one in any of these instances. Again, if one examines the Holocaust and the terrible sins committed against the Jews, did the majority of the German population respond properly? Could this decision have been correct? By all means no! In this same exact sense, it is incorrect to point to the verdict of those living in the same time period as Jesus and then assume that their decision was the right one.

The second factor mentioned here, "the traitor-complex," is stated by Jewish writers David Berger and Michael Wyschogrod. In attempting to discourage Jews away from receiving Jesus, they argue,

> You were born a Jew because your ancestors clung to their faith. Often, they had to give their very lives when misguided Christians forced the choice of baptism or death on them. You were born a Jew because your ancestors had the supreme courage to choose death. Had they chosen baptism, you would not have been born a Jew. Their readiness to make the ultimate sacrifice creates a special obligation for their descendants not to render that sacrifice meaningless. Before abandoning the Judaism of your ancestors, you must make an all-out effort to study it, to know it, to live it.[22]

This appeal is understandable in light of the injustices and wrongs that have been carried out against the Jewish people in the name of Christ and the Church. Nevertheless, it is not true that to become a Christian one abandons his or her Jewishness. The Christian faith is truly Jewish and completes and fulfills the faith of Abraham, Isaac and Jacob. When a Jewish person accepts Jesus as Messiah, it is a coming home, not a forsaking. It must also be pointed out that no genuine Christian would harm or hurt the Jewish people. Christians should be the best friends that the Jewish people have.

These are the basic factors that effect the present-day view of Jesus. There are most certainly other reasons that could be cited that serve as obstacles to the Jewish reception of the Gospel, but these are the primary ones.

Conclusion

The key for a Christian answer to the Jewish community is to recognize the factors that have contributed to the Jewish problem regarding Jesus and then approach the objections and arguments with this awareness. The goal of apologetics is not to "win the fight," but rather to remove obstacles that hinder the Jewish response to Jesus as Messiah. The Jewish tradition must be respected, yet carefully corrected and the unbelief and un-Biblical concepts must be gently but firmly removed.

It is easy for the Christian to be offended by the unkind and in some cases, derogatory remarks made concerning Jesus within Judaism. But the principles of the New Testament compel Christians to love the Jewish people and to reach out to them with the powerful message of Jesus and His love. The Jewish arguments can be refuted and the questions answered, but this must be done with the proper goal in mind—to lead Jewish people to Jesus.

Ø ⅗

ENDNOTES — CHAPTER 3

1. David Baron, *Types, Psalms and Prophecies* (London, England: Morgan and Scott LTD., 1924), p. 331.
2. Joseph Klausner, *Jesus of Nazareth*, translated by Herbert Danby (New York: Macmillan Company, 1925), p. 19.
3. Jakob Jocz, *The Jewish People and Jesus Christ*, (Reprint ed.; Grand Rapids: Baker Book House, 1979), p. 59.
4. *Ibid.*, p. 63.
5. Thomas Walker, *Jewish Views of Jesus* (London, England: George Allen and Unwin LTD., 1931), pp. 21,22.
6. Moses Maimonides, *Guide For the Perplexed. I, Chapter 71.*
7. Samuel Levine, *You Take Jesus, I'll Take God* (Los Angeles: Hamoroh Press, 1980), p. 77.
8. Jacob B. Agus, *The Jewish Quest* (New York: KTAV Publishing House Inc., 1911), p. 239.
9. Louis Goldberg, *Our Jewish Friends* (Neptune, New Jersey: Loizeaux Brothers, 1977), pp. 14,15.
10. Jacob Neusner, *Between Time and Eternity—The Essentials of Judaism* (Encino, Calif: Dickenson Publ. Co., 1975), p. 8.
11. *Ibid.,* p. 53
12. Goldberg, op. cit., p. 16.
13. Trude Weiss-Rosmarin, *Judaism and Christianity—The Differences* (New York: Jonathan David Publishers, 1943), p. 130.
14. Jocz, *op. cit.*, p. 59.
15. Samuel Umen, *Links Between Judaism and Christianity* (New York: Philosophical Library Pub., 1966), p. 43.
16. Dennis Prager and Joseph Telushkin, *The Nine Questions People Ask About Judaism* (New York: Simon and Schuster Inc., 1975), p. 87.
17. David Berger and Michael Wyschogrod, *Jews and Jewish Christianity* (New York: KTAV Publishing House Inc., 1978), p. 20.
18. Jocz, *op. cit.*, p.9.
19. Traditional Judaism does recognize the grace of God and does emphasize His mercy and forgiveness. However, salvation is based in man rather than in God: for further information, see Louis Goldberg, *Our Jewish Friends* (Neptune, New Jersey: Loizeaux Brothers, 1977), pp. 75-03.
20. Jocz, *op. cit.*, p. 11.
21. Levine, *op. cit.*, p. 69.
22. Berger and Wyschogrod, *op. cit.*, p. 68.

CHAPTER 4

Jewish Polemics and Hebrew Messianic Prophecy

Introduction to Hebrew Scripture and Messianic Prophecy

he Christian faith has continuously pointed to fulfilled Old Testament prophecy as proof of the Messianic claims of Jesus. Throughout the Gospels, statements are made regarding the fulfillment of the Old Testament prophecies in His person and ministry (Matthew 5:17; Luke 24:27, 44; John 15:25; Luke 22:37; Luke 4:20-21; Matthew 11:10; Matthew 13:14).

The apostles in the Book of Acts preached Jesus as the Messiah, evidenced by His resurrection and fulfillment of Old Testament prophecy (Acts 3:18; 10:43; 13:29). The entire New Testament endorses this same view regarding the Messianic predictions centering in Jesus (1 Corinthians 15:3, 4; Romans 1:2; 1 Peter 2:5, 6).

The early Church Fathers carry on this prophetic and apologetic appeal, as men such as Justin Martyr (AD 150-165), Irenaeus (AD 130-202), Origen (AD 185-254), Tertullian (AD 160-220) and others preached Jesus as Messiah founded upon His fulfillment of Messianic prophecy. Throughout the history of the Church to the present, the fulfillment of Old Testament prophecies in Jesus is a standard Christian apologetic. Yet the basis of Biblical Messianic prophecies pointing to the Messiah of Israel did not originate with the Christian faith. Jakob Jocz states,

> The method of finding the Messiah predicted in the Old Testament is not a Christian invention. It belongs to the ancient tradition of the Synagogue. The Rabbis held that 'all the prophets prophesied only of the days of the Messiah.'[1]

The search for the Messiah within Judaism has been a long and sorrowful endeavor. Jewish scholar Raphael Patai says concerning this,

> The number of men, who in the course of the long Diaspora history, claimed to be the Messiah is unknown and cannot even be estimated for those who left their traces in historical records can only be a fraction of the many who arose, created a stir, gathered a following and then met a violent end or disappeared.[2]

An example of this is found in the greatest Messianic movement in the Diaspora history which took place under a Sephardi Jew, Shabbatai Zevi (1626-1676). After accumulating a tremendous Jewish following, he was forced to convert to Islam, and abandoned all of his Messianic expectations.

For traditional Judaism, the Scriptures and tradition form the all important key in understanding the coming of the Messiah. Some by reading the Scriptures have set time periods for the date of Messiah's appearance. The great Jewish scholar Maimonides (1135-1204) succumbed to this and dated the Messiah's arrival at 1210 AD. Maimonides died in 1204 at the age of 69, just six years before the date he had set.[3] Even though Judaism has failed to produce the Messiah, the search continues and the Messianic prophecies of the Hebrew Scripture and tradition form the basis upon which the identification of the Messiah rests. The Christian presentation of Jesus as Messiah stresses the primary importance of the Scriptures, and upon this prophetic evidence, the Messianic claims of Jesus find support.

The following is a list of Messianic prophecies that find their fulfillment in Jesus of Nazareth.

1.	*Genesis 3:15	Messiah to be born of the seed of a woman.	Galatians 4:4 Matthew 1:18
2.	Isaiah 7:14	Messiah to be born of a [the] virgin.	Matthew 1:18-25 Luke 1:26-38
3.	*Psalm 2:7 Proverbs 30:4	Messiah to be the Son of God.	Matthew 3:17
4.	*Genesis 22:18	Messiah to be a descendant of Abraham.	Galatians 3:16 Matthew 1:1
5.	Genesis 35:10-12 *Numbers 24:17	Messiah to be a Son of Jacob.	Luke 1:33, 3:23-24
6.	*Genesis 49:10	Messiah to be born of the tribe of Judah.	Luke 3:23-33; Matthew 1:2; Revelation 5:5
7.	*Isaiah 11:1	Messiah to be from the family line of Jesse.	Luke 3:23, 32
8.	*Jeremiah 23:5	Messiah to be of King David's lineage.	Luke 1:32-33; Acts 13:22; Mark 9:10
9.	*Micah 5:2	Messiah to be born in Bethlehem.	Matthew 2:1-6 Luke 2:4-7
10.	*Psalm 72:10 *Isaiah 60:6	Messiah to be presented with gifts at his birth.	Matthew 2:1, 11
11.	Jeremiah 31:15	Messiah to be part of a destruction of children.	Matthew 2:16
12.	Hosea 11:1	Messiah to go into Egypt.	Matthew 2:13-15
13.	*Micah 5:2 *Isaiah 9:6	Messiah to be pre-existent.	Colossians 1:17 John 1:1-4, 8:38
14.	*Psalm 110:1 *Jeremiah 23:5-6	Messiah to be called Lord.	Luke 2: 11 Matthew 22:43-45

15. *Isaiah 7:14*	Messiah to be Immanuel (God with us).	Matthew 1:23
16. **Deuteronomy 18:18*	Messiah to be a prophet.	Matthew 21:11
17. **Psalm 110:1-4*	Messiah to be a priest.	Hebrews 10:10-12
18. *Isaiah 33:22*	Messiah to be a judge.	John 5: 30
19. **Psalm 2:6*	Messiah to be a king.	Matthew 27:37
20. **Isaiah 11:2*	Messiah to have special enduement of the Holy Spirit.	Matthew 3:16-17
21. **Isaiah 42:1-8* **Isaiah 61:1-3*	Messiah to come in righteousness to deliver those in the prison of spiritual darkness.	Luke 4:18 John 8:12
22. **Isaiah 40:3*	Messiah to be preceded by a messenger.	Matthew 3:1-2 Luke 1: 17
23. *Isaiah 9:1*	Messiah's ministry to begin in Galilee.	Matthew 4:12-13, 17
24. **Isaiah 35:5-6*	Messiah to be a miracle worker.	Mark 7:33-35 Matthew 9:35
25. *Psalm 78:2*	Messiah to speak by parables.	Matthew 13:34
26. **Zechariah 9:9*	Messiah to enter Jerusalem on a donkey.	Acts 19:35-37
27. **Isaiah 60:3* **Isaiah 49:6* **Psalm 36:9*	Messiah to be the light to all nations.	Acts 13:47-48
28. **Psalm 118:22*	Messiah to be a stone of stumbling to the Jews.	1 Peter 2:7
29. *Daniel 9:26*	Messiah to be killed "cut off."	John 19:30-33
30. *Psalm 49:1*	Messiah to be betrayed by a friend.	Matthew 10:4
31. **Zechariah 11:12*	Messiah to be sold for 30 pieces of silver.	Matthew 26:15
32. *Psalm 35: 11*	Messiah to be accused by false witnesses.	Matthew 26:59-60
33. *Isaiah 50:6*	Messiah to be smitten and spit upon.	Matthew 26:67
34. **Psalm 22:7-8*	Messiah to be mocked.	Matthew 27:31-43

35. *Psalm 22:16	Messiah's hands and feet to be pierced.	John 20:25 Mark 15:20-25
36. Psalm 69:4	Messiah to be hated without a cause.	John 15:25
37. Psalm 38:11	Messiah's friends to stand afar off.	Luke 23:49
38. Psalm 109:25	Messiah to be insulted and reproached by people shaking their heads at Him.	Matthew 27:39
39. *Psalm 22:17 40 *Psalm 22:18	Messiah to be stared upon.	Luke 23:35
40. *Psalm 22:18	Messiah's garment to be gambled away.	John 19:23-24
41. Psalm 69:21	Messiah to suffer thirst and be given gall and vinegar.	John 19:28-29 Matthew 27:34
42. *Psalm 22:1	Messiah to give a forsaken cry.	Matthew 27:46
43. Psalm 31:15	Messiah to commit His Spirit to God.	Luke 23:46
44. Psalm 34:20	Messiah's bones not broken.	John 19:33
45. *Psalm 22:14	Messiah's heart to be broken.	John 19:34
46. Zechariah 72:10	Messiah's side to be pierced.	John 19:34
47. Isaiah 25:8	Messiah to defeat man's greatest enemy–death.	John 11:25, 8:52 John 10:18
48. Amos 8:9	Messiah's death to be accompanied by darkness.	Matthew 27:45
49. Psalm 16:10	Messiah to rise again from the dead.	Acts 2:31
50. Psalm 68:18 *Psalm 110:1	Messiah to ascend and be seated at the right hand of God.	Acts 2:34-35 Acts 7:56 Hebrews 1:3
51. *Jeremiah 31:31	Messiah to be the establisher of a New Covenant.	Hebrews 8:6-13 Hebrews 9:12-22 Matthew 26:17, 22-29

In addition to these prophecies there is a prophetic passage in the Book of Isaiah (Isaiah 52:14 through Isaiah 53:12), which contains a very strong Messianic appeal to the suffering sin-bearing Servant, fulfilled in the Lord Jesus Christ.

52. *Isaiah 52:14	Messiah's face and bodily form to be marred and bruised.	John 19:1-2 Matthew 26:67-68 Matthew 27:27-30
53. *Isaiah 53:1	Messiah is not believed even though His miracles attest to who He is.	John 12:37-39
54. *Isaiah 53:2	Messiah to grow up in a humble home; no special beauty in him.	Luke 2:12, 40 Matthew 13:55-56
55. *Isaiah 53:3-4	Messiah despised and rejected by his own people.	John 1:11 John 7:46-48
56. *Isaiah 53:5-6	Messiah to bare all men's sins.	John 1:29; 11:49-52; 1 Corinthians 15:3-4
57. *Isaiah 53:7	Messiah to be silent before his accusers.	Matthew 25:59-63 Matthew 27:12-14
58. *Isaiah 53:8	Messiah to die for men's sins and transgressions.	Matthew 27:1-12
59. *Isaiah 53:9	Messiah to be buried with the rich.	Matthew 27:57-60
60. *Isaiah 53:10	Messiah to offer Himself as a sin offering.	Hebrews 2:10
61. *Isaiah 53:11	Messiah to be the justifier of many.	Romans 3:22-26 Ephesians 2:8-9
62. *Isaiah 53:1	Messiah to intercede for transgressors.	Luke 22:34 Hebrews 9:26, 28 1 Peter 3:18
63. *Isaiah 53:12	Messiah to be put to death among transgressors and law breakers (thieves).	Matthew 27:38 Luke 15:27-28

*Messianic application in Rabbinic writings.

With these standard Old Testament prophecies there are also additional prophecies that relate specifically to the time of the Messiah's coming. Malachi 3:1 (along with Zechariah 11:13; Haggai 2:7-9; Psalm 118:26) states that the Messiah must come while the Temple is still in existence. Since the Temple was destroyed in AD, 70 by the Roman leader Titus, the Messiah had to come prior to this event. This puts the Messiah's coming into the time period of Jesus, who lived approximately 40 years before the destruction of the Temple.

Isaiah 11:1 says that the Messianic King will come after the Davidic dynasty has fallen (or been "cut down"). The coming of Jesus occurred about 600 years after the downfall of David's throne.

Genesis 49:10 states, that soon after the arrival of the Messiah (Shiloh), the tribal identity (scepter) will be removed from Judah. After the coming of Christ, the tribe of Judah did lose its distinction and has remained in this condition until the present. This again places the arrival of the Messiah into the period of the life of Christ.

Daniel 9:24-27 deals specifically with the date of the Messiah' arrival. Depending on what starting date is chosen, all good Orthodox scholarship puts the predictive arrival of Messiah into the time period of AD 30-50. Scholar H. Hoehner, who did considerable research regarding this prophecy, dates the predictive arrival of the Messiah as taking place on Nisan 10, in AD 33. This date is the day of the triumphal entry of Jesus into Jerusalem. This is a very solid Messianic prophecy pointing to Jesus of Nazareth as being the predicted Messiah.

There are other prophecies in the Old Testament that have found their completion in Jesus and in the New Testament. Floyd Hamilton states in his book *The Basis of Christian Faith*,

> Canon Lidden is authority for the statement that there are in the Old Testament 332 distinct predictions which were literally fulfilled in Christ.[4]

Judaism's Position

When Judaism is faced with the abundance of Messianic prophecies which have found fulfillment in Jesus, the typical response is to affirm that Christians do not have a proper understanding of these passages of Scripture. Judaism has historically stated that the Christian interpretation and exegesis and the Hebrew Scriptures is fallacious. They affirm that Christians read the passage incorrectly and take it out of its context. Jewish scholar Daniel J. Lasker elaborates on Judaism's historical approach regarding the Christian understanding of the Hebrew Scriptures;

> Even when Jews and Christians agreed on the text, they disagreed on its exegesis. One important point of difference centered on the question whether the text was to be understood literally or figuratively, the Jews usually opting for the former, the Christians for the latter. Another important issue concerned the question whether or not the prophecies of the Hebrew Bible were indeed fulfilled by the advent of Jesus. Disagreements arose also as to the exact meaning of specific terms, e.g., "almah" in Isaiah 7:14 or whole passages, e.g., the identity of the suffering servant in Isaiah 53.[5]

There would be some real questions among Christians regarding the correctness of Mr. Lasker's appraisal of the Christian and Jewish methods of interpreting the Hebrew Scriptures. Nevertheless, this does affirm the general approach that Judaism has taken toward the Christian understanding of the Scriptures. Jewish writer Gerald Sigal in his book *The Jew and the Christian Missionary,* says,

Missionary Christianity starts with the thesis that the Jewish Bible is the revealed Word of God, but that Judaism went astray two thousand years ago. The missionaries claim that Christianity then became the true continuation of the Jewish spiritual past. To support that contention, they cannot attack the Hebrew Bible. Instead, in order to arrive at the theological concepts they desire, missionaries propose their own radically altered constructions of the meaning of biblical verses. These altered constructions bear no relation to any of the beliefs taught by priest and prophet, the authentic teachers in ancient Israel.[6]

He goes on to say,

... the Hebrew Bible is used and misused, by today's Christian missionary movement ...[7]

Throughout the history of Jewish polemics against the Christian faith, Jewish polemicists have appealed to the exegetical argument that Christianity errs in its understanding and interpretation of the Hebrew Scriptures (Old Testament).

Hebrew Prophetic Passages

A full presentation of prophetic passages in the Hebrew Scriptures pointing to Jesus as Messiah is beyond the limits of this thesis. However, eight of the major Messianic predictions will be examined and compared with the Jewish exegesis and application. This will be followed by a list of Jewish and Talmudic references regarding Messianic passages that have found fulfillment in Jesus. In the examination of Jewish objections to these passages, Isaac Troki's work, *Hizzuk Emunah,* and Gerald Sigal's book, *The Jew and the Christian Missionary,* will be used as primary sources. Other Jewish sources such as *The Nizzahon Vetus*, along with authors Samuel Sandmel and Samuel Levine, will also be referred to.

1. *Isaiah 7:14*

"Therefore the Lord himself shall give you a sign; Behold, a [the] virgin shall conceive, and bear a son, and shall call his name Immanuel" (Isaiah 7:14)

Christians have long interpreted this passage as referring to the birth of Christ, based on the New Testament writings, which declare that Jesus was born of a virgin (Matthew 1:18-25; Luke 1:26-35).

The Jewish objections to this verse are fourfold. a) The word translated "virgin" is the Hebrew word "almah" and it is mistranslated. It does not mean "virgin" but rather "young woman." b) The context of the prophecy refers to the time period of King Ahaz, not to Jesus who lived 600 years later. c) Jesus was not given the name Immanuel, as the verse declares. d) This "virgin myth," comes from Greek and Roman legends, not the Hebrew Scriptures.

a) Isaac Troki supports the *first argument*:

> The word "almah" (young woman) used in this verse, does not mean a virgin, as they (Christians) maintain, but signifies merely young woman.[8]

Passages such as Genesis 19:14, Genesis 24:43, Exodus 2:8, do reveal that "almah" can and does refer to a "young woman of marriageable age" and not strictly to "a virgin." On this point, Jewish scholars rest their case. Gerald Sigal continues this theme:

> The Hebrew for virgin is 'bethulah.' The Torah clearly indicates the unequivocal meaning to be 'a virgin,' Leviticus 21:14, Deuteronomy 22:15-19, 23, 28. The word 'bethulah' is used in an explicit legal sense leaving no question as to its meaning. While 'almah' does not define the state of virginity of a woman, 'bethulah,' by contrast, does. One would, therefore, reasonably expect that if Isaiah 7:14 refers specifically to a virgin, the prophet would have used the technical term 'bethulah' so as to leave no doubt as to the significance of his words.[9]

The answer to this assertion is that *both* of these Hebrew words, "almah" and "bethulah" do convey the meaning of "virgin," and the word "almah" is the best word to be used in the context of Isaiah 7:14.

Scholar Franz Delitzsch qualifies these two words:

> 'Bethulah' signifies a maiden living in seclusion in her parents' house and still a long way from matrimony; 'almah' is applied to one fully mature, and approaching the time of her marriage.[10]

Arthur W. Kac gives further information regarding this.

> According to Cyrus H. Gordon, eminent Jewish scholar in Semitics, the commonly held view that 'virgin' is Christian, whereas 'young woman' is Jewish, is not quite true. The fact is that the Septuagint, which is the Jewish translation made in pre-Christian Alexandria, takes 'almah' to mean, 'virgin' here. Accordingly, the New Testament follows the Jewish interpretation of Isaiah 7:14. Little purpose would be served in repeating the learned expositions that Hebraists have already contributed in their attempt to clarify the point at issue. It all boils down to this: the distinctive Hebrew word for virgin is 'bethulah,' whereas 'almah' means a 'young woman,' who may be a virgin, but is not necessarily so. Dr. Gordon cites an excerpt from one of the recently discovered Ugarit texts dating back to around 1400 BC, celebrating the marriage of male and female lunar deities. In this particular text there is a prediction that the lunar goddess will bear a son. In one sentence the bride is called by a word which is the exact etymological counterpart of the Hebrew 'almah'; in another sentence she is called by the etymological counterpart of the Hebrew 'bethulah.' 'Therefore,' Dr. Gordon concluded, 'the New Testament rendering of 'almah' as virgin for Isaiah 7:14 rests on the older Jewish interpretation which in turn is now borne out for precisely this annunciation formula

by a text that is not only pre-Isaianic but is pre-Mosaic in the form that we now have it on a clay tablet.'[11]

There is also evidence that the word "bethulah," does not always definitely and consistently refer to a virgin or a pure, unmarried maiden in the Scriptures. In Joel 1:8, "Lament like a virgin girded with sackcloth for the husband of her youth." Here the word "virgin" is "bethulah," and refers to a married maiden. While it is true that in almost all cases the word "bethulah" does refer to "virgin," this is an example in which it does not.

There are instances in the Hebrew Old Testament where both the words "almah" and "bethulah" are used to designate a virgin. In Genesis 24:15-16:

> "... before he had done speaking, that, behold, Rebekah came out, who was born to Bethuel, son of Milcah, the wife of Nahor, Abraham's brother, with her pitcher upon her shoulder.
>
> "And the damsel was very fair to look upon, a virgin [bethulah], neither had any man known her: ..."

In this passage of Scripture, referring to the same maiden, Rebekah, the word "almah" is used to describe her as a virgin. Genesis 24:43:

> "Behold, I stand by the well of water; and it shall come to pass, that when the virgin [almah] cometh forth to draw water, and I say to her, Give me, I pray thee, a little water of thy pitcher to drink ..."

Other passages such as Exodus 2:7-8; Song of Solomon 1:2-3; 6:8 refer to young maidens, who according to the context, are obviously virgins, and in each passage the word "almah" is used. In its translation of Isaiah 7:14 the Greek Septuagint, which was the official translation of the Hebrew Scriptures into the Greek language, uses the Greek word "parthenos" which means "virgin" in its translation of the Hebrew word "almah." The Septuagint was translated by Jewish scribes in Alexandria, Egypt, in about 250 BC. It was translated for Greek-speaking Jews who wanted the Hebrew Scriptures in their Greek language. The New Testament followed the Septuagint rendering of Isaiah 7:14, as seen in Matthew 1:18, 24-25, Luke 1:26-35. From this perspective, it would seem reasonable that the Hebrew translators who lived within 350-400 years from the date of the writing of Isaiah would probably have a better understanding of the proper translation of "almah" in Isaiah 7:14, than scholars much farther removed in date. This in itself is a very solid evidence indeed for the translation of the Hebrew word "almah," to "virgin" in Isaiah 7:14. The fact is that both "almah" and "bethulah" can be rendered as virgin, "bethulah" more explicitly referring to a young girl who was a virgin, and "almah" referring to a young maiden of marriageable age or a young woman who is a virgin.

Another strong fact supporting the translation of "almah" as "virgin" is found with the framework of the verse itself. Verse eleven states that this child-bearing event will be a "sign" to Israel.

Christian writer Dr. Harry Rimmer makes a significant point:

> What sign would there be to a nation in a young woman becoming a mother? That has happened so many millions of times in past history no man can estimate their number. This birth is to be one that will startle the world and give evidence of the fulfillment of a covenant of God![12]

In other words, if this event is to be a sign, the only obvious conclusion is that the word "virgin" is the proper translation rather than "young woman." The conception of a virgin is a clearly miraculous sign of God's intervention, whereas a normal human-related birth does not fulfill this criteria.

Verse 14 states that the child is going to be an amazing child and His name will demonstrate this. He is to be called "Immanuel," which means "God with us." When people see the fulfillment of the sign (the birth), they will recognize the uniqueness of this child. Again, the virgin birth supplies the needed evidence to recognize the special quality of the child.

The question may still be asked why Isaiah used the word "almah" instead of "bethulah" in his description of the young maiden in this verse.

Arthur Kac affirms,

> Had the word 'almah' in the Immanuel prophecy been used to indicate a virgin, the only sense it would have conveyed was that the future Messianic King would be born out of wedlock, in which case it would have made no sense either to Isaiah or to King Ahaz or to anyone else of that day. In the context of the historical situation during which the Immanuel prophecy was given, this prophecy brought to Isaiah and his contemporaries a two-fold message. To the Davidic King Ahaz it announced God's judgment upon the Davidic dynasty whose failings were climaxed by the reckless decision of Ahaz to invite Assyrian intervention. The long-range effect of this policy was the destruction of the Judean state and the downfall of the Davidic dynasty. The after-effects of these tragic events upon the Messianic hope would be well-nigh disastrous.
>
> The Messianic Prince, who in accordance with God's promises must spring from David's house, will come at a time when the Davidic line will have been all but extinguished. The disinherited Messianic Prince will not be born in the proud royal city of Jerusalem, but, as indicated by Micah, in Bethlehem, the insignificant birthplace of Jesse, the father of David. Messiah's mother will not be as she would have been, had the Davidic dynasty remained faithful, a queen residing in the royal palace; instead, she will be just an 'almah,' some unnamed and insignificant maiden. This

essentially was the meaning which the word 'almah' conveyed to Isaiah and his contemporaries, the only meaning which at that particular time could have made sense.[13]

In summary, both words "bethulah" and "almah" are used to designate and describe a "virgin, a young woman of marriageable age." The case for the translation of "almah" in Isaiah 7:14 as "virgin," far outweighs the evidence for the translation "young woman." Therefore, the verse should read, "Behold a [the] *virgin* shall conceive and bear a son ...".

b)   The *second* Jewish argument regarding this verse is verbalized by Isaac Troki:

> Moreover, the sense of the chapter, [Isaiah 7], is altogether adverse to the exposition of the Christians. It refers to Ahaz, king of Judah who had been in great trouble and consternation on account of the confederacy which the monarchs (Pekah, king of Israel and Rezin, king of Syria) had determined on, namely to besiege and subjugate Jerusalem ... Had it been the purpose of inspired writ to announce, as the Christians maintain, the advent of Jesus, how could Ahaz be concerned in a sign that could only be realized many centuries after his death or how could any promise cheer his heart that was to be fulfilled in his own days?[14]

He goes on to state that the prophetic totality of chapter seven refers to the time period of Ahaz, not to any far reaching date, such as that of the birth of Jesus Christ. Upon a close examination of the verses in this chapter, this conclusion by Isaac Troki proves to be incorrect. This passage looks beyond the immediate time of Ahaz and gives predictive elements that most assuredly point to the Messiah King, the ruler of the house of David.

In verses 15-20, Isaiah does not give a certain date of the coming of "Immanuel." He does, however, give a clue that the destruction of the whole Davidic kingdom will take place before this child comes into the prophetic picture.

*"For before the child shall know to refuse the evil and choose the good, the land that thou abhorrest shall be **forsaken of both her kings**."*[15]

Isaiah continues by saying:

*"The Lord shall bring upon **thee** and upon thy people [Judah] and upon thy fathers house, days that have not come, from the day that Ephraim departed from Judah, even the king of Assyria."*[16]

Isaiah says that both Israel and Judah along with the Davidic dynasty will be destroyed before this "Immanuel" comes (Isaiah 7:17, 20). Israel was led into Assyrian captivity in 721 BC and Judah into Babylonian captivity in 586 BC Both of these dates then draw close to the coming and birth of the Lord Jesus Christ in 6-3 BC and most definitely away from the time period of Ahaz.

Scholar Dr. H.A. Ironside states regarding the time period and arrival of this child in Isaiah 7:14:

> *Thus before this child should come on the scene and grow up to years of maturity, not only the king of Israel but also the king of Judah would have ceased to reign, and the land would be left without a son of David sitting on the throne of Judah, or any representative sitting on the throne of Israel.*[17]

The main contention from Jewish polemicists that the setting of Isaiah could not be so far removed from the life of Ahaz, is that the sign was to assure Ahaz. In other words, the prophecy was directed to Ahaz and if it was to be fulfilled many years later, why would Isaiah give such a meaningless sign as this to Ahaz. Once again, a close examination of the passage reveals that this sign *was not* directed to Ahaz, but instead to the whole house of David (to Judah, those of David's throne). Isaiah asks Ahaz to ask for a sign (verse eleven), but Ahaz refuses (verse 12). Isaiah then says, "Hear ye now, O House of David" (verse 13). He is now *not* directing the prophecy to Ahaz who refused to ask for the sign. Instead, Isaiah directs the sign to all those who are of the *house of David*. From this verse he goes on to describe the One who will come, the Son of David, the Messiah-King, and states that His coming will be *after* the land of Israel, north and south, have been devastated and the Davidic Dynasty is ended. George Adam Smith, and Dr. Franz Delitzsch, cover this material in a very exhaustive manner and for further study these men should be read as sources regarding the prophetic details in Isaiah 7.[18]

c) The ***third*** argument directed against the Christian exegesis of Isaiah 7:14, is based on the name "Immanuel" and the name given to the Lord Jesus. Jewish polemicist, Gerald Sigal, gives the main assertion of this argument:

> Strangely enough, nowhere in the New Testament do we find that Jesus is called Immanuel ... All the evidence thus indicates that Immanuel was a different individual from Jesus since Jesus was never called Immanuel.[19]

Samuel Levine states regarding this:

> How does that make sense—they were to call his name Immanuel and instead they called him Jesus![20]

Isaac Troki also appeals to this argument:

> From this it appears that Emanuel was a different individual from Jesus, for Jesus was in no instance called Emanuel—as to the name Jesus, it was given him by mere chance; there were many other Jews named Jesus.[21]

David Baron, a Jewish-Christian writer and missionary gives a very clear explanation and defense against the argument listed above:

> An objection has been raised why Jesus, if Isaiah 7:14 was really a prophecy of Him, was not called Immanuel. But the truth is

Immanuel was to be no more the actual name of Messiah than Wonderful, Prince of Peace, Desire of all nations, Shiloh or Jehovah Tsidkenu. All Messiah's titles were intended only as descriptions of His character, but His real name was, in the providence of God, concealed till his advent to prevent imposture on the part of pretenders, who would easily have taken advantage of it. But Jesus is really the best commentary on Immanuel, Immanuel—"God with us"; Jesus-Saviour. But how could God come near us except as Saviour? and how could Jesus be Saviour except as Immanuel, in Whom dwelt the fulness of the Godhead bodily? [22]

David Baron appeals to Isaiah 9:6, Jeremiah 23:6 and Haggai 2:7. In these Messianic passages (which are even recognized by many within Judaism as referring to the Messiah), the names given to the Messiah are obviously not to be his actual names, but rather are descriptions of his character and nature. Throughout the Hebrew Old Testament, names are ascribed to people and places that are not intended as personal names, but rather are given to reflect a God-given purpose or quality (Numbers 3:30; 2 Kings 3:11; Isaiah 20:22; 1 Samuel 1:4). This name of "Immanuel" is exactly that. It describes the fact that the Messiah would be "God with us." In Matthew 1:23, the Apostle Matthew asserts that *Jesus is this one* called "Immanuel," and this settles all doubt as to whom this name belongs as far as the New Testament is concerned.

d) *The last part* of this Jewish polemic against the New Testament interpretation of Isaiah 7:14 is verbalized by Samuel Levine. He argues:

Lastly, it is important to recognize the origin of the theory of the virgin birth. The Jews never had such a theory so why did the Christians invent it? The answer is clear: the Jews rejected Jesus and the Gentiles were about to do the same. So Paul did two things— he issued an order saying that to be a Christian one no longer had to obey the 613 commandments of the Torah that the Jews had to observe, and in addition, Paul introduced a few pagan myths into the new Christian religion so that it would appeal to the pagan Gentiles.[23]

Mr. Levine goes on to describe the pagan mythology of a god called Attis that was worshipped in Western Asia. He was said to be born of a virgin and was later killed and resurrected. He then adds:

The Christian religion is so similar to the worship of Attis that it cannot be considered a coincidence. Rather, Paul introduced the pagan ideas of his neighborhood into the worship of Jesus and made a new religion which would be perfectly acceptable to the Gentile pagans in his neighborhood. Paul simply switched Jesus for Attis, put a little Judaism in, and then called it Christianity.[24]

Gerald Sigal relates regarding this,

Many pagan religions believed in the idea of the impregnation of virgins by gods resulting in the birth of heroes. Stories of divine humans sired by the gods are told in several myths and legends ... The Pagan concept of divine birth, a concept alien to Judaism, entered Christianity through the Greco-Roman mythology then current in the western world.[25]

Both of these authors describe the link between Christian holidays such as Christmas and Easter and pagan holidays that were a part of the Roman Empire. They attempt to demonstrate that the Roman Catholic Church taught and endorsed beliefs of pagan origin. As can be readily seen, this argument moves away from any exegetical interpretation of Isaiah 7:14 and instead, ascribes to a totally different line of attack. This is a very old argument and is by no means original with Jewish polemics.

In response to these statements, it must be recognized that there is evidence that the Roman Catholic Church has adopted different pagan concepts into some of their forms of worship and belief. The dates of Christian "holidays" can be traced back to different forms of the Roman cultural background.[26] This requires a defense of the Roman Catholic Church and a study of just this subject matter in itself. But what took place in the association between Greek/Roman culture and the Roman Catholic Church did not begin to transpire until AD 350-400, and it has absolutely nothing to do with the New Testament and the teaching of the Lord's apostles.[27] It is incorrect to point to these matters that involve the historical background of the Roman Catholic Church and then go back 250-300 years earlier to the apostolic Church and assume that the foundations of the Christian faith took part in some type of pagan culture. This argument will be examined in detail in chapter 12.

Summary

When each of these objections espoused by Jewish polemicists are examined, it is evident that the Christian understanding of Isaiah 7:14 most certainly stands on a solid foundation. This verse is a definite prophetic passage which points to the virgin birth of the Lord Jesus Christ.

2. *Psalm 2:7*

"I will declare the decree: the Lord hath said unto me, Thou art my Son; this day have I begotten thee" (Psalm 2:7).

In the New Testament the apostles appeal to this verse as a prophetic passage of which Jesus, the Son of God, is the fulfillment (Acts 13:33; Matthew 3:17).

The basis of the Jewish argument concerning this verse is that the passage refers to King David, not Jesus. Isaac Troki states,

The reference to that psalm [Psalm 2] is objectionable, since the royal psalmist spoke here of his own person. It was against himself that the Gentiles raged, and carried on their warfare, when he had commenced his government.[28]

To respond to this, it should be stated that this entire Psalm has long been interpreted by Jewish sources to be Messianic in nature. E.W. Hengstenberg relates,

It is an undoubted fact, and unanimously admitted even by the recent opposers of its reference to Him [Jesus], that the Psalm [Psalm 2] was universally regarded by the ancient Jews as foretelling the Messiah. ... In the older Jewish writings also, there is a variety of passages in which the Messianic interpretation is given to this Psalm. Even Kimchi and Jarchi [Jewish polemicists] confess, that it was the prevailing one among their forefathers; and the later very honestly gives his reason for departing from it, when he says he preferred to explain it of David for the refutation of the heretics, that is, in order to destroy the force of the arguments drawn from it by the Christians.[29]

The Midrash Tehillim on Psalm 2 states,

And when the hour comes, says the Holy One, blessed be He, to them: I must create Him [Messiah] *a new creation, as even it is said, 'this day have I begotten you.'*[30]

From the *Yalkut:*

If I shall find the son of the King, I shall lay hold on him and crucify him and kill him with a cruel death. But the Holy Spirit mocks at him, 'He that sits in the heavens laughs, Jehovah has them in derision' [Psalm 2:4].[31]

Even the great Jewish scholar of the Middle Ages, Moses Maimonides, affirms:

The prophets and saints have longed for the days of the Messiah, and great has been their desire towards him, for there will be with him the gathering together of the righteous and the administration of goodness and wisdom and royal righteousness, with the abundance of his uprightness and the spread of his wisdom, and his approach to God, as it is said: Jehovah said unto me, 'Thou art my son, today have I begotten thee.'[32]

It is quite obvious that not only do Christians recognize that the passage is Messianic but so do the Jewish sources themselves. Other passages from Midrashic and Jewish writings could be cited; however, the point is well established. Mr. Levine even recognizes this and explains the Jewish interpretation of Psalm 2 as Messianic in this light:

According to those Jewish commentaries which say that Psalm 2 refers to the Messiah specifically, and not to David, that still leaves the issue open, for we still cannot know who the Messiah is. To say that Psalm 2 points necessarily and exclusively to Jesus, because he called himself the son of God is really absurd.[33]

There is no doubt here that the case for Psalm 2, as referring to David has no merit. The ancient Jewish sources themselves recognized and considered this Psalm as Messianic. It points to and finds fulfillment in the Messiah, the King of Israel.

Summary

The fact that this Psalm is Messianic, and that it states that the Messiah will be the Son of God, is clear. As a reaction against the Messianic claims of Christ, it has found a different interpretation within Judaism. The New Testament asserts that Jesus is the Son of God and the fulfillment of Psalm 2.

"God hath fulfilled the same unto us their children, in that he hath raised up Jesus again; as it is also written in the second Psalm, 'Thou art my Son, this day have I begotten thee'" (Acts 13:33).

Only Jesus meets and fulfills the criteria of this Psalm. He not only claims to be the Son of God, but He proves and verifies His claim by His resurrection from the dead:

"Jesus Christ ... declared to be the Son of God with power, according to the spirit of holiness, by the resurrection from the dead" (Romans 1:3-4).

3. Daniel 9:24-27

"Seventy weeks [490 years] *are determined upon thy people and upon thy holy city, to finish the transgression, and to make an end of sins, to make reconciliation for iniquity, and to bring in everlasting righteousness, and to seal up the vision and prophecy and to anoint the most Holy.*

Know therefore and understand, that from the going forth of the commandment to restore and to build Jerusalem unto the Messiah the Prince shall be seven weeks [49 years], *and threescore and two weeks* [434 years] *the street shall be built again and the wall even in troublous times.*

And after threescore and two weeks shall Messiah be cut off, but not for himself: and the people of the prince that shall come shall destroy the city and the sanctuary; and the end thereof shall be with a flood, and unto the end of the war desolations are determined.

And he shall confirm the covenant with many for one week: and in the midst of the week he shall cause the sacrifice and the oblation to cease, and for the overspreading of abominations he shall make it desolate, even until the consummation and that determined shall be poured upon the desolate (Daniel 9:24-27).

This is an extremely important prophecy relating to the time period of the Messiah. The key for this presentation, is to establish that the passage is Messianic in nature and that it points to the time period of Jesus Christ.

The basic exegesis of this passage is as follows: The word "weeks" (Daniel 9:24) comes from the Hebrew term "shavuim," which is rendered as "heptads" meaning "units or periods of seven."[34] It is describing a period of 70 units of sevens or 490 years. There is not much argumentation from Hebrew scholars that this is the correct understanding of the term "weeks" and even the Jewish polemicists referred to here agree on this point.

The prophecy asserts that this 490 year time span will begin with the commandment to restore and rebuild Jerusalem (verse 25). There are four dates that have been suggested as the starting date referred to in this prophecy: The decree of Cyrus—539 BC; The decree of Darius—519 BC; The decree of Artaxerxes to Ezra—457 BC; The decree of Artaxerxes to Nehemiah—444 BC. There is at this point some question as to which decree Daniel is referring as the "commandment to restore and build Jerusalem" (Daniel 9:25a). The two most feasible dates are the decrees given by Artaxerxes in 457 BC and 444 BC. The decree of Artaxerxes to Ezra in 457 BC is found in Ezra 7:11-16 and the decree to Nehemiah in 444 BC is found in Nehemiah 2:1-8. When these passages are examined, the decree to restore and to build Jerusalem is the decree given to Nehemiah in 444 BC. All of the other decrees refer to the rebuilding only of the Temple. None give permission to repair or restore the city except the Nehemiah decree in 444 BC. Therefore, the proper starting date should be 444 BC.

The Christian exegesis of Daniel 9:24-27 is as follows. The 490 years are divided up into three time segments: seven weeks (49 years), 72 weeks (434 years), and one week (seven years).

The first seven weeks in verse 25 refer to the time span used to restore the city. Biblical scholar Adam Clarke states,

> To the first period of seven weeks the restoration and repair of Jerusalem are referred, and so long were Ezra and Nehemiah employed in restoring the sacred constitutions and civil establishments of the Jews, for this work lasted forty-nine years after the commission was given by Artaxerxes.[35]

This time segment of seven weeks (49 years) is then added to 62 weeks (434 years) and together refer to the time period of the coming of the Messiah. Daniel 9:25 says,

> *"Know therefore and understand, that from the going forth of the commandment to restore and build Jerusalem unto the Messiah the Prince shall be seven weeks, and threescore and two weeks ..."*

By subtracting the 483 years (49 + 434) from the starting date set in this prophecy (444 BC), the time period of Jesus (AD 30) becomes the obvious prophetic intention.

Harold Hoehner, a Biblical scholar, provides a logical step by step approach demonstrating the means by which this is done.

Multiplying the sixty-nine weeks by seven years for each week by 360 days [length of a prophetic year] gives a total of 173,880 days. The difference between 444 BC [the decree to Nehemiah] and AD 33 [Jesus entry into Jerusalem] then is 476 solar years. By multiplying 476 by 365.24219879 or by 365 days, 5 hours, 48 minutes, 45.975 seconds, one comes to 173,855 days, 6 hours, 52 minutes, 44 seconds or 173,855 days. This leaves only 25 days to be accounted for between 444 BC and AD 33. By adding the 25 days to March 5 (of 444 BC), one comes to March 30 (of AD 33) which was Nisan 10 in AD 33. This is the triumphal entry of Jesus into Jerusalem.[36]

There are, of course, some Biblical scholars who feel that the decree to Ezra in 457 BC is the date Daniel refers to here and not the decree to Nehemiah of 444 BC used by Mr. Hoehner for this calculation. This understanding also has solid Scriptural support and could possibly be correct. Different calendars may also be used along with different culmination points, but both of the starting dates conclusively point to the the time period of Christ. Whether Christ's birth, baptism, or crucifixion is used as the finalization event, both dates lead to the time of Christ without manipulating or forcing any of the factors.

The last week referred to in this passage (verse 27), has some variation in interpretation. However, a particularly astute opinion is that verbalized by Adam Clarke; he says,

From the coming of our Lord, the third period is to be dated, viz. 'He shall confirm the covenant with many for one week,' that is seven years. This confirmation of the covenant must take in the ministry of John the Baptist with that of our Lord, comprehending the term of seven years during the whole of which he might be well said to confirm or ratify the new covenant with mankind. Our Lord says, 'The law was until John,' but from his first public preaching the Kingdom of God, or Gospel dispensation commenced. These seven years, added to the four hundred and eighty-three, complete the four hundred and ninety years, or seventy prophetic weeks, so that the whole of this prophecy, from the times and corresponding events has been fulfilled to the very letter.[37]

Daniel 9:27 states,

"And he [the Messiah] *shall confirm the covenant with many for one week: and in the midst of the week he shall cause the sacrifice and the oblation to cease, and for the overspreading of abominations he shall make it desolate, even until the consummation, and that determined shall be poured upon the desolate."*

Clarke affirms concerning this:

"... in the latter three years and a half in which he exercised himself in the public ministry, he caused by the sacrifice of himself, all other sacrifices and oblations to cease, which were instituted to signify his.[38]

On this basis, all three time segments were fulfilled in the coming of Jesus the Messiah.

Verse 24 speaks of six events that will transpire in the coming of the Messiah. Clarke expounds on each of these events and their significance in the life of Jesus of Nazareth.

In verse 24, there are six events mentioned which should be the consequences of the incarnation of our Lord.

I. To finish (*lechalle*; to restrain) the transgression which was effected by the preaching of the Gospel and pouring out of the Holy Ghost among men.

II. To make an end of sins; rather (*ulehathem chataoth* to make an end of sin offerings; which our Lord did when he offered his spotless soul and body on the cross once for all.

III. To make reconciliation; (*ulechapper*), to make an atonement or expiation) for iniquity; which he did by the once offering up of himself.

IV. To bring in everlasting righteousness (*tsedek olamin*); that is, the righteousness or the righteous One of the ages; that person who had been the object of the faith of mankind, and the subject of the predictions of the prophets through all the ages of the world.

V. To seal up (*velachtom*; to finish or to complete) the vision and the prophecy; that is, to put an end to the necessity of any further revelations by completing the canon of Scriptures, and fulfilling the prophecies which related to his person, sacrifice, and the glory that should follow.

VI. And to anoint the most Holy (*kodesh, kodashim*—the Holy of Holies; *mashiach* "to anoint" which comes from *mashiach*, the Messiah, "the anointed one"); signifies in general to consecrate or appoint to some special office. Here it means the consecration or appointment of our blessed Lord, the Holy One of Israel, to be the Prophet, Priest, and King of mankind.[39]

The total of these six events were uniquely completed by the Messiah, the Lord Jesus.

"to finish the transgression," Matthew 11:13, Jeremiah 31:31-34.
"to make an end of sin [sin offerings]," Hebrews 9:25-28.
"to make reconciliation for iniquity," 2 Corinthians 5:17-21.
"to bring in everlasting righteousness," Romans 10:1-13; 3:20-28
"to seal up the vision and the prophecy," Galatians 1:6-9
"to anoint the most Holy," Hebrews 9:1-15.

There are two factors found in verses 26 and 27 that also confirm that this passage has found fulfillment in Jesus. Daniel 9:26a states,

> *"And after threescore and two weeks shall Messiah be cut off* [an idiom for His death], *but not for himself."*

Daniel asserts that the coming of the Messiah will be climaxed by His death. The New Testament teaches this very truth regarding the life and ministry of Jesus. Christ's death on the cross was the redemptive price paid for the sin and iniquity of mankind. His death (and resurrection) was the climax of His life just as Daniel predicted in Daniel 9:24-27 (Matthew 26:28; Acts 2:22-39; 1 Peter 2:20-25).

In verse 26, the second factor which indicates that this prophecy is referring to Jesus is stated.

> *"... and the people of the prince that shall come shall destroy the city and the sanctuary; and the end thereof shall be with a flood, and unto the end of the war desolations are determined"* (Daniel 9:26b).

This verse refers to another prince whose people will destroy Jerusalem and the Temple. The fulfillment to this occurred in AD 70 when the Roman ruler, Titus sent his armies into Jerusalem and destroyed the city and the Temple, a little less than forty years after Christ's death and resurrection.

In summary, the prophecy in Daniel 9:24-27, finds the following fulfillments in Jesus of Nazareth.

1) The prophecy establishes that the time period from "the going forth of the commandment to restore and to build Jerusalem unto the Messiah the Prince, shall be seven weeks and threescore and two weeks (total 69 weeks or 483 years)." From either of the two possible starting dates of 457 BC or 444 BC, this points directly into the time period of Christ.

2) The six events characterizing this Messianic event in Daniel 9:25 were all uniquely fulfilled in Jesus of Nazareth.

3) The death of the Messiah which is one of the key elements mentioned in Daniel 9:24-27, corresponds to the centrality of the death on the cross in Christ's life (Matthew 16:21; Luke 9:51).

4) The destruction of Jerusalem and the Temple is said to be an event related to the coming of the Messiah, and in AD 70, the city and the Temple were destroyed.

On these factors, the Christian exegesis of this passage rests. None other than the Messiah, Jesus of Nazareth is the intended fulfillment.

Of all the arguments raised by Jewish polemicists examined in this thesis, this is by far the most unconvincing. The Jewish argument concerning Daniel 9:24-27 and its reference to Jesus has three main parts. a) The passage is not Messianic in nature. b) The time period is divided into two segments. The first seven weeks culminate in a prince and the second threescore and two weeks refer to the time in which the city remains built. c) Jesus does not fit the description of the prince referred to.

a) The Jewish sources maintain that this passage is not Messianic in nature. Gerald Sigal argues,

> The original Hebrew text does not read, 'the Messiah the Prince,' but having no article, it is to be rendered 'a mashiach' (an anointed one, messiah) a prince, i.e. Cyrus (Isaiah 45:1, 13; Ezra 1:1-2). The word 'mashiach' is nowhere used in Scripture as a proper name, but as a title of authority of a King or high priest. Therefore, a correct rendering of the original Hebrew should be: 'an anointed one, a prince.'[40]

In response to this argument, it should be said that the correct reading of the text is just as is stated here. It does not read "the Messiah" but rather "an anointed one, a prince." However, this does nothing in proving that the passage is not Messianic in nature. Dr. E.W. Hengstenberg affirms regarding this,

> An Anointed One, in accordance with the whole character of the prophecy, is intentionally left indefinite, with no article to indicate his identity with the Messiah, a Prince. It was the less necessary to point out this identity, because the careful and unprejudiced reader might easily determine this from the context. As an Anointed One of itself implied a king of Israel; as this designation was made still clearer by its being opposed to a Prince who was to come; so the reader would necessarily be led at once to think of the Messiah, because prophecy knows no other king of Israel after the exile.[41]

The entire context of the passage along with all that is related in verses 24-27 affirm that this Anointed One is a king of Israel. The 70 weeks are applied to "thy people" (Israel) and "thy holy city" (Jerusalem). To say that this Prince is someone not related to Israel violates the entire context of the prophecy. Since no one in Israel held the position of king after the exile, this clearly points to the King-Messiah, the only one who could possibly culminate all that is said to occur here. The Jewish objection that this passage is not Messianic has no basis. The reference to the Jewish King-Messiah is the obvious intention of the writer.

b) A second position espoused by Jewish polemicists asserts that there is a division in the outline of time (49 years and 434 years) in Daniel 9:24-27. In verse 25, the first seven weeks are set over against the last 62 weeks. Concerning this Sigal says,

> The 'atnah' is the approximate equivalent of the semicolon in the modern system of punctuation. It thus has the effect of separating the seven weeks from the sixty-two weeks ... By treating the sixty-two weeks as a distinct period, this verse, in the original Hebrew, shows that the sixty-two weeks mentioned in verse 25 are correctly

separated from the seven weeks by the 'atnah.' Hence, two anointed ones are spoken of in this chapter, one who comes after seven weeks, and the other after a further period of sixty-two weeks.[42]

There is no point in arguing over Hebrew punctuation at this point. It is true that verse 25 has two separate periods of time (seven weeks and 62 weeks). Nevertheless, verse 26 ascribes the totality of this time to the "cutting off" of the Messiah. Any attempt to validate a theory of two Messiahs proves worthless when verse 25 is examined in the light of verse 26. Dr. Hengstenberg gives a very satisfactory explanation for the two time segments in verse 25.

> Accordingly he, [Daniel] here designates the whole distance 'from the going forth of the word, until the Anointed One,'... by a two-fold determination of time. Sixty-nine weeks in all, shall elapse. Seven until the completed restoration of the city, sixty-two from that time until the Anointed One, the Prince. ... according to our interpretation of the words, 'from the going forth,' etc., the two-fold division of the time period is already contained in these words, and therefore, a two-fold determination of the time must naturally be expected.[43]

The theory of two Messiahs forces and twists the evident intent of this passage. Isaac Troki recognizes this and interprets this passage differently. He says,

> The seventy weeks are evidently a given period of time elapsing from the destruction of the first to the destruction of the second temple.[44]

Rather than seeing two Messiahs as Mr. Sigal does, Isaac Troki interprets the seven weeks as first referring to an "anointed one," whom he names as Cyrus (Isaiah 45:6) and the 62 weeks as the time in which the Temple remains built. With its destruction in AD 70 by Titus, the 62 weeks or 434 years finds an approximate fulfillment. He says,

> If the Christians take an impartial view of this chapter of Daniel, they cannot possibly imagine that it alludes to Jesus, who suffered on the cross nearly a half a century before the exile of Israel.[45]

The problem with both of these two Jewish interpretations is that neither one of them consider or even refer to verse 26. This verse states what the 62-week period refers to.

"And after threescore and two weeks shall Messiah be cut off ... "
(Daniel 9:26a)

The culmination of these time periods is found in the coming of the Messiah. This is the express reading of the context of Daniel 9:24-27. Throughout this passage the theme that is repeated is the "Messiah."

c) The last argument advanced against this passage and its reference to Jesus is given by Gerald Sigal:

The words 'v'ayn lo' (9:26) are incorrectly translated by the King James Version as "but not for himself." It should be translated as 'he has nothing' or 'he shall have nothing.' How can Christian missionaries apply this verse and Isaiah 53:12 where 'God's servant receives a portion with the great' to Jesus? ... One who has nothing' (Daniel 9:26) does not receive 'a portion with the great' (Isaiah 53:12), does not rise bodily to heaven (Acts 1:9) and does not sit at the 'right hand of the throne of the Majesty' (Hebrews 8:1). It is precisely with his death that Jesus was allegedly able to attain his rewards. Therefore, 'he shall have nothing' cannot refer to the Jesus of Christian missionary theology.[46]

It has long been acknowledged by scholars that a literal reading of verse 26 should be "shall have nothing" instead of "not for himself." On this there is solid agreement between both the Christian and Jewish scholarship. However, to go from this more literal reading of verse 26 to establishing that Jesus therefore could not possibly be the "anointed one" who is "cut off" or "killed," is a very weak argument. W.E. Biederwolf says regarding this,

Verse 26 'and shall have nothing'—all Hebrew scholars agree with this reading. The meaning is that He shall then possess nothing; He shall not possess the Kingdom or be the acknowledged King.[47]

In other words, the passage simply refers to the fact that the Messiah will not establish His earthly kingship and authority at the time referred to in Daniel 9:24-27. His earthly rulership will not be recognized and He "shall have nothing." This is exactly what transpired with the fulfillment of this prophecy in the Messiah, the Lord Jesus Christ (Luke 17:20-37; Acts 1:6-9). The Second Coming of Jesus is what will bring the realization of His earthly kingship and rule (Matthew 24:27-31; 2 Thessalonians 1:5-12; Revelation 20). Isaiah 53:12 refers to the spiritual realm and the exaltation of the Messiah through His accomplishments on the cross, and in no way contradicts the phrase "he shall have nothing" (Daniel 9:24-27).

Summary
When each of the objections raised by Jewish polemicists are examined, the shallowness of their position becomes clear. No effort is made to examine the passage carefully because the obvious conclusion is that the time period of 490 years leads to the Messiah who was "cut off" (killed).[48] Who else but Jesus fits into the time period and then satisfies all six descriptive events spoken of in verse 24? If this prophecy referred to someone else, he would have had to live in the same time period as Christ, been killed and then satisfied all that verse 24 attributes to him.

"... to finish the transgression, and to make an end of sins [sin offerings], *and to make reconciliation for iniquity, and to bring in everlasting righteousness, and to seal up the vision and prophecy, and to anoint the most Holy"* (Daniel 9:24).

In other words, he would have to be identical to Jesus, in his time period, in his death, and in his accomplishments. Yet there is none but Jesus of Nazareth who can possibly be referred to by Daniel. History is silent of any other claimant during AD 30-50 who could possibly have met the criteria mentioned in Daniel 9:24-27. As history has clearly demonstrated, this prophecy points to *none other* than the carpenter from Galilee—The Lord Jesus Christ.

4. *Micah 5:2*

"But thou, Bethlehem Ephratah, though thou be little among the thousands of Judah, yet out of thee shall he come forth unto me that is to be a ruler in Israel; whose goings forth have been from old, from everlasting" (Micah 5:2) [1st verse in the Hebrew text.]

This prophecy asserts that the birthplace of the Messiah will be the town of Bethlehem in Judaea and that this ruler (Messiah) will be of Divine origin. A.W. Kac states,

> Bethlehem was not large enough to have a thousand families or family clans, a truly insignificant town. The mention of Bethlehem was not merely to indicate Messiah's birthplace, but his lowly human background as contrasted with his exalted Divine origin, 'whose goings forth are from old, from everlasting.' The future Ruler in Israel, whose goings forth reach back into eternity is to spring from insignificant Bethlehem, like his ancestor King David.[49]

The New Testament affirms concerning the birthplace of Jesus,

"Now when Jesus was born in Bethlehem of Judaea in the days of Herod ... " (Matthew 2:1).

"And Joseph also went up from Galilee, out of the city of Nazareth, into Judaea, unto the city of David, which is called Bethlehem; (because he was of the house and lineage of David)" And she brought forth her firstborn son, ... " (Luke 2:4, 7a).

The New Testament also states that Jesus was indeed Divine and that His "coming forth" was from everlasting.

"In the beginning was the Word, and the Word was with God and the Word was God ...

"And the Word became flesh and dwelt among us ... " (John 1:1, 14).

"Jesus said unto them, Verily, verily, I say unto you Before Abraham was, I am " (John 8:58).

The objections to this prophecy as it relates to Jesus are fourfold:

a) The passage does not describe the birthplace of the Messiah.

b) The New Testament is unclear regarding the birthplace of Jesus.

c) Even if Jesus was born in Bethlehem, so were thousands of others who were not the Messiah.

d) This passage does not indicate the Divine origin of the Messiah.

a) Samuel Levine describes the *first argument*;

> The verse seems to refer explicitly to David, since it parallels 1 Samuel 17:12. Now David was the son of that Ephrathite of Bethlehem ...
>
> This verse is saying, You, David, though you ought to be the little among the thousands of Judah, yet from you will come ... Messiah. It does not say that the Messiah will be born in Bethlehem, but that the father (the distant father) will be born in Bethlehem.[50]

Isaac Troki relates the same explanation of Micah 5:2. He says,

> But the sense of the verse is this: Thou, Bethlehem, although one of the minor localities among the cities of Judah, from thee a man shall come forth, (i.e., trace his descent back to thee), who shall be ruler in Israel, and that same man will be a descendant of David who came from Bethlehem.[51]

The problem with this interpretation is that Micah 5:2 is not describing the 'birthplace of the father of the Messiah,' but rather is referring to the birthplace of the Anointed One Himself as the obvious and clear reading of the context indicates. If this passage were referring to the family line of the Messiah, the reading would state that. But no mention is made that would indicate that the Messiah "traces His descent back" to Bethlehem. An examination of ancient rabbinic exegesis of Micah 5:2 reveals that Bethlehem was considered the birthplace of the Messiah.[52] Therefore, to interpret this passage in this manner is not only faulty exegesis, is is not even proper Jewish exegesis.

b) The *second Jewish argument* is stated by Gerald Sigal;

> Christian missionaries allege that Jesus fulfilled Micah's prophecy in that he was supposedly born in Bethlehem. Matthew's claim that Jesus was born in Bethlehem (Matthew 2:1) is supported by Luke 2:4-7. Mark is silent on the matter. John relates that some people believed that the Messiah will come from Bethlehem (John 7:42), but does not take advantage of the opportunity to demonstrate that Micah's prophecy was fulfilled by claiming that Jesus was actually born there. This is highly unusual and leads one to suspect that John did not agree with the assertion that Jesus was a Bethlehemite. He lets stand the opposing assertion that Jesus was really of Galilean origin, (John 1:46, 7:41). Except for the references found in Matthew and Luke, all indications, even in the writings of these two evangelists, point to the fact that Jesus was from Nazareth.[53]

Both of the Gospels, which deal with the birth narrative of Jesus (Matthew and Luke), state that Jesus was born in Bethlehem (Matthew 2:1; Luke 2:4-7). The Gospel of Mark does not state that Jesus was born in Bethlehem for the simple reason that it does not deal at all with the subject of Christ's birth; therefore, there is no reason to mention Bethlehem as Jesus' place of birth. The Gospel of John also does not mention Bethlehem as Jesus' birthplace because, like the Gospel of Mark, it does not deal with any discussion regarding the birth of Christ.

According to Mr. Sigal, the Gospel of John implies that Jesus was born in Nazareth. Here, Mr. Sigal reveals a lack of knowledge concerning the New Testament. All four Gospels and the Book of Acts affirm that Jesus grew up and lived the major portion of His life in Nazareth. The Gospel of Luke states that Joseph and Mary left their hometown of Nazareth and traveled to Bethlehem for a special Roman taxing and while they were there, Jesus was born (Luke 2:1-7). Luke 2:39 states that some time after Jesus' birth, they returned to Nazareth. Matthew also relates that Jesus was born in Bethlehem and later returned to Nazareth (Matthew 2:1, 19-23). This is indeed an interesting but extremely invalid argument.

c) Regarding the *third* objection to this prophecy, Isaac Troki argues;

> The birth of Jesus in Bethlehem does not entitle him to the claim of being the Messiah, for hundreds and thousands of children were born at Bethlehem, and that causality did not constitute them Messiahs. [54]

Obviously, by simply being born in Bethlehem, one does not thereby demonstrate to be the Messiah. However, this prophecy does eliminate every other city in the world and states that from the small town of Bethlehem, the Messiah will be brought forth. Jesus' birth in this location is then extremely important, for had he not been born in Bethlehem, He would have had no right to make any further Messianic claims.

d) The *last argument* against the Christian exegesis of Micah 5:2 deals with the last sentence in the verse; "whose goings forth have been from old, from everlasting." The Christian understanding of this phrase is that it refers to the Divine, eternal pre-existence of the Messiah. The word "everlasting," "olam," in Hebrew, is used numerous times in the Old Testament. It translates as "everlasting" or "age-lasting" and is applied to the everlasting, eternal nature of God (Genesis 21:33; Deuteronomy 33:27; Psalm 41:13 90:2; Jeremiah 10:10).[55] It is also used to describe God's covenant with Abraham (Genesis 17:13,19), God's righteousness and salvation (Psalm 119:144; Isaiah 45:17), and everlasting life (Daniel 12:2).

The Jewish rejection of the Christian interpretation of the last phrase of Micah 5:2 is given by Isaac Troki;

> ... nor can it be asserted that an allusion to the Eternal God is implied by 'and his coming forth is from ancient time from the days of old.' We cannot possibly attribute to the Infinite Being a coming forth ...[56]

The answer to this is that the term "coming forth" is the appropriate term to be used in describing the Divine qualities of the Messiah and His pre-existence. J.B. Payne states,

Attempts have been made to minimize either the uncreatedness or the eternity of the One whose coming forth is here anticipated: the RSV, for example, reads that from Bethlehem 'shall come forth for me one whose origin (not, coming forth) is from ancient days' (not, from everlasting). Yet the nouns 'mosa' and 'mosa a' 'coming/going forth' are never found at any other point in Scripture to signify 'origin' and their verbal root, in the line just preceding, clearly maintains the standard meaning of 'come forth.'[57]

The Christian doctrine of the Messiah agrees with this term "coming forth." There was never a moment or time when Messiah was not God. He has always existed. This term "coming forth" in no way means "origin," but rather it refers to the ongoing existence of the Messiah. Just as:

the sun goes forth—Genesis 19:23 ... morning by morning, but it does not begin to be each morning, so with the Messiah.[58]

There is good evidence that the Talmudic view of this portion of Scripture interpreted it to indicate the pre-existence of the Messiah. Raphael Patai, a professor at the Hebrew University of Jerusalem stated,

... the concept of the pre-existence of the Messiah accords with the general Talmudic view which holds that 'The Holy One, blessed be He' prepares the remedy before the wound.[59]

He continues by saying,

The names by which Messiah is called are revealing. In the *First Book of Enoch*, he is called 'Head of Days' ... alluding to his pre-existence ... He is also called the 'Son of Man,' others applied to him the name of God, a daring procedure in the Jewish context.[60]

The Targum Jonathan, a Second Century Aramaic paraphrase of the Scriptures interprets Micah 5:2 by saying:

And you, O Bethlehem Ephrath, you who were still too small to be numbered among the thousands of the house of Judah, from you shall come forth before Me the Messiah, to exercise dominion over Israel, he whose name was mentioned from before, from the days of creation.[61]

From these citations it is evident that the Christian exegesis of Micah 5:2 is not far removed from the Talmudic and traditional interpretation. However, the New Testament goes beyond the traditional Jewish view of the Messiah and teaches the deity of Christ. When this is coupled with Old Testament passages such as Isaiah 9:6, Proverbs 30:4 and Jeremiah 23:5-6, the case for the Messiah's deity and pre-existence is strengthened.

Summary
When Micah 5:2 is examined in the light of the New Testament account of Christ's birth, another prophetic element finds its fulfillment in Jesus of Nazareth. Jewish polemicists offer no evidence to refute this prophetic fulfillment primarily because there is none. They just simply try to pass this prophecy off as unimportant. Yet the fact remains, Jesus met the requirements of this Messianic prediction.

5. Isaiah 9:6-7

"For unto us a child is born, unto us a son is given: and the government shall be upon his shoulder; and his name shall be called, Wonderful, Counsellor, the mighty God, the everlasting Father, the Prince of Peace. Of the increase of his government and peace there shall be no end, upon the throne of David, and upon his kingdom, to order it, and to establish it with judgment and with justice from henceforth even for ever. The zeal of the Lord of hosts will perform this" (Isaiah 9:6-7).

These verses have long been held by Christians to refer to the Divine Sonship and deity of the Lord Jesus Christ. There is no other figure in all of Jewish history, outside of Jesus, who has claimed the type of characteristics outlined in this verse, and then fulfilled each detail in such a remarkable manner. Jesus was born of a Jewish woman (Luke 2:1-7), son of man (Luke 9:22), yet also the Son of God (Mark 1:1). He is the Governor over all, with total power and authority in heaven and earth (Matthew 28:18; Philippians 2:11). His government will increase until all enemies are subdued to Him (1 Corinthians 15:24-28). He is wonderful in His birth (Matthew 1:23-25), His miracles (Mark 2:5-12), His preaching (Matthew 7:28-29), His death (John 19:30-37; Matthew 26:28), His resurrection and ascension (Matthew 28:5, 6; Acts 1:1-9). He is the Counsellor, expounding and revealing God's laws and purposes as none other (Hebrews 1:1-3). He is the mighty God, God manifest in the flesh (John 1:1-6, 14). He is the Father of eternity, the origin and cause of all existence (Colossians 1:13-19). He is the Author and Giver of peace (John 14:27). In His Second Coming, He will establish the visible realization of an everlasting government (Revelation 21, Isaiah 11). He will judge and rule the world in justice and judgment (John 5:24-29; 2 Thessalonians 1:8-10; Psalm 72). The Lord Jesus Christ is truly the fulfillment of this prophecy.

Jewish polemicists, of course, reject the Christian exegesis of Isaiah 9:6. There are basically three arguments. a) This prophecy refers to King Hezekiah. b) The "birth" referred to is in the past tense, referring to someone already born. c) Jesus did not fulfill any of these characteristics.

a) Isaac Troki states regarding the first argument,

> Those passages refer to Hezekiah, King of Judah, during whose government Israel experienced, through a divine intercession, a signal deliverance from Sennacherib, king of Assyria ...[62]

Gerald Sigal continues to expound on the manner in which Hezekiah fulfilled this prophecy;

> Hezekiah is called 'a wonderful counselor' because this name is a sign which foretells God's design for him ...
> Hezekiah is called 'the mighty God' because this name is a sign which foretells God's defense of Jerusalem through the miraculous sudden mass death of Sennacherib's army ...
> Hezekiah is called 'the everlasting Father' because this name is a sign which foretells that God will add years to his life ...
> Hezekiah is called 'ruler of peace' because this name is a sign which foretells that God would be merciful to him ...
> Hezekiah's Kingdom is declared to be forever, for through his efforts to cleanse the Temple ritual of idolatry, even though apostasy followed under his son Menasseh, the Davidic dynasty was once more confirmed as the only true kingly rule that God would accept over his people 'from henceforth and forever.' The greatness of Hezekiah lies in his setting the stage for Israel's future.[63]

The problem with the application of Isaiah 9:6,7 to Hezekiah is that in none of these descriptive instances would any mere man suffice. These verses clearly call for a Divine Being, based upon the nature of the names attributed to this "son." Hebrew scholar Delitzsch states regarding the name "mighty God" ("El Gibbor") in Isaiah 9:6:

> There is no reason why we should take 'El' in this name of the Messiah, in any other sense than in 'Immanu-El,' not to mention the fact that 'El' in Isaiah is always a name of God, and that the prophet was ever strongly conscious of the antithesis between 'El' and 'Adam,' as chapter 31:3 clearly shows. And finally 'El Gibbor' was a traditional name of God, which occurs as early as Deuteronomy 10:17, Jeremiah 32: 18, Nehemiah 9:32, Psalm 24:8. The name 'gibbor' is used here as an adjective like 'shaddai' in 'El Shaddai.' The Messiah, then, is here designated 'mighty God'...[64]

Dr. E.W. Hengstenberg maintains:

> But had Isaiah called an earthy King, God, or given him Divine predicates, he would have acted in direct opposition to his duty to defend the rights of God from every encroachment, and have rendered himself unworthy of the dignity of a prophet."[65]

Elsewhere he says,

> How could he [Isaiah] ascribe Divine attributes to Hezekiah, a feeble mortal, and thus insult the majesty of God, whose servant he was ... Even among the idolatrous heathen, the practice of ascribing divine names and predicates to kings did not originate till a later

and corrupt age; and in what light this practice was viewed by the Jews, let the example of Josephus show, who regards the death of Agrippa as a punishment for not disapproving the conduct of the people, who cried out to him as god.[66]

Throughout the Book of Isaiah, the prophet carefully distinguishes between men and Jehovah and never does he confuse this situation. To suppose then that a man-king Hezekiah, is the person referred to in this passage goes against the entire tenor of the Hebrew Scriptures and the Jewish faith.

There is no question that in the Old Testament, human names with a reference to God were designated to men such as Elihu—"My God is He," Eliab—"God is my Father," Eliada—"God knows," Elisha—"God is salvation," Eliezer—"God is my help."[67] However, these are *not* names that ascribe a quality of God and then refer directly to God as the name "El Gibbor" does (Deuteronomy 10:17; Jeremiah 32:18). Isaiah 9:6 refers to the "son" as "the mighty God, the everlasting [or eternal] Father," depicting Divine qualities that can be applied only to God Himself.

Another problem with the application of Isaiah 9:6-7 to King Hezekiah is found in the fact that his government by no means lasted forever. After Hezekiah's death, his son Menasseh took the throne and was a evil, ungodly king. Less than 100 years later, the Babylonian captivity of Judah took place and the kingly throne of Judah ended. The king referred to in Isaiah 9:7 is stated to have a Kingdom that will "have no end." To suppose that in any possible way, Hezekiah met this criteria of Isaiah 9:7 is to exegete Scripture fallaciously.

b) Isaac Troki gives the second Jewish argument:

... that this great miracle, namely, the fall of the camp of Sennacherib, referred to in the verses under consideration, was occasioned from the regard entertained by the Almighty for 'the virtue of the child born unto us' and which at the time of the prophecy, was already 'given unto us.'[68]

Mr. Troki asserts that since verse six states "a son *is* given" (present tense), any future application to Christ must be rejected. Dr. Hengstenberg says concerning this,

The Prophet beholds the great Redeemer as already born. If anyone chooses to infer from thence that the subject of the prophecy must, at that time, have been actually born, he must also, on account of the preterities, in the first and following verses assume, what no interpreter has done, that the predicted prosperity had already been conferred upon the Israelites.[69]

In other words, if the prophet meant that this "son" was already born, then the results of his kingship mentioned in verse seven would also have transpired. But history clearly reveals that this has not taken place. The tense of the first part of the passage is not to be considered as a vital factor in the exegesis of these verses, for the remaining sentences clearly demonstrate that the events are future. Hengstenberg continues and says,

> The distance of time does not thereby come into consideration, because it is neither known, nor regarded by the Prophets, who hold all events of futurity combined in one picture.[70]

c) The last argument discussed here is stated by three of the four Jewish sources referred to in this chapter. *The Nizzahon Vetus* states,

> For unto us a child is born, Isaiah 9:5 [9:6 in English KJV]. The heretics [Christians] say that this is the one descended from that defiling union. Answer them: It says of his son that he will establish the throne of David and his Kingdom. If so, then their words contradict each other, for they say that the verse, 'the scepter shall not depart form Judah ... until Shiloh comes' Genesis 49:10, means that the power and kingdom shall not pass from Judah until Shiloh, i.e., the messenger, or Jesus, shall come, and then the kingdom and power shall pass from the house of Judah. Furthermore, they interpret the verse, 'With the coming of the Most High ... the Messiah shall be cut off'—Daniel 9:24,26 in a similar way. Thus, he does not establish the kingdom of Judah but rather destroys it. [71]

The objection raised by *The Nizzahon Vetus* put in simple terms asks this question. Christians interpret Genesis 49:10 to mean that the tribal authority and judicial system (scepter and lawgiver) of Judah will cease immediately following the coming of the Messiah (Shiloh). If after Jesus came, Judah lost its power and kingdom, how can Jesus establish the throne of David mentioned in Isaiah 9:7? Secondly, how can the Messiah establish David's kingly throne if he is cut off (dies) as stated in Daniel 9:24-27? It seems like a circular contradiction. The answer to this can only be found in the two appearances of Jesus the Messiah.

In His first coming the death spoken of in Daniel 9:24-27 took place (Mark 15:33-39). However, the Messiah rose from the dead and later ascended back to Heaven (Acts 1:1-11). His promise was that He would one day return to establish His visible earthly Kingdom (Matthew 25:31-33). When this great event takes place, the unending Kingdom, spoken of in Isaiah 9:7 will be established. Genesis 49:10 in no way confuses this prophetic situation. Soon after Messiah's first coming, the tribal identity and authority of Judah did cease and it has remained that way unto the present. Genesis 49:10 also states that the Messiah must be able to identify Himself as a descendant of the tribe of Judah. With the destruction of the Temple in AD 70 and subsequent loss of genealogical records, the Messiah had to come prior to AD 70. This again points to the first coming of the Messiah, the Lord Jesus, who was born of the tribe of Judah (Luke 3:23, 33) and lived in Israel between 6-3 BC and AD 30.

Genesis 49:10 and Daniel 9:24-27 have therefore been fulfilled in Messiah's first coming. When Messiah returns, the throne of David mentioned in Isaiah 9:7 will once again be established and He (Messiah) will rule and reign as King, fulfilling the great Messianic promises of the Hebrew Scriptures. There is nothing contradictory in any of these prophecies.

Any other attempt to fulfill these prophecies would result in a contradiction. In contrast, the manner by which Jesus fulfills these prophecies does *no* such thing. This demonstrates the remarkable manner in which the Messiahship of Jesus finds perfect agreement with the truthfulness of the Hebrew Scriptures, for in no other way could all of these prophecies be fulfilled.

Isaac Troki presents another form of this argument;

> To give Jesus the above appellations is altogether incompatible with his own history. How can he claim the names 'Wonderful' and 'Counsellor,' when it is remembered that one of his disciples frustrated his designs, and betrayed him to his enemies? How can he merit the title, 'Powerful' or 'Omnipotent God,' who suffered an unnatural death? How can he be the 'Father of Eternity,' who did not attain even half of the natural period of human life? How can he be distinguished as the 'Prince of Peace'? whereas, no peace existed in his days: and as he himself asserted, by saying 'I am not come to bring peace into the earth, but the sword.'[72]

Isaac Troki's argument reveals a misunderstanding regarding the life and ministry of Jesus. Judas did not frustrate the "designs" of Jesus. According to the New Testament, Jesus predicted his death on numerous occasions prior to the actual event (Luke 12:50; John 10:17; 19:11; Matthew 26:24; 20:17-19), and He stedfastly asserted that His death on the cross was the stated purpose of His coming (Matthew 20:28). Though Judas did plot against Jesus, Jesus was well aware ahead of time of the purposes and motives of Judas' heart, and by no means were any of Messiah's designs frustrated by him (Matthew 26:21-25; John 13:2-30). Jesus stated that "no man taketh it [my life] from me, but I lay it down of myself"—John 10:18. The New Testament therefore, presents the foreknowledge and determinate plan of God for the crucifixion of the Messiah, and in no way did any failure of this express purpose take place (Hebrews 9:26-28; 1 Peter 1:18-20; Revelation 13:8). This argument, therefore, has no basis.

Troki continues by asking, how can God die? To answer this it must be stated that since Troki has rejected the incarnation and the authority and teaching of Jesus the Messiah, probably no answer will suffice him. Nevertheless, the evidence of the New Testament demands the acknowledgment that Jesus was indeed God, and that the only method of saving men was for God to pay the penalty for the sin of mankind Himself, which occurred with Christ's death on the cross (Romans 6:23; 1 Peter 1:18-20; Colossians 2:9-15). The New Testament teaches that "God was in Christ, reconciling the world unto Himself" (2 Corinthians 5:18).

A further problem with Troki's objection is found in a faulty understanding of what death is. Death is not cessation of being, but rather only separation of the spirit from the body (Ecclesiastes 8:8; 12:7; Amos 2:27; John 19:30; Luke 23:46). Jesus, who was God, never ceased from being God in death, but rather experienced a separation between His body and spirit. Jesus who was truly God and truly man, experienced the common enemy of all men, death, demonstrating that He was a man and in addition He defeated death by rising from the dead, demonstrating that He was God. You either accept this evidence or reject it; however, you reject it at your own peril.

Lastly Troki asks, how can Jesus be the Prince of Peace when he brought no peace? Again, the New Testament gives the answer. Jesus did indeed bring peace, but His peace is first the peace *with* God (Romans 5:1), and secondly, the peace *of* God (John 14:27; 2 Timothy 1:7; Philippians 4:6, 7).

Through Christ's work on the cross, the sin which kept man separated from God (Isaiah 59:1; Romans 3:23), was removed and forgiven (Acts 3:19; Isaiah 1:18). When men receive Jesus as Lord and Savior the result is peace with God (Romans 5:1). Secondly, freedom from fear and anxiety are the by-products of the Christian life. As the believer grows in his walk of discipleship with Christ, the peace *of* God is included in his life. And thirdly, the New Testament teaches that at the Second Coming of the Messiah a political realm of peace will be established through His earthly rulership. This of course is the type of peace that Troki is referring to in his objection, but Isaiah's reference to "the Prince of Peace" goes beyond this singular aspect of peace and refers to the Author and Giver of peace which includes all three of the areas discussed here. Jesus is truly the Author and Giver of peace that Isaiah 9:6 points to.

Lastly, Samuel Levine states,

> Jesus was never called these names; i.e., Wonderful, Prince of Peace, etc., even in the New Testament, and yet the verse says explicitly that the person referred to will be called those names ...

> Furthermore, 9:6 says that there will be no end of the government of this person, and no end to the peace. How can this refer to Jesus? His government never began, let alone had any peace. Thus, this verse refers to someone, but surely not to Jesus, who was not called the Father, nor any of those names, nor had a government, nor peace. [73]

Mr. Levine's argument attempts to make this verse mean that this "king" had to be explicitly called the names referred to in Isaiah 9:6. But this is not the intent of the author. The five names given are not to be the literal names of this "king." As noted in the section dealing with the Isaiah 7:14 prophecy, the names "Shiloh," "Desire of Nations," "Jehovah Tsidkenu," "Immanuel," were never intended as Messiah's real name, but rather as titles describing His character. Dr. Delitzsch states concerning this,

> The name Jesus is the combination of all the Old Testament titles used to designate the Coming One according to His nature and His works. The names contained in ch. 7:14 and 9:6 are not thereby suppressed; but they have continued from the time of Mary downwards, in the mouths of all believers. There is not one of these names under which worship and homage have been paid to Him.[74]

Nowhere in all of the Hebrew Scriptures is the personal name of the Messiah given. Instead God has given descriptive titles throughout the Old Testament that describe and reveal the character and nature of the Messiah. If Messiah's name were given, it would be easy for imposters to assume his name. For example Bar Kochba, in AD 132 assumed the name "son of a star" (Numbers 24:17) and claimed to be the Messiah. The result was a terrible destruction and elimination of much of the Jewish community. This most certainly was not God's desire; therefore the personal name of the Messiah was withheld from the Scriptures for this purpose.

Lastly, the argument concerning the establishment of the government referred to in Isaiah 9:7 is easily answered. This objection has been examined earlier in this thesis, and it will be dealt with in greater detail in chapter 7. A short presentation here will suffice.

Jesus asserted early in His ministry, that His first coming was to take Him to the cross, and that a return to the earth later would be the culmination of His Messianic mission (Luke 19:27, 1:32, Matthew 25:31, 26:64). In the Second Coming of Christ the realization and full establishment of His government will be openly revealed. The literal establishment of the Messianic-ruled government is the clear teaching of both the Old Testament and New Testament and none other than Jesus the Messiah will be the Ruler. This is the New Testament answer to Mr. Levine's argument.

Summary

It is interesting to note the differences in the Jewish polemicists discussed here. Isaac Troki and Gerald Sigal state that the names listed in Isaiah 9:6 are only figurative in nature, yet Samuel Levine demands a literal application. Troki and Sigal make no personal link between Hezekiah and the unending government of verse seven, yet Levine establishes that it must be a part of this person's credentials. Dr. Hengstenberg states concerning these Jewish polemicists and their lack of harmony,

These are unanimous only in their opposition to the Messianic interpretation: in all other respects the greatest difference prevails among them.[75]

The fulfillment of this prophecy in the person of Jesus of Nazareth is the clearest and most natural exegesis of this passage. With an understanding of the New Testament teaching concerning the First and Second Comings of the Messiah the Lord Jesus, none other than Jesus fits the characteristics described in Isaiah 9:6-7.

6. Psalm 22

This Psalm contains prophetic passages which, according to the New Testament, have found fulfillment in Jesus.

"My God, my God, why hast thou forsaken me? why art thou so far from helping me" (Psalm 22:1).

"All they that see me laugh me to scorn: they shoot out the lip, they shake the head, saying,

He trusted on the Lord that he would deliver him: let him deliver him, seeing he delighted in him" (Psalm 22:7-8).

"I am poured out like water, and all my bones are out of joint: my heart is like wax; it is melted in the midst of my bowels.

My strength is dried up like a potsherd; and my tongue cleaveth to my jaws; and thou hast brought me into the dust of death.

For dogs have compassed me: the assembly of the wicked have inclosed me: they pierced my hands and my feet.

I may tell all my bones: they look and stare upon me.

They part my garments among them, and cast lots upon my vesture" (Psalm 22:14-18).

This Psalm speaks of a number of details that depict the events of the crucifixion of Christ.

"And about the ninth hour Jesus cried with a loud voice, saying, Eli, Eli, lama sabachthani? that is to say, My God, my God, why hast thou forsaken me?" (Matthew 27:46).

Jesus uttered the very words of Psalm 22:1 during His suffering upon the cross. In the Gospel of Matthew, the following is stated:

"Likewise also the chief priests mocking him, with the scribes and elders, said,

He saved others; himself he cannot save. If he be the King of Israel, let him now come down from the cross, and we will believe him.

He trusted in God; let him deliver him now, if he will have him: for he said, I am the Son of God" (Matthew 27:41-43).

This passage identifies Psalm 22:7-8 with the words of the chief priests who looked upon Jesus as He died on the cross and uttered these words. In the Gospel of John there are additional similarities listed between Psalm 22 and the crucifixion of Jesus.

"After this, Jesus knowing that all things were now accomplished, that the scripture might be fulfilled, saith, I thirst" (John 19:28).

And he bearing his cross went forth into a place called the place of a skull, which is called in the Hebrew Golgotha: Where they crucified him, and two other with him, on either side one, and Jesus in the midst" (John 19:17-18).

"They said therefore among themselves, Let us not rend it, but cast lots for it, whose it shall be: that the scripture might be fulfilled, which saith, They parted my raiment among them, and for my vesture they did cast lots ..." (John 19:4).

"But one of the soldiers with a spear pierced his side, and forthwith came there out blood and water" (John 19:34).

It is evident from these passages that the sufferings described in Psalm 22:14-18 closely resemble the Crucifixion events. A short summary of these verses reveal the fulfillment of Psalm 22 in Jesus' death and resurrection.

1) A forsaken cry—Psalm 22:1; Matthew 27:46
2) Mocking by the crowd—Psalm 22:7, 8; Matthew 27:41-43
3) Heart is broken—Psalm 22:14; John 19:34
4) Intense suffering—Psalm 22:15; John 19:17,18
5) Suffering thirst—Psalm 22:15; John 19:28
6) Piercing of hands and feet—Psalm 22:16; Luke 23:33, John 20:25
7) Stared upon—Psalm 22:17, Luke 23:35
8) Garments parted and lots cast—Psalm 22:18; John 19:24
9) Suffering ends in victory—Psalm 22:22-25, Matthew 28:1-6, Hebrews 2:12-13

Based on this evidence, the New Testament writers affirm, that the fulfillment of Psalm 22 is found in the crucifixion sufferings of Jesus.

The Jewish objection to this Psalm as referring to Jesus rests on four primary arguments. a) The early Christian writers of the Gospels altered the details of Christ's crucifixion in order to fit and coordinate them to this Scriptural reference. b) Psalm 22 ends with joy; if Jesus fulfills all of this Psalm, why did His life end in death and defeat. c) The Christian translation of Psalm 22:16 is incorrect. d) This Psalm refers to King David only.

a) The first argument is disputed by Gerald Sigal;

The early Christians, in interpreting and expanding the accounts of Jesus' death, sought confirmation of their claims in the Hebrew Scriptures. Believing Jesus to be the fulfillment of biblical prophecy, they proclaimed him the Messiah. The Scriptures were searched for evidence which could be used to demonstrate the truth of their hypothesis. This was especially true for the crucifixion since such a fate does not easily fit into the prophetic visions of a triumphant Messiah. That is why early Christianity inserted many scriptural references within the account of the crucifixion, altering at the same time some of the details of the crucifixion story in order to coordinate them with these scriptural references. In this effort, Psalm 22 played a crucial role. Indeed, it has become, for Christianity, a major proof-text for the most important elements of the several crucifixion accounts.[76]

Samuel Levine also states this argument:

> ... the only reason we would think that this Psalm refers to Jesus is because the history described in the New Testament seems to indicate a similarity between the crucifixion story and this Psalm. But the problem remains, how can we know if the history of the New Testament is true? Or was it doctored to make Jesus look the subject of Psalm 22.[77]

When other explanations regarding a prophecy are inadequate, this argument becomes the last objection that can be raised. However, the New Testament documents are very reliable historical records. There will be an examination of the New Testament later in chapter 13; but, a short examination will be appropriate here. The Gospels appeal to firsthand, eyewitness testimony concerning events that occurred in the full vision of the public. These records (the Gospels) were written within 20-50 years of the death of Christ and were written when eyewitness knowledge of the events was still available. If the recorded facts of the Gospel were not truthful, the corrective element of these eyewitnesses would have served to remove any nonfactual material. Moreover, history is silent concerning negative testimony regarding the Gospel related events of Christ's life. When historical testing methods are applied to the New Testament records, they prove to be extremely reliable and trustworthy documents. This entire Jewish argument lacks any evidence to substantiate these claims, and in fact, it is proven to be a totally fallacious position.

b)   The second argument is stated by Mr. Sigal:

> Psalm 22 cannot be made to apply to the life of Jesus. Jesus' life ends on a note of disappointment, whereas the psalmist, after describing metaphorically his trials and tribulations, concludes on a positive note. No such positive position is taken by Jesus. If he fulfilled literally all of Psalm 22, instead of selective parts, the logical order of development would be for depression to give way to joy as he realizes God's purpose has been attained through his act of sacrificial death.[78]

It is amazing that this objection could possibly be raised concerning this Psalm as it applies to Jesus. Any examination of the Gospels should reveal that the crucifixion of Christ comes to a great climax of joy in the resurrection and ascension. What greater climax could possibly take place after the death of the Messiah than a resurrection where death is defeated and the claims of the Messiah verified?

After Jesus' resurrection the following event took place:

"And he led them out as far as to Bethany, and he lifted up his hands, and blessed them.

And it came to pass, while he blessed them, he was parted from them, and carried up into heaven.

And they worshipped him, and returned to Jerusalem with great joy:

And were continually in the temple, praising and blessing God. Amen" (Luke 24:50-53).

If the life of Christ does not end on a positive note, it must be asked what more could occur to make it that way? The resurrection of Christ stands as the cornerstone of the joy and triumph of the Christian faith.

c) The third argument concerning this Psalm is given again by Sigal;

Christian missionary apologists assert that the Hebrew word (*ka-ari*) in verse 17 (16 in some versions) should be translated as 'pierce.' They render this verse as: 'They pierced my hands and my feet.' This follows the Septuagint version, used by the early Christians, whose error is repeated by the Vulgate and Syriac. This rendering contains two fallacies. First, assuming that the root of this Hebrew word is *krh* 'to dig,' then the function of the 'aleph' in the word *ka-ari* is inexplicable since it is not part of the root. *Karah* consists only of the Hebrew letters *kaph*, *resh*, and *he*, whereas the word in the Hebrew text, *ka-ari*, consists of *kaph-aleph*, *resh*, and *yod*. Second, the verb *krh*, 'to dig,' does not have the meaning 'to pierce.' *Karah* generally refers to the digging of the soil, and is never applied in the Scriptures to the piercing of the flesh.[79]

He continues by saying,

The correct interpretation of the verse must be based on the elliptical style of this particular psalm. The text should read, in effect: 'Like a lion (they are gnawing at) my hands and my feet.'[80]

Hebrew scholar Franz Delitzsch states regarding the argument against the Septuagint rendering of Psalm 22:16,

... nothing of any weight can be urged against the rendering of the LXX (Septuagint).

... the fulfillment in the nailing of the hands and (at least, the binding fast) of the feet of the Crucified One to the cross is clear.[81]

In *The Pulpit Commentary* the following is stated concerning the Christian translation which is based on the Septuagint:

There are no sufficient critical grounds for relinquishing this interpretation. It has the support of the Septuagint, the Syriac, the Arabic and the Vulgate version. Whether the true reading be *kaaru* or *kaari*, the sense will be the same.[82]

Dr. Gill explains how this Jewish reading of Psalm 22:16 came into being;

> In this clause there is a various reading; in some copies in the margin it is, 'as a lion my hands and my feet,' but in the text, 'they have dug or pierced my hands and my feet,' both are joined together in the Targum, 'biting as a lion my hands and my feet.' The modern Jews are for retaining the marginal reading, though without any good sense, and are therefore sometimes charged with the wilful and malicious corruption of the text, but without sufficient proof, since the different reading in some copies might be originally occasioned by the similarity of the letters ׳ and ׀ and therefore finding it in their copies or margins ... have chosen that which best serves their purpose.[83]

The answer to this argument is simple. The Christian translation follows the Septuagint, Arabic, Syriac, Ethiopic, Greek, and Latin Vulgate versions which read: "they dug [pierced] my hands and my feet." It is true that there are manuscript readings which cause eminent critics to divide into one of the two positions regarding the proper rendering of this verse. The whole difference lies between the ׳ (yod) and ׀ (vaw) which can be easily confused, with the former reading "like a lion" and the latter "they pierced." What probably happened is that through the period of textual transmission, a scribe changed the text by mistake and inserted a "yod" and failed to attach a vertical line so that it would become a "vaw." It therefore reads "like a lion," instead of "they pierced." The Septuagint, which was established before the time of Jesus, retains the correct textual phrase—"they pierced," and the Gospel of John (AD 90-95) confirms this rendering. Along with this, by examining the passage, the reading which most easily adapts into the context is the reading "they pierced." "Like a lion my hands and my feet" does not fit into a context that is expressing agony and suffering but "they pierced my hands and my feet" seems to fit with much greater ease. There is evidence from a 13th Century Rabbinical work entitled *Yalkut Shimoni,* that the reading of Psalm 22:16 as "pierced" was accepted by certain rabbis. Rabbi Nehemiah states,

> They pierced my hands and my feet in the presence of Ahasuerus [when commenting on Psalm 22].[84]

The support for the rendering of the passage in the New Testament manner is sufficiently strong to validate the Christian translation "they pierced my hands and my feet."

d) The fourth argument asserts that King David is the one referred to here. Jewish sources by no means are in agreement on this understanding of Psalm 22. Some Jewish polemicists apply this Psalm to the Jewish people; others to Hezekiah or another subject in Jewish history, and still others to the Messiah himself. The *Nizzahon Vetus* relates the argument that King David is the subject of Psalm 22.

The true explanation of the psalm is that David said it of his war with the Amalekites after they invaded and despoiled both the land of the Philistines and that of Judah and left Ziklag in flames.[85] The problem with this explanation is that King David does not fit the criteria of Psalm 22. Dr. Hengstenberg states concerning King David,

That he was never in such distress as is here described ... In this Psalm the sufferer appears alone, the object of universal scorn, forsaken of every helper, given up to the violence of blood-thirsty enemies, and at the point of death; there David was in the midst of a brave and numerous host, and in no danger of his life ... To this it must be added that, while this description of suffering contains much which does not suit David, there is, on the other hand, among so many particulars, nothing which gives intimation of the event or the time to which this lamentation of David belongs. In other Psalms, which are less circumstantial than this, we can often tell whether they were composed in the flight before Saul or in that before Absalom, and can readily decide with precision concerning them. But this Psalm, abounding as it does in particulars, does not afford us a single trace to lead us to the words in the history of David's misfortunes to which it relates.[86]

To ascribe this Psalm to David when he in *no* way meets the criteria of this Psalm is improper exegesis of the Hebrew Scriptures. With this type of interpretation of the Scriptures, anyone in Jewish history who has suffered at all in life could be viewed as the subject referred to here. Yet the particulars and details mentioned in this passage do not allow for this. This Psalm is a clear prophetic passage that has found fulfillment in the Messiah, the Lord Jesus, for no one else can satisfy this Psalm as He has.

Summary

The Jewish polemic regarding this Psalm offers many weak objections against its fulfillment in Jesus of Nazareth. However, no alternative explanation worthy of credit is given. An examination of the Rabbinic interpretation of Psalm 22 reveals that it was considered by many rabbis to refer to the suffering of the Messiah. Information regarding this is provided at the end of this chapter.

When Jewish polemicists offer the above noted arguments, they are contradicting an ancient Messianic interpretation given to it by early Jewish rabbis. Jesus, who claimed to be the Messiah, fulfilled the details of this Psalm in a remarkable manner. To reject its application to Jesus is to ignore the plain facts of history.

7. *Isaiah 52:13-53:12*

This passage is possibly the strongest Messianic portion of Scripture which has found fulfillment in Jesus of Nazareth. It uniquely describes the crucifixion suffering of Christ and His death for the redemption of mankind. Because of its length, a short verse by verse Christian exegesis will be provided.

"Behold, my servant shall deal prudently, he shall be exalted and extolled and be very high" (Isaiah 52:13).

This verse refers to the exaltation of the Servant, the Lord Jesus (Matthew 28:18; Colossians 1:13-19), which has in part taken place by His resurrection from the dead. The full unveiling of His majesty is still to come (Philippians 2:5-11; 2 Thessalonians 1:8-12).

Verse 14 states that before this exaltation, there would be a period of suffering and humiliation.

"As many were astonied [astonished] *at thee; his visage was so marred more than any man, and his form more than the sons of men"* (Isaiah 52:14).

The Lord Jesus was stricken and smitten in His pre-crucifixion proceedings, until he was fully marred and bruised (John 19:1-3).

"So shall he sprinkle many nations; the kings shall shut their mouths at him: for that which had not been told them shall they see; and that which they had not heard shall they consider" (Isaiah 52:15).

"So shall he sprinkle many nations ..." was fulfilled in Christ's redemptive achievements (Hebrews 12:24). His death and resurrection have brought about the preaching of the good news of salvation in all the world so that all men may know and serve the Lord (Luke 24:46, 47; Acts 1:8).

"Who hath believed our report? and to whom is the arm of the Lord revealed?

For he shall grow up before him as a tender plant; and as a root out of dry ground: he hath no form nor comeliness; and when we shall see him, there is no beauty that we would desire him.

He is despised and rejected of men; a man of sorrows and acquainted with grief: and we hid as it were our faces from him; he was despised, and we esteemed him not" (Isaiah 53:1-3).

These verses speak of the universal rejection of the Servant of the Lord. Jesus was rejected by His own family (John 6:66; 7:1-5), and Jewish people (Matthew 13:55-56; John 1:11). He grew up within the Jewish race and faith which anticipated the glorious coming of the Messiah, yet because of His absence of pomp and splendor, Jesus was despised and rejected (John 19:14-15).

"Surely he hath borne our griefs, and carried our sorrows: yet we did esteem him stricken, smitten of God, and afflicted.

But he was wounded for our transgressions, he was bruised for our iniquities: the chastisement of our peace was upon him; and with his stripes we are healed.

All we like sheep have gone astray; we have turned every one to his own way; and the Lord hath laid on him the iniquity of us all" (Isaiah 53:4-6).

The Servant bore the sins of all; He took upon Himself the sin and iniquity of the world (John 1:29; Matthew 26:28). Jesus, the Savior, was smitten of God and afflicted and through this suffering, which ultimately led to death on the cross, He provided forgiveness and salvation for mankind (1 Peter 2:22-24; 2 Corinthians 5:17-21).

"He was oppressed, and he was afflicted, yet he opened not his mouth: he is brought as a lamb to the slaughter, and as a sheep before her shearers is dumb, so he openeth not his mouth.

He was taken from prison and from judgment: and who shall declare his generation? for he was cut off out of the land of the living: for the transgression of my people was he stricken" (Isaiah 53:7-8).

In His trial Jesus was oppressed and judged wrongly, yet he remained silent. He literally was "led as a lamb to the slaughter," and died for the transgressions of men (Matthew 26:59-63, 27:12-14).

"And he made his grave with the wicked, and with the rich in his death; because he had done no violence, neither was there any deceit in his mouth" (Isaiah 53:9).

This verse refers to the death of Jesus in which He was crucified with evildoers (two thieves) (Matthew 27:38; Mark 15:27-28). He also was buried in a tomb provided by a rich man, Joseph of Arimathea (Matthew 27:57:60). These two minute details concerning the death and burial of the Suffering Servant found perfect fulfillment in Jesus Christ.

"Yet it pleased the Lord to bruise him, he hath put him to grief: when thou shalt make his soul an offering for sin, he shall see his seed, he shall prolong his days, and the pleasure of the Lord shall prosper in his hand.

He shall see of the travail of his soul, and shall be satisfied: by his knowledge shall my righteous servant justify many; for he shall bear their iniquities.

Therefore will I divide him a portion with the great, and he shall divide the spoil with the strong; because he hath poured out his soul unto death: and he was numbered with the transgressors; and he bare the sin of many, and made intercession for the transgressors" (Isaiah 53:10-12).

Verse 10 states that it was God's will to bruise His Servant and to put Him to grief. The Jewish rulers and Roman authorities responsible for the crucifixion of Jesus were only instruments used by God (Hebrews 9:26-28; Revelation 13:8; 1 Peter 1:18-20). All of mankind's sin put the Servant there, and the responsibility for His death rests with every person individually. Verse 10 culminates by describing Christ's resurrection, "... he shall prolong his days ..." (Isaiah 53:10d), and the establishment of the Church, "... he shall see his seed (Isaiah 53:10c). Verses 11 and 12 describe the salvation from sin provided by Jesus' death and resurrection, "... he hath poured out his soul unto death: and he was numbered with the transgressors; and he bare the sin of many, and made intercession for the transgressors" (Isaiah 53:12).

When all of these predictive factors of Isaiah 52 and Isaiah 53 are brought together, the fulfillment of this prophetic passage by the Lord Jesus is astounding. The following list, gives a summary of the fulfillment of Isaiah 52:13-53:12 in the life and ministry of Jesus.

1) Servant's body and face beaten: Isaiah 52:14–John 19:1, 2.
2) Servant is not believed in: Isaiah 53:1–John 1:11, 12:37-39.
3) Servant comes from a humble background: Isaiah 53:2–Luke 2:12, 40.
4) Servant rejected by his people: Isaiah 53:3-4; John 7:46-48.
5) Servant is the sin-bearer: Isaiah 53:5-6; John 1:29; 11:49-52.
6) Servant is righteous: Isaiah 53:11; John 8:46.
7) Servant is silent before accusers: Isaiah 53:7; Matthew 26:59-63.
8) Servant dies for men's sin: Isaiah 53:8; Matthew 27:1, 2.
9) Servant buried in rich man's grave: Isaiah 53:9; Matthew 27:57-60.
10) Servant dies with criminals, lawbreakers: Isaiah 53:12; Matthew 27:38
11) Servant justifies many people: Isaiah 5:12; Romans 3:22-26.
12) Servant intercedes for sinners: Isaiah 53:12; Luke 23:34, Hebrews 7:25.

It is totally impossible that all of these events literally took place in the Crucifixion by mere chance. Only the supernatural prophetic nature of God's Word could produce a passage as predictively perfect as this.

The position held by Judaism regarding Isaiah 52:13-53:12 is quite different than that of the Christian faith. There are numerous Jewish arguments brought against this passage and its reference to Jesus.

Four major Jewish objections will be examined thoroughly here. a) This passage does not refer to the Messiah but rather to the nation of Israel. b) The Gospel accounts of Jesus' death were made to fit the descriptive language of Isaiah 53. c) A careful examination of the life of Jesus does not agree with the Isaiah passage. d) The interpretation of certain verses in Isaiah are not to be taken literally; they are to be understood as metaphors only.

a) The *first* Jewish argument states that instead of referring to the Messiah, Isaiah 52:13-53:12 refers to the Jewish people. This has by no means been the opinion of the older Jewish sources, but rather has become the modern exegesis of Isaiah 53, in order to refute the claims of Christ. Dr. Hengstenberg says,

The Jews in more ancient times unanimously referred this prophecy to the Messiah.[87]

Arthur Kac relates concerning this,

Rashi, the Jewish Biblical and Talmudic commentator of the eleventh century, was the first one to suggest that the Suffering Servant of Isaiah 53 represents Israel. It is thought that the suffering inflicted on the Jews by the crusaders was a determing factor in Rashi's interpretation. Until then the Suffering Servant of Isaiah 53 was almost universally understood by the Jews as referring to the Messiah. ... Rabbi Moshe Cohen Iben Crispin (fourteenth century) states that those who for controversial reasons apply the prophecy of the Suffering Servant to Israel, find it impossible to understand the true meaning of this prophecy, 'having forsaken the knowledge of our teachers, and inclined after the stubbornness of their own opinions.' Their misinterpretation, he declares, 'distorts the passage from its natural meaning, 'for it was given of God as a description of the Messiah, whereby, when any should claim to be the Messiah, to judge by the resemblance or non-resemblance to it whether he were the Messiah or no.' [88]

In spite of this, 99 out of 100 Jewish polemicists today interpret the totality of this passage as referring to the Jewish people. Samuel Levine gives the essential elements of this argument,

Many Jewish commentators feel that it refers to the Jewish people on the whole. We find many instances in the Bible where the Jewish people on the whole are addressed to, or are described, in the singular, such as the very famous, 'Hear O Israel, the Lord who is our God, is one' (Deuteronomy 6:4); the verb 'hear' there is singular in the Hebrew original. See also, in the Hebrew, Deuteronomy 4:10 ('omadtah'). The Ten Commandments in Exodus 20 are in the singular, in the Hebrew, and yet were addressed to the entire people. Exodus 18:13 'the nation stood'—in the singular, again, Exodus 19:2—'camped,' in the singular, again. There are many such instances like this in Isaiah as well, if you look at the original Hebrew. Thus, while you will find many places where the plural is used, you will also find many places where the singular is used to describe the entire people.[89]

He states further,

Thus, in Isaiah 49:6, Isaiah says that the Jews are to be a light to all of the nations, and are therefore more responsible, and therefore Isaiah points out in chapter 53 that the Jews will bear the iniquity of the world. This is a very simple, unforced, smooth understanding of the verses.[90]

Gerald Sigal also points out that Isaiah 52:13-53:12 calls the subject being referred to "the servant." He follows this by saying, "Israel is often spoken of as the servant of the Lord (e.g., Isaiah 41:8-9; 44:1-2; 21, 45:4; 48:20; 49:3)."[91]

Upon an examination of all the passages mentioned by these two men, the context of each verse either names "Israel" or makes it clear that the whole Jewish nation is being referred to. The author makes it obvious in the context what the intended meaning is, and *never* is any guess work involved. The singular or plural in each case also makes no difference. For instance, in Exodus 18:13, the people "stood" is stated in the singular. But the context makes it clear that more than one person is standing and that the entire congregation of people is the subject matter.

> *"But thou, Israel, art my servant, Jacob whom I have chosen, the seed of Abraham my friend"* (Isaiah 41:8).

Again in this verse the clear intent is demonstrated. Israel is referred to as the "servant" only after the author actually names Israel as the subject. This same type of contextual clarity is found in all of the passages in the Old Testament where Israel is spoken of in this manner. However, *no* such possible application to the Jewish people can be found in Isaiah 53. Dr. Hengstenberg says regarding interpreting Isaiah 53 as referring to the Jewish people,

> It is true, that the Jewish people are sometimes personified as a unity, and called servant of Jehovah. But such a personification extended through a whole section, without the slightest intimation that the discourse does not relate to one individual, can be confirmed by no analogous example. In the third verse the subject is termed 'he,' in the tenth verse a soul is attributed to him; grave and death are used in reference to a subject of the singular number. Did the Prophet wish to be understood, he must have given at least some hint as to his meaning. The Servant suffered voluntarily—vs. 10, innocent—bears all men's sins, suffered quietly and patiently; Israel— they did not go voluntarily into the Babylonian exile,— carried away in violence. They did not suffer innocently, but bore in the exile the punishment for their own sins as spoke Moses. [92]

This Jewish interpretation of Isaiah 53 ignores the clear context and meaning of this chapter. In verse three, the Servant is referred to as "a man of sorrows"; in verse four, "he" carries "our" sorrows and bears "our" grief. Here the prophet is referring to his own Jewish people when he says "our" griefs and sorrows, and thus makes a distinction between the Jewish people and "he" the Servant. In verse 9, the Servant is said to be a perfectly innocent person:

> *"... he had done no violence* [wrong], *neither was any deceit in his mouth"* (Isaiah 53:9b).

In no way could this apply to Israel who throughout the Old Testament is stated to be neither sinless or righteous (Deuteronomy 9:4-6; Joshua 24:9; Ezra 9:6-7; Psalm 14:2-3; Isaiah 1:4; 1:13; 6:1-6; 64:6; 65:7; Ecclesiastes 7:20; Daniel 9:4-6).

The prophet states in verse 6, that the Servant will bear all of mankind's sin, which of course, includes the Jewish people. The whole concept of substitution eliminates the Jewish people, seeing that it is impossible Biblically to bear one's own sins (Psalm 49:7, 8; Ezekiel 18:10; Leviticus 26:14-15). The words "we" and "he" are also separated from one another in verses 5 and 6. The "we" refers to Isaiah and the rest of Israel; the "he" therefore refers to the individual who is to be the Suffering Servant. The culmination of the suffering that the Servant goes through is his own death. The nation of Israel has suffered, but she has never died.

The passage mentions the "mouth" of the Servant, his "visage," "form," "soul," "death" and "grave" (Isaiah 53:7-12). These singular and human-related terms make clear the simple intent of the author. The Servant is *not* the Jewish people, but rather was a man chosen of God to fulfill the subject matter of Isaiah 52:13-53:12. Why else would the Prophet Isaiah include terms that apply only to an individual? This is the simple, straight forward, Messianic exegesis of Isaiah 52:13-53:12, and the Jewish polemicists know it! No one else in all of Jewish history fulfills the details of this prophecy like that of Jesus of Nazareth. Mr. Levine makes this very point when he states,

> Perhaps Isaiah 53 refers to the Messiah, and perhaps the Messiah will be despised, etc.—but perhaps this Messiah has not come yet? So what if Jesus suffered, perhaps the real Messiah will also suffer, and so perhaps Isaiah 53 refers to the future Messiah. There is no proof that it refers to Jesus even if the passage refers to a Messiah. [93]

In other words, what Mr. Levine is saying is that whoever the Messiah is, he will be exactly like Jesus in all these details, yet of course, not Jesus. Why not just face the facts, that Jesus is the Servant to whom Isaiah refers? Forget the argument from the silent future and deal with the fulfilled facts of history. Jesus is the Suffering Servant-Messiah of whom Isaiah speaks, and the facts of history bear this out in ever so clear consistency.

b) The *second* argument is stated by both Levine and Sigal. Mr. Levine says,

> Isaiah 53 seems to resemble the crucifixion, but only if the history of the Jesus story is honest and correct. That, however, is very questionable. Read *The Passover Plot* by Schonfield; keep in mind that if you were making up a story about someone whom you thought was the Messiah, you would try to doctor the story so that it resembled the description written hundreds of years before, in the book of Isaiah, about the Messiah, if indeed, (it is talking about the Messiah in the first place). [94]

Mr. Sigal reinforces this same argument;

> It is well known that much of what the New Testament claims concerning Jesus was added after his death, as his followers began

combing the Scriptures in search of proof-texts. They seized upon Isaiah 53 and built the claims of their faith around it. Stories concerning Jesus were adjusted to agree with Isaiah 53. ... Early Christianity filled in certain elements in the life of Jesus so that Jesus could fulfill all the biblical passages that the early church considered to contain messianic prophecies. The events of Jesus' life have been arranged and amplified to accord with early Christian doctrines and to serve apologetic needs. [95]

This argument is used by Jewish polemicists whenever the prophetic passage seems quite clearly to point to Jesus. This has to be the weakest and most unfounded in all of the Jewish polemic arsenal. The Gospel documents are very reliable historical records, written by eyewitness sources. To call into question the events of the New Testament is to call all of ancient history into question. This is truly an argument from silence, for it is based on absolutely *no facts whatsoever.* It is noteworthy that as often as this argument is expressed by Jewish polemicists, not once are facts supplied along with it to substantiate the claims. In Chapter 13 a full examination demonstrating the trustworthy character of the New Testament will be provided. The Gospel narrative is reliable and of the highest quality. This argument against the historical reliability of the Gospels is wholly fallacious and incorrect.

c) The *third* Jewish argument concerning the Isaiah 52:13-53:12 passage states that if one examines the life of Jesus, the results will demonstrate that in no way could Jesus have been the Servant of whom Isaiah speaks, for the events of Jesus' life and the criteria of the passage oppose one another. There are four areas mentioned by Jewish polemicists in which these so-called "differences" occur. (1) His physical appearance. (2) His blasphemy. (3) His violence. (4) His offspring.

(1) *His physical appearance:* The Servant is depicted in this passage of Scripture as "despised," "rejected," "a man of sorrows" (Isaiah 53:3). It also says that "there is no beauty that we should desire him" (Isaiah 53:2). It is consummated by stating, "we hid as it were our faces from him, he was despised and we esteemed him not" (Isaiah 53:3). Concerning this description Sigal says,

> Does this description fit the one of Jesus as depicted by the evangelists? Was he a frail, unsightly child? Was he a repulsive adult? According to them, he was, throughout his entire lifetime, greatly desired by an ever growing multitude of people, as is strikingly illustrated in Luke's summation of Jesus' formative years: 'And Jesus kept increasing in wisdom and in physical growth and in favor with God and men'–Luke 2:52. ... There is simply no indications in the Gospels that Jesus, as he grew up, could in any way be likened to a 'tender plant' , i.e., stunted, or to a 'root out of dry land,' i.e., withered or that he was extremely repulsive to look at, as the servant was said to be by his many enemies. We are thus

compelled to conclude that the life of Jesus, as portrayed in the Gospels, does not at all fit that of the suffering servant of the Lord as portrayed in Isaiah.[96]

The fallacy of this argument lies in a misinterpretation of what Isaiah is referring to. Isaiah is not in any manner describing the physical features of the Servant as a child or as an adult, nor is he depicting the response of the multitudes to his physical appearance. Instead, he is referring to the basic rejection of the Servant by His Jewish people. Jesus was not born in a royal, kingly setting, but rather He was born into the humble home of a Galilean carpenter (John 1:45-46; 7:45-49; Matthew 13:54-56). He did not align himself with any of the political, Messianic ideas that were contemporary with His day and people. Jesus preached repentance of sin and total commitment to the salvation and right-standing with the Father, that only He personally could provide. There was no great political attractiveness in this, nor did it fit with the prevalent national needs of the Jewish community. Jesus was never hailed by the Jewish authorities and political powers as the Messiah-King of Israel, but instead, He was crucified as a blasphemous, deceiver who attempted to lead Israel astray. The New Testament makes this point abundantly clear. This is exactly what Isaiah the prophet is referring to and the attempt by Sigal to confuse this clear intent of the author is unexcusable. In Isaiah 52:14 and Isaiah 53:3 the physical appearance of the Servant is mentioned; however, this applies to the suffering and torment that He is to endure which results in His marred and broken condition. The fact that Jesus was a "man of sorrows," "rejected," "despised," with no special beauty or kingly attractiveness is the clear picture that the New Testament presents of Him.

(2) *His blasphemy:* Samuel Levine verbalizes the second part of this objection;

> Isaiah says that the person referred to 'is brought as a lamb to the slaughter, and as a sheep before her shearers is dumb, so he openeth not his mouth' (verse 7). Now, whoever this verse is referring to, one thing is certain—it certainly is not referring to Jesus. If you look in Matthew 27:46, you will see that Jesus, while he was crucified, not only was not silent, but he even seems to be blaspheming, for he cried out with a loud voice 'My God, My God, why hast Thou forsaken me?' Jesus is crying out to God, and he accuses God of forsaking him. That certainly is not the silent sheep of Isaiah 53, who was not to cry out in a loud voice, nor was he to blaspheme and accuse God in public.[97]

Mr. Levine refers to Isaiah 53:7 which deals with the voluntary character of the Servant's suffering. The Servant is willingly to give His life and die for the sins of mankind. In each of the Gospel accounts, this is exactly the manner in which Jesus was led to His death (Matthew 26:24; 39-54; Mark 14:35-36; Luke 9:51; 22:42; John 10:17; 18:5; 19:11). In *no* account of Jesus' trial does He offer speech that was defensive or that resisted the verdict of His judges. Jesus' trial and death perfectly agree with the description given by Isaiah 53:9. When Jesus uttered the words, "My God, my God, why hast thou forsaken me?", He was by no means blaspheming the Father. Throughout the Gospels the relationship between Jesus and the Father is described as that of perfect unity (John 10:30; 14:9-10; 17:21-24). But on the cross Jesus bore the sin of the world, and experienced the only moment when the Father turned His back on the Son. He had literally become "sin for us" (2 Corinthians 5:21), and felt the awful rejection that would accompany such an event. At that point in time, He uttered these words, which are more than perfectly fitting. To suppose that by this utterance, Jesus blasphemes the Father and demonstrates His unwillingness to die is extremely incorrect. The New Testament affirms the obedience of Jesus to do the will of the Father throughout the sufferings of the Crucifixion. In Luke 22:42 Jesus states, "... Father, if thou be willing, remove this cup from me: nevertheless not my will, but Thine be done."

(3) *His violence:* The third Jewish objection deals with the description of the Suffering Servant in Isaiah 53:9, which states, he had done no violence neither was any deceit in his mouth." Regarding this, Sigal states,

> Violence may be defined as causing injury or damage by rough or abusive treatment. If the New Testament account is true, Jesus did commit certain acts of violence. Whip in hand, he attacked the merchants in the Temple area, causing a fracas (Matthew 21:12, Mark 11:15-16, Luke 19:45, John 2:15). He caused the death, by drowning, of a herd of swine by allowing demons to purposely enter their bodies (Matthew 8:32, Mark 5:13, Luke 8:33) and destroyed a fig tree for not having fruit out of season (Matthew 21:18-21, Mark 11:13-14). ... Whatever the reason for Jesus' action, it was an act of violence, which is not in conformity with the picture of the nonviolent suffering servant of the Lord as portrayed in Isaiah 53:9.[98]

When Isaiah speaks of the Messiah as one who "had done no violence," he is referring to evil, cruel or wrong acts. The Hebrew word "chamas," used here for violence, employs exactly this kind of meaning. Jesus never committed evil violence as the word "chamas" implies. Throughout the Hebrew Scriptures, God, at times, had to employ violent acts, such as drowning the Egyptian army in the Red Sea (Exodus 14:26-31), disciplining the nation of Israel for their disobedient and sinful acts (Leviticus 10:1-5), judging wicked, evil nations (Nahum 1:1-6). Yet, in none of these instances was the violence of God evil or wrong. Instead, God's holiness and righteousness was maintained and exalted. The fact that God was wholly without sin, even though violent acts were committed would be strongly supported by these Jewish polemicists. In this exact same sense, Jesus committed acts that were violent; however, they were violent in a Godly, righteous manner, and dealt with spiritual principles totally within His authority and power to enforce.

The cleansing of the temple exemplified God's concern that His Temple be not profaned with thievery and commercial gain. It was to be a place of prayer and worship, giving help and strength to the needy. On this basis, He drove the money-changers and merchants out of the Temple area.

The casting out of the demons from the demoniac of Gadara (Mark 5:1-20) and the destruction of the herd of swine which followed, also had a purpose behind it. Jesus permits the demons to enter the swine to demonstrate what type of anger demons would inflict upon humans if left to their own liberty and evil. Satan's total purpose is to destroy mankind, and the demon influence that he exercises in people's lives has this one goal in mind. Jesus does allow the swine to be destroyed. But through this loss a picture is conveyed relating how small a value temporal riches have in God's estimation. When the city heard of this apparent disaster, they came to Jesus and asked Him to leave their area (Matthew 8:34). This action demonstrates that the value system of men places swine above *salvation*, for they would rather have had their swine than the Savior. Jesus permitted this event to show to His disciples and all who would read of this event within the Scriptures, the importance of the salvation of a human soul against the value of earthly possessions.

The destruction of the fig tree (Matthew 21:18-21), was also neither a thoughtless or evil violent act. The tree was on the way side; therefore it was not private property, and on this basis any traveler had the right to pick fruit from it. Jesus' cursing of this fig tree was not based on resentment or disappointment for not finding any fruit on it. Rather, this action was emblematical in nature. Jesus has been preaching the truths of repentance and salvation in Israel for over two and one half years. But, by and large, the Jewish nation and leadership had not responded to His message. The fig tree, which is very common in Palestine, is used here to represent the nation of Israel. Scholar Adam Clarke states that this cursing of the tree,

> ... was intended to point out the state of the Jewish people. 1) They made a profession of the true religion. 2) They considered themselves the peculiar people of God, and despised and reprobated all others. 3) They were only hypocrites, having nothing of religion but the profession: leaves, and no fruit. [99]

The literal withering away of Israel as a nation, which is what is being depicted in this passage, took place in the destruction of Jerusalem and the eventual dispersion of the Jewish people from their land in AD 70. The time period in which God had required good fruit from Israel produced only leaves. This is what Jesus is referring to in this "violent" event.

Isaiah 53:9 refers to the Messiah as "one who had done no violence," and by this statement refers to evil, malicious actions, which result in hurtful, harmful destruction. In none of the cases mentioned by Jewish polemicists, does Jesus commit evil violence. Instead, throughout His life, He suffered the hate and malice of others, culminating in the death on the cross, where He states; "Father forgive them for they know not what they do" (Luke 23:34).

(4) *His offspring:* Regarding this last objection, Levine states,

> In Isaiah 53:10, it says that 'he shall see his seed, he shall prolong his days.' This means that the subject of Isaiah 53 will have children and live a long life. Since neither of these was true in the life of Jesus, Isaiah 53 cannot refer to Jesus. It could, however, refer quite easily to the Jewish people.[100]

The word "seed" that is used in Isaiah 53:10 is the Hebrew word "zera," and it is used numerous times throughout the Scriptures. It is translated to mean "seed" or "offspring,"[101] and implies a literal application. However, there are instances throughout the Hebrew Scriptures where the word does not follow the strict meaning of physical seed or offspring. In passages such as Malachi 2:15, Proverbs 11:21, Psalm 22:31, Isaiah 1:4, 57:4, Genesis 3:15, 38:8, Jeremiah 2:21, a somewhat different meaning is employed for the word "zera." For example in Genesis 3:15, "the seed of the serpent" hardly refers to a literal serpent and its offspring, but rather it refers to Satan and his spiritual followers or offspring. In this same manner, Isaiah 53:10 is not to have the strict physical offspring interpretation, but rather applies to a spiritual seed or offspring.

This word "zera" is the proper word to be used in Isaiah 53:10. If we examine the New Testament, we discover that God raised the Messiah from the dead and made Him the head of the new creation or spiritual offspring (2 Corinthians 5:17; Romans 6:4; Galatians 6:15; Ephesians 2:15; 4:21-24; 1 Corinthians 15:45-50; John 3:1-18). Isaiah used this word *zera* to convey exactly this type of meaning, namely that Jesus would "see his seed" or His Church birthed and then grow and expand (Matthew 16:18; 28:18, 20). The word *travail*–"amal" (Isaiah 53:11), although not strictly referring to birth pains, most certainly adds to this exegesis of the passage in reference to the spiritual rebirth that faith in Jesus as Lord and Savior brings.

When all four of these objections are examined carefully, no evidence is presented that invalidates the fulfillment of the "Servant" in Jesus' life and ministry. The life, character and ministry of Jesus perfectly fits with the description of the Suffering Servant of Isaiah 52:13-53:12.

d) The last Jewish argument regarding Isaiah 52:13-53:12 is given by Mr. Sigal;

The Christian missionary interpretation of Isaiah 53 posits that such phrases as 'for he was cut off out of the land of the living' (verse 8), 'his grave was set' (verse 9), and 'in his death' (verse 9) refer to the death and burial of Jesus, with subsequent verses indicating his post-resurrection glorification. Actually, these phrases are not to be taken literally. The metaphor 'his grave was set,' describing an event in the life of God's suffering servant, is similar to the statement, 'for he was cut off out of the land of the living' (verse 8). Metaphors of this type used to describe deep anguish and subjection to enemies, are part of the biblical idiom. Similar metaphorical language is used, for example, in Ezekiel 37 to express the condition preceding relief and rejuvenation following the end of the exile. Ezekiel provides the clues needed for understanding the phraseology used by Isaiah. The metaphorical images employed by Isaiah– 'cut off out of the land of the living' and 'grave'–are also used in Ezekiel's description of the valley of the dry bones, where the bones symbolize the exiled Jewish people. Lost in an apparently hopeless exile, the Jewish people exclaim: 'we are clean cut off' (Ezekiel 37:11). ... It is now clear that Isaiah's phrase, for he was 'cut off' out of the land of the living', refers to the deadly condition of exile. Similarly, the term 'grave' in Isaiah–1'And his grave was set with the wicked'–refers to life in exile as used in Ezekiel: 'I will open your graves, and cause you to come up out of your graves' (Ezekiel 37:12), where 'graves' is a metaphor for the lands of exile.[102]

The basic reason for the non-literal, metaphorical application of the phrase "he was cut off out of the land of the living" and the words "death" and "grave," is that a literal exegesis would eliminate the Jewish people as being the Servant referred to in Isaiah 53. The Jewish people have had many terrible periods of persecution and violence, but they have never died or ceased to be. Because of this clear historical fact, a different exegesis for Isaiah 53, other than the obvious, is the only option for Jewish polemicists. There is no question that in the Scriptures, the use of metaphors or figures of speech are employed. However, the principles of Biblical hermeneutics (rules of interpretation) prove very helpful in relationship to this type of Scriptural problem.

The following five rules of hermeneutics are listed here to clarify this issue. These principles which are employed by Jewish and Christian scholars, are based on the fact that the writers of the Scriptures wrote with the intent of being understood. These five rules are progressive in nature and must be applied to a passage or phrase in the listed order. They are as follows:

1. It is necessary, so far as possible, to take the words in their usual and ordinary sense.

2. It is necessary to take a word or words in the sense which the setting of the phrase indicates.

3. It is necessary to take the words in the sense which the context indicates, that is, the verses which precede and follow the text that is being studied.

4. It is necessary to take into consideration the object or design of the book or passage in which obscure words or expressions occur.

5. It is necessary to consult parallel passages explaining spiritual things by spiritual. This includes parallels of words, ideas and general teachings.[103]

The problem with the Jewish exegesis of Isaiah 53:8-9 is that it passes by the first four principles and uses only the last rule as it relates to the terms, "death," "grave" and "cut off." This procedure proves to be fallacious for it violates the intended order by which these rules are applied. Only when the first three rules cannot render the obvious intent of the author, do the last two become relevant. In this case, if the first three principles are applied to Isaiah 53:8-9, the literal intended meaning is self-evident. The first rule states that if possible, we are to take the words in their usual and ordinary sense. The second rule demands that the setting of the phrase be examined and the third rule asserts that the context must be allowed to dictate the intention of the author. By taking the words in their ordinary sense within the setting of the context, a literal interpretation of Isaiah 53 is arrived at. No need for a cross-reference or parallel passage such as Ezekiel 37 is needed. The suffering, "the death," "the grave" and the "cutting off" (an idiom of death) of the Servant, work together within this context to make it clear that a literal death is being referred to.

As stated earlier, the Servant in Isaiah 53 is referred to in the singular "he" and "him," and is contrasted over against "us," referring to the Jewish and Gentile people (Isaiah 53:3-6). Isaiah 52:14 states that the Servant has a "visage" (appearance) and a "form." and that these were marred and beaten "more than any man" (Isaiah 52:14). Isaiah 53:10 affirms that the Servant has a soul and continues by saying that He will offer His soul as an "offering" "asham" (a guilt offering) for sin.[104] An offering for sin throughout the Hebrew Scriptures in which an animal was used, was accompanied by the literal death of a sacrifice victim (Exodus 24:5; Leviticus 1:2,10; 4:23-32). Can it ever be said that the Jewish people have offered themselves as a "asham" by literally dying as a sacrifice victim? All of these factors point to a singular individual and a literal death.

Lastly, when Isaiah 53:8-9 is coupled with Daniel 9:26, which states that the Messiah will be "cut off," the literal death and grave of the Servant in Isaiah 52:13-53:12 is strengthened. The Hebrew word used in Daniel 9:26 for "cut off" is the term "karath," which implies a sudden, violent end.[105] Throughout the Hebrew Scriptures, this term refers to a literal, sudden death (Genesis 17:14; Exodus 12:15; 31:14; Leviticus 7:20-25; Numbers 9:13; Psalms 37:9; Proverbs 2:22;

Zechariah 14:2). This is exactly the type of death that Jesus went through in His crucifixion. The literal interpretation of the death of the Servant in Isaiah 53 is the only conclusion that an honest examination of Isaiah 52:13-53:12 can render.

Summary

The case for the Messianic nature of Isaiah 52:13-53:12, is self evident. It has long been considered a Messianic passage within Judaism. However, because of the obvious similarities between this passage and the life of Jesus, a non-literal exegesis has become the standard Jewish view of Isaiah 52:13-53:12.

The Jewish polemicists really cannot make up their mind how to refute the Christian position on Isaiah 53. One argument states that in *no* way do the events of Christ's life agree with the facts mentioned in the passage. But a second argument asserts that the agreement between the life of Jesus and Isaiah 53 was the result of proof-texting. The contradictions of the Jewish objections to Jesus as the subject of Isaiah 52:13-53:12 are made strikingly clear by the extreme lack of solid reasoning, exemplified by the above noted arguments.

An honest search of the subject matter referred to within this passage will lead one to the Messiah, the Lord Jesus Christ.

8. Zechariah 12:10

"And I will pour upon the house of David, and upon the inhabitants of Jerusalem, the spirit of grace and of supplications: and they shall look upon me whom they have pierced, and they shall mourn for him, as one mourneth for his only son, and shall be in bitterness for him, as one that is in bitterness for his firstborn" (Zechariah 12:10).

The 12th through 14th chapters of Zechariah speak of the last days and the culmination of world history. The prophet speaks of the trials and temptations that will plague the Jewish people at this time. It is stated that during this time the Jewish people will call upon the Lord for deliverance (Zechariah 13:9), and it is then that the Messiah comes and delivers them (Zechariah 14:4). Zechariah 12:10 states that when the coming of the Messiah occurs, great lamentation and sorrow will be the result. The Jewish people will "look upon me whom they have pierced, and they shall mourn for him, as one mourneth for his only son ..." At this time, the Jewish people will recognize that Jesus is their long awaited Messiah who was rejected in His first appearance on the earth.

The Jewish objection to this exegesis of Zechariah has three main positions. a) The person "pierced" here is the warrior Messiah of Israel, not Jesus of Nazareth. b) God cannot be pierced. c) The spirit of grace and supplication referred to in verse 12 never occurred in Christ's lifetime.

a) The first argument is given by Gerald Sigal;

> On that day, they (the nation of Israel i.e., the house of David and the inhabitants of Jerusalem ...) shall look to me (God) whom they (the nations spoken of in verse 9, that shall come up against Jerusalem) have pierced; then they (Israel) shall mourn for him (the slain of Israel as personified by the leader of the people, the warrior Messiah who will die in battle at this time. ...[106]

He continues;

> All of the nation's dead will be mourned, but the mourning over the death of the warrior Messiah symbolizes the collective grief as the people mourn for the fallen of Israel.[107]

There are two problems with this Jewish interpretation of Zechariah 12:10. First, the word "they," used all three times in verse 10, refers to Israel. Verse 10 begins by stating explicitly, "the house of David," and the "they" used throughout this verse obviously refers to "the house of David" (Israel). In no way can the "they" in "whom *they* have pierced" refer to the Gentile nations without totally confusing the intent of the verse. If the author had this as his intention, he would have distinguished the second reference of "they" from Israel, by referring to the Gentile nations directly. But he does not do this, thereby applying the entire verse to the people of Israel. This is an important distinction, because by designating the word "they" to the Gentiles, the relationship of Christ's death and the Jewish rejection of Him as Messiah, is sidestepped.

The second problem with this interpretation of Zechariah 12:10 is that it attributes the subject "me whom they have pierced" to the "warrior Messiah." Who is the warrior Messiah? Sigal makes no effort to give theological support for this person. Where in the Scriptures does it speak of the coming "warrior Messiah"? He gives no Scriptural support, but states that the Talmud saw this person as the "warrior Messiah, the son of Joseph who will be slain at this time (B.T. Sukkah 52a)." Jewish scholar Raphael Patai explains how the concept of this "warrior Messiah" came into being. He says,

> Scholars have repeatedly speculated about the origin of the Messiah ben Joseph legend and the curious fact that the Messiah figure has thus been split in two. It would seem that in the early legend, the death of the Messiah was envisaged, perhaps as a development of the Suffering Servant ...[108]
>
> When the death of the Messiah became an established tenet in Talmudic times, this was felt to be irreconcilable with the belief in the Messiah as the Redeemer who would usher in the blissful millennium of the Messianic age. The dilemma was solved by splitting the person of the Messiah in two: one of them, called Messiah ben Joseph, was to raise the armies of Israel against their enemies, and, after many victories and miracles, would fall victim to Gog and Magog. The other, Messiah ben David, will come after

him and will lead Israel to the ultimate victory, the triumph, and the Messianic era of bliss.[109]

There is no possible way that the Scriptures can be twisted to teach of such a person. The book of Zechariah is Messianic in nature. It is the Messiah that causes the "house of David" to "mourn for him, as one mourneth for his only son." No such allusion to a "warrior Messiah" will ever find agreement with the Messianic teachings of the Hebrew Scriptures.

b)   The second argument is related again by Mr. Sigal;

Of course, God cannot be literally pierced. The idea of piercing God expresses the fact that Israel stands in a very special relationship to God ... To attack (pierce) Israel is to attack God. That is why God says: 'Me whom they have pierced.'[110]

There is no question that throughout the Hebrew Scriptures God identifies Himself with Israel. In each case the context makes this intention clear (Exodus 23:22; Isaiah 49:25). But in the Zechariah 12:10 passage, the Lord Jehovah expressly states that the one pierced is to be literally applied to Himself. The Lord speaks in the exact same sense as other instances in the Old Testament (Exodus 20:3, 5-7; Ezekiel 6:3, 4; Amos 8:9; Jeremiah 7:19-23).

If one questions Zechariah 12:10 and the direct reference of the Lord to "me," then every passage in the Scriptures where the Lord communicates to mankind and then refers to Himself must likewise be questioned. To hold to such a position is untenable. Based on what criteria does one determine when the Lord speaks and refers to Himself and when He does not? A position such as this leads to total confusion.

If Mr. Sigal understood properly the incarnation, he would recognize that the God-man, Jesus Christ, was indeed pierced. With a clear understanding of this New Testament truth, He would not have to opt for a distorted and strained interpretation of Zechariah 12:10. This passage is strong evidence for not only the death and piercing of the Messiah, but also for His deity.

c)   The third Jewish argument is stated by Samuel Levine;

Now, if this refers to the first coming of Jesus, then what was the spirit of grace and supplication? It never seemed to have occurred. In addition, there certainly was no great mourning in Jerusalem and throughout the land by all of the Jewish families after the death of Jesus. On the contrary, since many Jews, according to the Gospels, encouraged the crucifixion, if anything there was a great rejoicing, rather than mourning. Thus, without any doubt, Zechariah 12:10 does not refer to Jesus.[111]

This objection is based on a simple mistake on Mr. Levine's part. Zechariah 12:10 was not fulfilled in Christ's first appearance and subsequent death on the cross. Instead it refers to His Second Coming in which He will usher in the events and the kingdom described in

Zechariah 12-14. The "spirit of grace and supplication" is an event that is yet to occur. When the Messiah, the Lord Jesus returns, the Jewish people will recognize Him as the "pierced one," who was slain in history past on the cross. They will then weep and mourn for Him, recognizing fully that Jesus is their Messiah, whom they rejected.

Summary

This prophecy is indeed a strong source of prophetic evidence for the piercing and slaying of the Messiah. The Hebrew word "dagar," which means "pierced or thrust through,"[112] is used 10 times in the Hebrew Scriptures, and in eight of those 10 times it refers to the piercing of a sword or spear with an accompanying death. There is no question that the piercing in Zechariah 12:10 refers to the death of the subject. With this evidence, tied to the fact that this entire portion of Scripture is Messianic in nature, the evidence for its fulfillment in Jesus Christ is very strong. But just as other Scriptural passages that refer to Jesus are rejected by Jewish polemicists, Zechariah 12:10 is found to be no exception. This rejection will continue until the day when the actual realization of Zechariah 12:10 is fulfilled. In the meantime, hundreds of Jewish people face God and eternity apart from the Savior of all men, the Messiah, the Lord Jesus.

"Behold, he cometh with clouds, and every eye shall see him, and they also which pierced him: and all kindreds of the earth shall wail because of him. Even so, Amen" (Revelation 1:7).

Rabbinic Writings and the Messianic Prophecies

One of the main points of the Jewish argument against the Christian faith is that the Christian exegesis of the Hebrew Scriptures is erroneous. The Medieval period was the fortifying time for most of this type of prophetic objection. However, by appealing to early Jewish traditional writings, the case for the Messianic application of numerous Old Testament prophecies can be demonstrated. The following is a very short compilation of a few citations demonstrating this. The dating of the material from which these quotations are taken is as follows:

Targum Onkelos	(AD 100-200)
Babylonian Talmud	(AD 200-500)
Targum Jonathan	(AD 100-150)
Targum Pseudo-Jonathan	(AD 600-700)
Midrash Tehillim	(AD 900-1000)
Targum Yerushalmi	(AD 600-700)
Pesikta Rabbati	(AD 600-900)[113]

Genesis 3:15–*Targum Pseudo-Jonathan*;

And I will put enmity between thee and the woman, and between the seed of your offspring and the seed of her offspring; and it shall be that when the offspring of the woman keep the commandments of the law, they will aim right (at you) and they will smite you on the head; but when they abandon the commandments of the law, you will aim right (at them), and you will wound them in the heel. However, for them there will be a remedy, but for you there will be none, and in the future they will make peace with the heel in the days of the king, Messiah.[114]

Genesis 35:11-12–*Targum Jonathan;*

And the Lord said to him, I am El Shaddai: spread forth and multiply; a holy people, and a congregation of prophets and priests, shall be from thy sons whom thou hast begotten, and two kings shall yet from thee go forth. And the land which I gave to Abraham and to Izhak will I give unto thee, and to thy sons after thee will I give the land.[115]

Genesis 49:10–*Targum Jonathan;*

Kings shall not cease, nor rulers, from the house of Jehuda, nor sapherim teaching the law from his seed, till the time that the king, the Meshiha, shall come, the youngest of his sons; and on account of him shall the peoples flow together. How beauteous is the King, and Meshiha who will arise from the house of Jehuda.[116]

Genesis 49:10–*Targum Yerushalmi;*

Kings shall not cease from the house of Judah, nor scribes who teach the Torah from his children's children, until the time of the coming of the King Messiah to whom belongs the kingdom, and to whom all dominions of the earth shall become subservient.[117]

Numbers 24:17–*Targum Onkelos;*

I see him, but not now; I behold him, but not nigh. When a King shall arise out of Jakob, and the Meshiha be anointed from Israel ...[118]

Deuteronomy 18:18; Isaiah 11:3–*Maimonides;*

Messiah will be a very great Prophet, greater than all the Prophets with the exception of Moses our teacher ...

His status will be higher than that of the Prophets and more honourable, Moses alone excepted. The Creator, blessed be He, will single him out with features wherewith He had not singled out Moses; for it is said with reference to him, 'And his delight shall be in the fear of the Lord; and he shall not judge after the sight of his eyes, neither decide after the hearing of his ears.'[119]

Psalm 2–*Midrash Tehillim;*

The sufferings are divided into three parts: one for David and the fathers, one for our own generation, and one for the king Messiah, and this is what is written, 'He was wounded for our transgression ...'[120]

Psalm 22–*Pesikta Rabbati;*

'My strength is dried up like a potsherd'—(Psalm 22:15). Then the Holy One—blessed be He!—says to Him; Ephraim, my righteous

Messiah, you took all this upon yourself from the six days of creation; now your suffering shall be like my suffering; ...'.[121]

Psalm 22–*Pesikta Rabbati, Piska* 36:1-2;

(When the Messiah comes), the Holy One, blessed be He, will tell him in detail what will befall him: There are souls that have been put away with thee under my throne, and it is their sins which will bend thee down under a yoke of iron and make thee like a calf whose eyes grow dim with suffering ... iron beams will be brought and loaded upon his neck until the Messiah's body is bent low ... It was because of the ordeal of the son of David that David wept saying, 'My strength is dried up like a potsherd'–Psalm 22:16.[122]

Psalm 21:1–*Midrash Tehillim;*

God calls King Messiah by His own name. But what is His name? Answer; Jehovah is a man of war—Exodus 15:3.[123]

Psalm 72:12, 17–*Babylonian Talmud*–Sanhedrin 98b;

O God, give thy judgments to King Messiah ... May his name [Messiah] be Yinnon as long as the sun.[124]

Psalm 118:22 (Isaiah 8:13-15)–*Targum Isaiah;*

The Lord of hosts, him shall ye call holy; and let him be your fear and let him be your strength. And if ye will not hearken, his Memra shall be amongst you for vengeance and for a stone of smiting, and for a rock of offence to the houses of the princes of Israel, for a breaking, and for a stumbling; ...[125]

Isaiah 9:6–*Targum Isaiah;*

The prophet saith to the house of David, a child has been born to us, a son has been given to us; and He has taken the law upon Himself to keep it, and His name has been called from of old, Wonderful, Counsellor, Mighty God, He who lives forever, the Anointed one [Messiah], in whose days peace shall increase upon us.[126]

Isaiah 11:1–*Targum Isaiah;*

And a King shall come forth from the sons of Jesse, and an Anointed One from His son's sons shall grow up. And there shall rest upon him a spirit from before the Lord, the spirit of wisdom, and understanding, the spirit of counsel and might, the spirit of knowledge, and of the fear of the Lord.[127]

Isaiah 11:1-4–*Babylonian Talmud;*

Sanhedrin II—The Messiah—as it is written, and the spirit of the Lord shall rest upon him, the spirit of wisdom and understanding, the spirit of counsel and might, the spirit of knowledge, and of the fear of the Lord.[128]

Isaiah 11:2–*Targum Isaiah;*

And a King shall come forth from the sons of Jesse, and an Anointed One [Messiah] from his son's son shall grow up.[129]

Isaiah 33:22–*Targum Isaiah;*

For the Lord is our judge, who brought us out of Egypt by his might; the Lord is our teacher, who gave us the instruction of his law from Sinai; the Lord is our King, he shall deliver us, and execute a righteous vengeance for us on the armies of Gog.[130]

Isaiah 44:6–*Targum Isaiah;*

Thus saith the Lord, the King of Israel, and his saviour the Lord of hosts, I am He, I am He that is from of old; yea, the everlasting ages are mine, and beside me there is no God.[131]

Isaiah 52:13-53:12–*Targum Jonathan;*

Behold, My servant the Messiah shall prosper; he shall be exalted and great and very powerful.[132]

Isaiah 53:6–*Targum Jonathan;*

All of us were scattered like sheep, we were exiled, each in his own direction, but it is the will of God to pardon the sins of all of us on his [Messiah's] account.[133]

Isaiah 53–*Rabbi Moshe el Sheikh* (Chief Rabbi of Safed) in the 16th Century;

Our Rabbis with one voice accept and affirm the opinion that the prophet is speaking here of the King Messiah, and we shall ourselves also adhere to the same view.[134]

Isaiah 53:5–*Machzor* in the *Musaf;*

Our righteous anointed [Messiah] departed from us: horror hath seized us, and we have none to justify us. He hath borne the yoke of our iniquities, and our transgression, and is wounded because of our transgression. He beareth our sins on his shoulders that he may find pardon for our iniquities. We shall be healed by his wound, at the time that the Eternal will create him as a new creature. O bring him up from the circle of the earth. Raise him up from fear, to assemble us the second time on Mount Lebanon, by the hand of Yinon [a rabbinic name for Messiah].[135]

Jeremiah 23:6, Lamentation 1:16–*Echa Rabbathi;*

What is the name of the Messiah? R. Abba ben Cahana (AD 200-300) has said: Jehovah is His name, and this is proved by 'This is His name.'[136]

Daniel 7:13, Zechariah 9:9–*Babylonian Talmud, Sanhedrin 98a;*

R. Joshua opposed two verses: it is written, 'And behold, one like the son of man came with the clouds of heaven'; whilst it is written, (behold, thy King cometh unto thee ...) 'lowly, and riding on an ass'. If they are meritorious, (he will come) with the clouds of heaven; if not, lowly and riding upon an ass.[137]

Daniel 9:24-27–*Megillah 3a Babylonian Talmud;*

The Targum of the Prophets was composed by Jonathan ben Uzziel under the guidance of Haggai, Zechariah and Malachi ... and a Bath Kol came forth and exclaimed, who is this that has revealed My secrets to mankind? ... He further sought to reveal a targum of the Hagiographa [part of the Scriptures that contain Daniel], but a Bath Kol went forth and said; Enough! What was the reason? Because the date of the Messiah is foretold in it. [138]

Micah 5:1–*Targum Jonathan;*

And you, O Bethlehem Ephrath, you who were too small to be numbered among the thousands of the house of Judah, from you shall come forth before Me the Messiah, to exercise dominion over Israel, he whose name was mentioned from before, from the days of creation. [139]

Zechariah 9:9–*Babylonian Talmud—Ber. 56b*;

If one sees an ass in a dream, he may hope for salvation, as it says; 'Behold thy King cometh unto thee; he is triumphant and victorious, lowly and riding upon an ass.' [140]

Zechariah 12:10–*Sukkah 52a Babylonian Talmud*;

What is the cause of the mourning ... It is well according to him who explains that the cause is the slaying of Messiah the Son of Joseph since that well agrees with Scriptural verse, 'And they shall look upon me because they have thrust him through, and they shall mourn for him as one mourneth for his only son.' [141]

Jewish-Christian scholar, Alfred Edersheim gives a fully documented list of Messianically-applied Old Testament passages in the Rabbinic writings. Concerning this he states;

The following list contains the passages in the Old Testament applied to the Messiah or to Messianic times in the most ancient Jewish writings. They amount in all to 456, thus distributed: 75 from the Pentateuch, 243 from the Prophets, and 138 from the Hagiographa, and supported by more than 558 separate quotations from Rabbinic writings. Despite all labor and care, it can scarcely be hoped that the list is quite complete although, it is hoped, no important passage has been omitted. [142]

He adds,

The Rabbinic works from which quotations have been made are: the Targumim, the two Talmuds, and the most ancient Midrashim. [143]

A careful examination of this list reveals that 45 of the 63 prophetic proclamations listed on pages 36-39 were found to be Messianically applied in the Rabbinic writings. Of the eight Hebrew prophetic passages examined in this chapter, 22 of the 26 predictions fulfilled by Jesus of Nazareth, were considered by Rabbinic sources to be clear Messianic qualifications. Along with these citations, numerous other Hebrew Scriptural references that have found fulfillment in Jesus can be found within the Rabbinic writings. Indeed, the argument that the Christian exegesis of the Hebrew Scriptures is erroneous, does not stand up in the light of Jewish history and ancient Messianic thought.

Conclusion

Through the long process of polemic activity, Judaism has narrowed down its scope of the Hebrew Scriptures until very few passages are considered Messianic. The early Jewish Messianic thought was quite different from this. As demonstrated earlier, much of the material covered in this chapter was traditionally accepted as Messianic in nature by the ancient interpreters. It is therefore evident that the Christian exegesis of the Hebrew prophecies was not a Gentile invention, but rather was in agreement with these older Rabbinic sources. The present Jewish polemic material which denies these passages and their Messianic application, is not only attacking Christianity but ancient Judaism as well.

Judaism has learned in its struggle with Christianity that the most successful way to resist the evidence for Jesus' Messiahship is to deny the Messianic nature of the Scriptures which have found fulfillment in Him. Many within Judaism (Reform Judaism) totally deny the personality of the Messiah, and instead view the Messianic prophecies as finding fulfillment in a Messianic Age or Influence. This has been, in their case, the easiest and most effective means of denying Jesus and His Messianic qualifications. Nevertheless, this does nothing to change the truly remarkable manner in which Jesus has completed and fulfilled many prophetic predictions. The Scriptures stand as a cornerstone of evidence revealing that Jesus is truly the Messiah, the King of Israel. If one honestly examines the passages presented in this chapter, the result will be that Jesus will be seen as the Anointed One, the Messiah of Israel.

ᵫ ᴣ

ENDNOTES — CHAPTER 4

1. Jakob Jocz, *The Jewish People and Jesus Christ* (Reprint ed.; Grand Rapids: Baker Book House, 1979), p. 205.
2. Raphael Patai, *The Messiah Texts* (Detroit: Wayne State Univ. Press, 1979), p. 43.
3. *Ibid.*, p. 39.
4. Floyd Hamilton, *The Basis of Christian Faith* (New York: Harper and Row Publishers, 1964), p. 160.
5. Daniel J. Lasker, *Jewish Philosophical Polemics Against Christianity in the Middle Ages* (New York: KTAV Publishing House Inc., 1977), p. 4.
6. Gerald Sigal, *The Jew and the Christian Missionary: A Jewish Response to Missionary Christianity* (New York: KTAV Publishing House Inc., 1981), p. XV of Introduction.
7. *Ibid.*, p. XVI of Introduction.
8. Isaac Troki, *Faith Strengthened* (New York: Hermon Press, 1970), p. 96.

9. Sigal, op. cit., p. 23.
10. Franz Delitzsch, *The Prophecies of Isaiah, Vol. I* (Grand Rapids: Wm. B. Eerdmans Pub. Co., 1949), p. 217.
11. Arthur W. Kac, *The Messianic Hope* (Grand Rapids: Baker Book House, 1975), p. 138.
12. Harry Rimmer, *The Magnificence of Jesus* (Grand Rapids: Wm. B. Eerdmans Pub. Co., 1947), pp. 124-125.
13. Kac, op. cit., p. 140.
14. Troki, op. cit., pp. 96-97.
15. Isaiah 7:16.
16. Isaiah 7:17.
17. H.A. Ironside, *Isaiah,* (Neptune, New Jersey: Loizeaux Brothers Inc., 1952), pp. 46-47.
18. These two sources provide excellent scholarship on this topic. Franz Delitzsch, *The Prophecies of Isaiah, Vol. I* (Grand Rapids: Wm. B. Eerdmans Pub. Co., 1949) and George Adam Smith, *The Book of Isaiah, Vol. I* (New York: Harper and Brothers, 1927).
19. Sigal, op. cit., p. 26.
20. Samuel Levine, *You Take Jesus, I'll Take God*, (Los Angeles: Hamoroh Press, 1980), p. 39.
21. Troki, op. cit., p. 104.
22. David Baron, *Rays of Messiah's Glory: Christ in the Old Testament* (Grand Rapids: Zondervan, 1955), p. 38.
23. Levine, loc. cit.
24. *Ibid.*, p. 41.
25. Sigal, op. cit., p. 20.
26. B.K. Kuiper, *The Church in History* (Grand Rapids:. Wm. B. Eerdmans Pub. Co., 1951), pp. 85-89.
27. *Ibid.*, p. 86.
28. Troki, op. cit., p. 274.
29. E.W. Hengstenberg, *Christology of the Old Testament* (Reprint ed.; Grand Rapids: Kregel Publications, 1970), p. 43.
30. Kac, op. cit., pp. 78,79.
31. Alfred Edersheim, *The Life and Times of Jesus the Messiah* (3rd ed.) Grand Rapids: Wm. B. Eerdmans Pub. Co., 1971), p. 716.
32. Kac, op. cit., p. 132.
33. Levine, op. cit., p. 49.
34. J. Barton Payne, *Encyclopedia of Biblical Prophecy* (Grand Rapids: Baker Book House, 1973), p. 383.
35. Adam Clarke, *Clarke's Commentary, Vol. IV* (New York: Abingdon Cokesbury Press, n.d.), p. 602.
36. Harold Hoehner, *Chronological Aspects of the Life of Christ* (Grand Rapids: Zondervan Publishing House, 1977), p. 138.
37. Clarke, loc. cit.
38. *Ibid.*, p. 603.
39. *Ibid.*, p. 602.
40. Sigal, op. cit., p. 110.
41. Hengstenberg, op. cit., p. 419.
42. Sigal, op. cit., pp. 110-111.
43. Hengstenberg, op. cit., p. 417.
44. Troki, op. cit., p. 200.

45. *Ibid.*, p. 204.
46. Sigal, op. cit., p. 111.
47. William E. Biederwolf, *The Second Coming Bible* (Reprint ed.; Grand Rapids: Baker Book House, 1977), p. 222.
48. Daniel 9:26.
49. Kac, op. cit., p. 34.
50. Levine, op. cit., p. 35.
51. Troki, op. cit., p. 164.
52. Edersheim, op. cit., p. 735.
53. Sigal, op. cit., pp. 76,77.
54. Troki, op. cit., pp. 163-164.
55. Robert Young, *Young's Analytical Concordance to the Bible*, Grand Rapids: Wm. B. Eerdmans Pub. Co., 1973), p. 311.
56. Troki, op. cit., p. 168.
57. Payne, op. cit., p. 431.
58. A. Lukyn Williams, *Christian Evidences For Jewish People, Vol I* (Cambridge: W. Heffer and Sons Limited, 1910), p. 188.
59. Patai, op. cit., pp. 16-17.
60. *Ibid.*, p. 17.
61. Samson H. Levey, *The Messiah: An Aramaic Interpretation; The Messianic Exegesis of the Targum* (Cincinnati: Hebrew Union College, 1974), p. 92
62. Troki, op. cit., p. 105.
63. Sigal, op. cit., pp. 29-31.
64. C.F. Keil and F. Delitzsch, *Keil and Delitzsch Commentaries on the Old Testament, Isaiah, Vol. I* (Grand Rapids: Wm. B. Eerdmans Pub. Co., 1949), p. 252.
65. Hengstenberg, op. cit., p. 179.
66. *Ibid.*, p. 182.
67. Young, *Young's Analytical Concordance to the Bible*, op. cit., pp. 294-295.
68. Troki, loc. cit.
69. Hengstenberg, op. cit., p. 178.
70. *Ibid.*, p. 183.
71. David Berger, the "Nizzahon Vetus" as found in *The Jewish Christian Debate in the High Middle Ages* (Philadelphia: The Jewish Publication Society of America, 1979), p. 102.
72. Troki, op. cit., p. 106.
73. Levine, op. cit., p. 54.
74. Keil and Delitzsch, op. cit., p. 251.
75. Hengstenberg, op. cit., p. 79.
76. Sigal, op. cit., p. 95.
77. Levine, op. cit., p. 34.
78. Sigal, op. cit., p. 97.
79. *Ibid.*
80. *Ibid*
81. Keil and Delitzsch, op. cit., p. 319.
82. Canon H.D.M. Spence and Joseph S. Exell, *Pulpit Commentary, Psalms, Vol. I* (New York: Funk and Wagnalls Co., n.d.), p. 153.

83. John Gill, *Dr. Gill's Commentary–Old Testament Judges–Psalms,
Vol. II* (Reprint ed.; London, England: William Hill Collingridge, 1954), pp.
950-951.
84. Rachmiel Frydland, *"Messianic Prophecy"* unpublished manuscript–
1980.
85. Berger, "Nizzahon Vetus" in *The Jewish Christian Debate in the
High Middle Ages,* op. cit., p. 155.
86. Hengstenberg, op. cit., p. 86.
87. *Ibid.,* op. cit., p. 247.
88. Kac, op. cit., pp. 75-76.
89. Levine, op. cit., pp. 24-25.
90. *Ibid.,* p. 25.
91. Sigal, op. cit., p. 37.
92. Hengstenberg, op. cit., p. 253.
93. Levine, op. cit., p. 253
94. *Ibid.* , pp. 27-28.
95. Sigal, op. cit. , pp, 66-67.
96. *Ibid.,* pp. 38-39.
97. Levine, op. cit., p. 28.
98. Sigal, op. cit, pp, 54-55.
99. Clarke, *Clark's Commentary, Vol. V.,* op. cit., p. 326.
100.Levine, loc. cit.
101.Young, *Young's Analytical Concordance to the Bible*, op. cit., p.
853.
102.Sigal, op. cit., pp. 53-54.
103.Edwin Oster, "Hermeneutics," unpublished material, 1974. Notes
to a lecture series on Biblical Hermeneutics at Seattle Bible Training School
[now Seattle Bible College], Seattle, Wa.
104.Young, *Young's Analytical Concordance to the Bible*, op. cit., p.
712.
105.*Ibid.* p.218.
106.Sigal, op. cit., p.80.
107.*Ibid.,* p.82.
108.*Ibid.*
109.Patai, op. cit., p.166.
110.Sigal, op. cit., pp. 80-81.
111.Levine, op. cit., p. 18.
112.Young, *Young's Analytical Concordance to the Bible,* op. cit., p.
752.
113.Geoffrey Wigoder ed., *Encyclopedia Dictionary of Judaica* (New
York: Keter Publishing House Jerusalem LTD., 1974), pp. 414, 584-586.
114.John Bowker, *The Targums and Rabbinic Literature* (London,
England: Cambridge University Press, 1969), p. 122.
115.J.W. Ethridge, *The Targums of Onkelos and Jonathan Ben Ussiel
on the Pentateuch, Vol. I* (New York: KTAV Publishing House Inc., 1968),
p. 279.
116.*Ibid.,* p. 331.
117.Samson H. Levey, *The Messiah: An Aramaic Interpretation; The
Messianic Exegesis of the Targum,* op. cit., p. 11.
118.Ethridge, op. cit., p. 309.

119. A. Cohen, *The Teachings of Maimonides* (London, England: George Routledge and Sons Ltd., 1927), p. 221.
120. Edersheim, op. cit., p. 716.
121. Kac, op. cit., p. 80.
122. William G. Braude, *Pesikta Rabbati* (New Haven, Conn: Yale University, 1968), pp. 678-680
123. Theodore Laetsch, *Bible Commentary: Jeremiah* (St. Louis: Concordia Pub. House, 1970), p. 193.
124. Edersheim, op. cit., p. 719.
125. J.F. Stenning ed., *The Targum of Isaiah* (London, England: Clarendon Press, 1949), p. 28.
126. *Ibid.*, p. 32.
127. *Ibid.*, p. 40.
128. "Seder Nezikin," *The Babylonian Talmud*, trans. I. Epstein, Vol. 3. (London, England: The Soncino Press, 1935), pp. 626-627
129. Stenning, loc. cit.
130. *Ibid.*, p. 110
131. *Ibid.*, p. 148.
132. Levey, op.cit., p. 63.
133. *Ibid.*, p.66.
134. Baron, *Rays of Messiah's Glory*, op. cit., p. 271
135. A. Phillips, *Machzor For Rash Hashana and Yom Kippur* (Revised ed.) New York: Hebrew Pub. Co., 1931), p. 239.
136. Laetsch, loc. cit.
137. "Seder Nezikin," *The Babylonian Talmud*, op. cit., p. 668.
138. "Seder Mo'ed," *The Babylonian Talmud*, trans. I. Epstein, Vol. 4 (London, England: Soncino Press, 1938), p. 10.
139. Levey, op. cit., p. 92.
140. "Seder Zeraim," *The Babylonian Talmud*, trans. I. Epstein (London, England: Soncino Press, 1938), p. 350.
141. "Seder Mo'ed," *The Babylonian Talmud*, trans. I. Epstein, Vol. 3 (London, England: Soncino Press, 1938), p. 246.
142. Edersheim, p. 710.
143. Ibid.

CHAPTER 5

Jewish Polemics and Anti-Semitism

Introduction

nti-Semitism is defined by Webster's dictionary as "prejudice against Jews" and "discrimination against or persecution of Jews."[1]

A Semite is defined as,

> one of the descendents of Shem. A member of a Caucasian race now chiefly represented by Jews and Arabs, but in ancient times including also the Babylonians, Assyrians, Aramaeans, Phoenicians, and various other people of southwestern Asia.[2]

Since other Semitic people have not been persecuted and hated historically like the Jews, a more exact description of this attitude would be to call it anti-Jewish or anti-Judaic. But because of the general use of this term and its basic application to Jews, anti-Semitism is the accepted description of the Gentile hatred toward the Jewish people.

Anti-Semitism is as old as the Jewish people themselves. It can be traced back to the Pharaoh and his hatred of Israel (Exodus 1-12). The Assyrian, Babylonian, Greek and Roman conquests have also added to the unjust treatment of the Jewish people.

Anti-Semitism is a highly complex movement and has taken many forms throughout history. Unfortunately, some within the Christian Church have contributed to this attitude and have played a part in the history of anti-Semitic persecution. The charges of being "Christ-killers" and "deicides" along with the accusation of "ritual murder (killing of Christians or Gentiles and then using their blood in the Passover service)" was directed toward Jews from "Christian" sources.[3]

> The popular literature produced during the Middle Ages was almost entirely dominated by a single point of view, that of Orthodox Christianity; mystery, miracles, and morality plays, chronicles, and legends, poems, folk tales and folk songs, all painted the Jew as the fount of evil, deliberately guilty of unspeakable crimes against the founder of the Christian faith and the Christian church.[4]

The anti-Jewish attitude can be traced back to Church Fathers such as Tertullian (AD 155-220), Hippolytus (AD 170-236), Cyprian (AD 195-258), and Chrysostom (AD 347-407), who each wrote divisive and anti-Biblical material concerning the Jews. The full force of the Church's anti-Semitic attitude was manifested in the years AD 1000-1500. These were the years in which the greatest Jewish atrocities were committed by the powerful Roman Catholic Church.

It is no exaggeration to say that the empirical Church, i.e., the Church of history; has shown herself the greatest enemy of the Jewish people. The Church has, therefore, been the first and foremost stumbling block in the Jewish appreciation of Jesus. In the words of Canon Danby, no mean authority on the subject: 'The Church, by its deliberate choice and conduct, has made itself one gigantic and seemly impenetrable obstacle between them and the figure of our blessed Lord.'

The memory of terrible wrongs suffered at the hands of Christians has deeply entered the Jewish consciousness. It could not have been otherwise. Crimes perpetrated in the name of one religion against another religion make victims into martyrs and martyrs are not easily forgotten.

The most eloquent witness of what the Jews thought about Christianity comes from a letter addressed to German Jewry by Isaac Zarphati, a fugitive from Christian Europe to Mohammedan, Turkey: 'I have been informed of the calumnies, more bitter than death, which has befallen our brethren in Germany; of the tyrannical laws, the compulsory baptisms and the banishments which daily take place. And if they flee from one place, greater misfortunes befall them in another ... the spiritual guides and the monks, false priests, rise up against the unhappy people and say, 'we shall persecute them to destruction, the name of Israel shall no longer be remembered. The Christians not only drive them from place to place, but lurk after their lives, brandish over them the sharpened sword, cast them into the flaming fire, into surging waters or into stinking swamps ... It is better to live among Mohammedans than among Christians ... All your days are gloomy, even your Sabbaths and festivals.'[5]

The Anti-Semitic Argument

The argument that Christianity has been the great enemy of the Jewish people, is a standard objection raised by Jewish polemicists. Samuel Levine states this anti-Semitic argument;

If Christianity is the religion of grace, brotherly kindness, and other nice qualities, as the Christians claim it is, then why have the Christians throughout history been so cruel and murderous, especially towards the Jews? If you would read, The History of Anti-Semitism by Leon Poliakov, and the book by Malcolm Hay, published under the titles of either The Foot of Pride or Europe and the Jews, you would see some shocking evidence of Christian behaviour throughout the centuries. Here are some examples from the two books: It was the annual custom at Toulouse to drag a Jew into the Church of St. Stephen and slap him on the face before the altar, occasionally with such force that, at least once, the Jew's brains and eyes were knocked out. In discussing the Crusades (which started in 1096), many non-Jewish history books choose to omit the fact that thousands of Jews were offered the choice of the cross or the sword. In refusing conversion, thousands of Jews were killed throughout France and Germany. The Crusaders themselves were promised eternal happiness by the Church for killing 'infidels' such as the Jews. In 1215, at the Fourth Lateran Council, Pope Innocent III decreed that Jews in Christian countries must wear something that readily identified them as Jews. Jews were forced to wear yellow circular forms, pointed hats, and similar disgracing items when they were in public. Hitler learned this piece of history well, and revived this Christian custom when he took control over Nazi Germany. If you read *A History of the Marranos* by Cecil Roth, you will see what Christian 'love' is about, in its true form. Roth describes the procedures of the Holy Inquisition in Spain, where, after totally secret trials, various tortures were used to elicit from the accused a confession that the person had been doing Jewish practices. In an earlier period, the most common torture would be to raise the accused, and then let him fall from a beam, to which he was attached by a short rope, so that when he fell, he would stop with a horrible jerk before he reached the ground.

... in 1391, Archdeacon Ferrand Martinez went throughout Spain, offering Jews the sword or the cross. Many accepted the cross in order to save their lives. In 1411, another Christian cleric called Ferrer did it again. Thus, there were at least 50,000 (some say more) Jews who accepted Christianity instead of the sword, and it was these pseudoChristians, who were called Marranos ('pigs' in Spanish), who were watched most carefully by the Holy Inquisition.

... and even in modern times, during the Nazi destruction of the Jews, the Pope remained silent the entire time, even when he knew what was happening and could have done something. This silence was perfectly consistent with the essence of the Christian attitude towards the Jews throughout history–either convert them or kill them, or watch them be killed. So the question remains—why were the Christians so terribly cruel to the Jews and how could one call Christianity a religion of love, when so many people have been murdered in the name of Jesus? [6]

Israeli religious scholar, Pinchas Lapide states regarding the subject of the Church and anti-Semitism:

When Christianity became the state religion of the Roman Empire, there was no room in the Church for the Jews. A dogmatism which would tolerate only one people of God, one kind of divine election and a single way of salvation, condemned all Jews as murderers of Christ—John 19:5-18, who had the devil for their father—John 8:44. The rabbis were damned as well, lumped together as the synagogue of Satan—Revelation 2:9; 3:9. In the period from the fourth to the sixteenth century no fewer than 106 popes and 92 church councils issued anti-Jewish laws and regulations. Exile and mass murder, compulsory baptism and kidnapping of children, suffering and torture made Israel a martyr, a figure of affliction among the Gentiles, and its Diaspora a bloody, thousand-year long Via Dolorosa. [7]

To Judaism, objections dealing with this issue, are possibly the most potent and forceful that can be aimed at the Christian faith. Even if all of the other Jewish arguments are proved to be fallacious, the arguments dealing with Christianity's murderous behaviour toward Jews still remain and from the Jewish perspective, they invalidate the entire faith in Jesus as Messiah. How can the true religion of the Messiah direct such vicious assaults against the Jewish people; the chosen of God? If Jesus is the builder of the Church (Matthew 16:18), the behavior of the His Church directly reflects upon Him. Therefore, to the Jew the atrocities of the Church become the atrocities of Christ. When all the evidence is brought forward, the Christian's basic response, is to stammer a humble apology and then attempt to offer some excuse. But, genuine answers can be given that help clear the Jewish confusion on this issue. In dealing with this problem, no quick and slight solutions are acceptable; however, there are answers that can be given which do relieve the misunderstandings held by Jews concerning the Christian faith and anti-Semitism. Three areas of evidence will be examined in dealing with this anti-Semitic problem.

1. *The Source of "Christian anti-Semitism" is not Found in the New Testament.*

Jewish scholarship has claimed that the basis of the anti-Semitism practiced by the Church throughout history is found within the teachings of the New Testament. Jewish scholar Samuel Sandmel, states concerning the New Testament and anti-Semitism.

> For the Jewish reader there are, in addition, some special problems. The tenor and tone of the New Testament are such that they put him immediately on the defensive. He reads what are no more and no less than direct or oblique attacks on Jews and on Judaism, for much of the New Testament was composed in a time of sharp conflict between Jews and Christians. As the Jewish reader identifies himself with his fellow Jews, he is apt to identify historical events, such as the Crusades, the Black Plague, the expulsion from Spain, Hitler, and the like, with sentiments to be found in the New Testament. Immediately an understandable bar to his sympathetic reading arises.[8]

Jewish sources point out New Testament references that allegedly are anti-Jewish in nature. In John 8:44, Jesus states concerning the scribes and Pharisees,

> *"Ye are of your father, the devil, and the lusts of your father ye will do ..."*

In Luke 10:25-37, the story of the good Samaritan, stated by Jesus is pointed out to be anti-Semitic. Mark 14:55-65 describes the trial of Jesus and is accused of having an anti-Semitic tone. Matthew 23:1-39 records Jesus' statements concerning the Jewish scribes and Pharisees;

"Woe unto you, scribes and Pharisees, hypocrites! for ye are like unto whited sepulchres, which indeed appear beautiful outwardly, but are within full of dead men's bones, and of all uncleanness" (Matthew 23:27).

"Ye serpents, ye generation of vipers, how can ye escape the damnation of hell?" (Matthew 23:33).

These verses are also considered hateful and anti-Jewish. In Acts 2:23, the Apostle Peter states concerning the death of Jesus,

*"Him, being delivered by the determinate counsel and foreknowledge of God, ye [Jews] have taken, and by **wicked** hands have crucified and slain"* (Acts 2:23).

This verse is accused of placing the blame for Christ's death on the Jewish people and as later serving as the basis for the attacks made by Christians upon Jews for killing the Messiah. The writings of the Apostle Paul, in which he discusses the Mosaic Law and Israel's spiritual blindness, are also stated to be anti-Semitic (Romans 4, 9-11; Galatians 3; 2 Thessalonians 2:14-16).

A number of points need to be established in order to clear up these allegations. First, the early apostolic Church was made up of Jews, not Gentiles. The writers of the New Testament were all Jewish believers in Jesus with the possible exception of Luke. The above noted passages, then, took place within the nation and family of the Jewish people, just as the books of the Old Testament were written within a Jewish framework. In Acts 7:51-53, Stephen makes a series of declarations which are considered by Jewish polemicists to be anti-Jewish in nature;

"Ye stiffnecked and uncircumcised in heart and ears, ye do always resist the Holy Ghost: as your fathers did, so do ye" (Acts 7:51).

Which of the prophets have not your fathers persecuted? and they have slain them which shewed before of the coming of the Just One; of whom ye have been now the betrayers and murderers:

"Who have received the law by the disposition of angels, and have not kept it" (Acts 7:52-53).

If one compares these verses with passages in the Old Testament, great similarity can be found.

"Ah sinful nation, a people laden with iniquity, a seed of evildoers, children that are corrupters; they have forsaken the Lord, they have provoked the Holy One of Israel unto anger, they are gone away backward" (Isaiah 1:4).

"That this is a rebellious people, lying children, children that will not hear the law of the Lord:" (Isaiah 30:9).

"For my people is foolish, they have not known me; they are sottish children, and they have none understanding: they are wise to do evil, but to do good they have no knowledge" (Jeremiah 4:22).

*"In vain have I smitten your children; they received no correction:
... your own sword hath devoured your prophets, like a destroying
lion"* (Jeremiah 2:30).

*"But they [Israel] mocked the messengers of God, and despised
his words, and misused his prophets, until the wrath of the Lord
arose against his people, till there was no remedy"* (2 Chronicles
36:16).

Since both the Old and New Testaments were written within the
Jewish community and both contain statements describing the sinfulness of Israel, both must be equally considered anti-Semitic. No
intelligent thinking Jew would ever endorse an idea that ascribed
anti-Semitism to the Hebrew Scriptures. Likewise, it is also incorrect
to label the New Testament as anti-Semitic literature, when one
recognizes that it is Jewish literature written within a Jewish context,
reporting prophetic pronouncements upon both Jewish and Gentile
sin.

Secondly, the New Testament does not teach that the Jews are
guilty of being "Christ-killers." Jesus says in John 10:17-18,

*"Therefore doth my Father love me, because I lay down my life,
that I might take it again.*

*No man taketh it from me, but I lay it down of myself. I have power
to lay it down, and I have power to take it again. This commandment have I received of my Father"* (John 10:17-18).

Jesus asserts here that His death was not the end result of a Jewish
conspiracy, but rather a part of His plan to redeem the world from
sin. In Matthew 20:18-19, Jesus states that His death involved both
Jews and Gentiles;

*"Behold, we go up to Jerusalem; and the Son of man shall be
betrayed unto the chief priests and unto the scribes, and they shall
condemn him to death,*

*"And shall deliver him to the Gentiles to mock, and to scourge,
and to crucify him; and the third day he shall rise again"* (Matthew
20:18-19).

The New Testament teaches that it was not the handful of Jewish
and Gentile executioners who caused Jesus' death, but rather the sin
of all mankind that led to the substitutionary death of the Messiah
(Isaiah 53:4-6; 1 Corinthians 15:3; Hebrews 2:9; John 3:16; 1 Timothy
2:6; 1 John 2:2; 1 John 3:16). To assume that the Jews are solely
responsible for the death of Jesus totally ignores the teaching of the
New Testament which teaches *no* such concept.

Thirdly, the New Testament view of the Jewish people is a
compassionate one. Paul states that his love for Israel and his country-
men is so great that he is willing to be "accursed from Christ," for
their sake (Romans 9:1-3; Romans 10:1-4; 3:1-2). In Matthew 23:37-
39, Luke 13:34-35, and Luke 19:41-44, Jesus weeps and laments over

Jerusalem and the Jews, demonstrating His deep love and concern for them. Throughout the Gospels, Jesus demonstrates His love and compassion for His people, the Jews (Matthew 9:36; 14:14; Matthew 15:32; Mark 6:34, 8:2).

Fourthly, in passages such as John 8:44 and Matthew 23:1-39, Jesus uses harsh words in speaking to the Jewish religious leaders. He is not directing these words to all Jews in general, but rather to the group of scribes and Pharisees who resisted Him and His message throughout His ministry. These words are not intended to be hateful or harmful but rather are corrective in nature. The stern rebukes do not constitute a basis for anti-Semitism anymore than Isaiah's or Ezekiel's warnings were anti-Semitic.

Lastly, the New Testament has high praise for the descendants of Abraham who loved and followed God, and includes them in the "hall of faith" (Hebrews 11:1-40). However, for those Jews who resisted God's laws, killed the prophets and rejected the Messiah, the New Testament writers had stern words of warning. These same warnings were also applied to Gentiles who resisted God's will. It is in this manner that the New Testament employs the words that are considered by Jewish polemicists to be anti-Semitic.

2. The Teachings of the New Testament Totally Deplore All Forms of Anti-Semitism.

The principles taught in the New Testament are those of love, forgiveness, kindness and mercy. No possible basis for hatred and violence toward Jews or Gentiles can be cited within the teaching of the Lord or His apostles. In Luke 23:34, Jesus prays for His executioners;

"Father, forgive them; for they know not what they do. ..."

This hardly gives credence to a directive of hatred and bitterness toward those who crucified Jesus. Jesus taught that true disciples and followers of His would be recognized by their love;

"A new commandment I give unto you, That ye love one another; as I have loved you, that ye also love one another.

By this shall all men know that ye are my disciples if ye have love one to another" (John 13:34-35).

The New Testament continues from this basis of love and describes the necessity of the following qualities to be a part of the life of a genuine believer of the Messiah. This list is representative of many more passages that could be given;

"Blessed are the merciful: for they shall obtain mercy" (Matthew 5:7).

"And when ye stand praying, forgive, if ye have ought against any: that your Father also which is in heaven may forgive you your trespasses" (Mark 11:25).

"Bless them which persecute you: bless, and curse not.

"Recompense to no man evil for evil ... avenge not yourselves, but rather give place unto wrath: for it is written, Vengeance is mine; I will repay, saith the Lord" (Romans 12:14, 17, 19, 21).

"... being reviled, we bless; being persecuted, we suffer it: Being defamed we entreat:" (1 Corinthians 4:12-13).

Charity suffereth long, and is kind; charity envieth not, charity vaunteth not itself, is not puffed up,

Doth not behave itself unseemly, seeketh not her own, is not easily provoked, thinketh no evil;

Rejoiceth not in iniquity, but rejoiceth in the truth;

Beareth all things, believeth all things, hopeth all things, endureth all things" (1 Corinthians 13:4-7).

Not rendering evil for evil, or railing for railing: but contrariwise blessing; knowing that ye are thereunto called, that ye should inherit a blessing" (1 Peter 3:9).

Above all things have fervent charity among yourselves: for charity shall cover the multitude of sins" (1 Peter 4:8).

The anti-Semitism practiced by "Christians" certainly finds no basis within the teachings of the New Testament. Instead, the New Testament pronounces judgment upon all hateful, murderous actions. For example;

"Ye have heard that it was said by them of old time, Thou shalt not kill; and whosoever shall kill shall be in danger of the judgment:

But I say unto you, That whosoever is angry with his brother without a cause shall be in danger of the judgment: and whosoever shall say to his brother, Raca, shall be in danger of the council; but whosoever shall say, Thou fool, shall be in danger of hell fire" (Matthew 5:21-22).

"For the wrath of God is revealed from heaven against all ungodliness and unrighteousness of men, who hold the truth in unrighteousness;" (Romans 1:18)

"Now the works of the flesh are manifest, which are these; Adultery, fornication, uncleanness, lasciviousness,

Idolatry, witchcraft, hatred, variance, emulations, wrath, strife, seditions, heresies,

Envyings, murders, drunkenness, revellings, and such like: of the which I tell you before, as I have also told you in the time past, that they which do such things shall not inherit the kingdom of God" (Galatians 5:19-21).

"Let all bitterness, and wrath, and anger, and clamour, and evil speaking, be put away from you, with all malice:" (Ephesians 4:31).

"Whosoever hateth his brother is a murderer: and ye know that no murderer hath eternal life abiding in him" (1 John 3:15).

"But the fearful, and unbelieving, and the abominable, and murderers, and whoremongers, and sorcerers, and idolaters, and all liars, shall have their part in the lake which burneth with fire and brimstone: which is the second death" (Revelation 21:8).

All of the above passages apply to the numerous types of persecution and mistreatment directed toward Jewish people from anti-Semitic groups. The New Testament calls all such action into judgment and makes it clear that no genuine Christian can practice this kind of behavior.

3. *The Source of Anti-Semitism is Found Within the Sinful Nature of Men:*

Anti-Semitism did not originate within any political, social or religious setting. Instead it was produced out of the heart of sinful mankind, and encouraged by Satan himself. The Hebrew Scriptures teach the awful wickedness of the human heart;

"The heart is deceitful above all things, and desperately wicked: who can know it" (Jeremiah 17:9).

All men are sinners, both Jews and Gentiles (Ecclesiastes 7:20; Romans 3:23), and anti-Semitism is one of the gross sins of the Gentile nations.

The name of Christianity has been blackened by people, who, under its banner, have committed atrocious actions to support their twisted philosophies and distorted ideas. Anti-Semitism is only one of the many goals of these imposters of the Christian faith. The Crusades, the Christian-Arab conflicts and the present religious wars of the Northern Ireland situation have no part of genuine New Testament Christianity, but rather use the Christian banner as a scapegoat for the evil deeds of political and social systems. History past has shown that the pagan rulers and kings who, under the guise of the Christian Church, practiced anti-Jewish actions had, as their goals, power, prestige and wealth and had no resemblance to the principles and purposes found in the New Testament. Even today, the so-called "Christian" organizations which encourage and practice anti-Semitism have these same types of goals in mind. These are sinful, wicked people, who share no spiritual kinship with born-again Christians. Each of these groups should be exposed and labeled correctly as "Hate Organizations," which share absolutely nothing with the teachings of the New Testament. The New Testament warns of this type of deception and false "Christianity."

"And Jesus answered and said unto them, Take heed that no man deceive you.

"And many false prophets shall rise, and deceive many" (Matthew 24:4, 11).

"A good tree cannot bring forth evil fruit, neither can a corrupt tree bring forth good fruit.

Every tree that bringeth not forth good fruit is hewn down, and cast into the fire.

Wherefore by their fruits ye shall know them.

Not everyone that saith unto me, Lord, Lord, shall enter into the kingdom of heaven; but he that doeth the will of my Father which is in heaven.

Many will say to me in that day, Lord, Lord, have we not prophesied in thy name? and in thy name have cast out devils? and in thy name done many wonderful works?

And then will I profess unto them, I never knew you: depart from me, ye that work iniquity" (Matthew 7:18-23).

"For such are false apostles, deceitful workers, transforming themselves into the apostles of Christ.

And no marvel; for Satan himself is transformed into an angel of light.

Therefore it is no great thing if his ministers also be transformed as the ministers of righteousness; whose end shall be according to their works" (2 Corinthians 11:13-15).

"They profess that they know God; but in works they deny him being abominable, and disobedient and unto every good work reprobate" (Titus 1:16).

The Apostle Paul warned of a departing from the Christian faith which found fulfillment within the Roman Catholic religious and political systems which enforced anti-Semitism in the Middle Ages. He stated,

"Now the Spirit speaketh expressly, that in the latter times some shall depart from the faith, giving heed to seducing spirits, and doctrines of devils:" (1 Timothy 4:1).

The erroneous teachings and anti-Jewish attitudes that have come out of the Catholic system and its departure from New Testament Christianity form much of the misunderstanding of Christianity on the part of Judaism.

Jewish scholars appear to see no distinction between the New Testament as represented today by Fundamental and Evangelical Christianity and the Roman Catholic Church. The differences, however, are massive in nature and the knowledge of these distinctions would prove very helpful in the understanding of the true nature of the Christian faith. Throughout Church history, many true Christians were persecuted and killed by the "Christian" powers, along with the Jews. These Christians were labeled as "heretics" by the Roman Catholic Church and experienced, as the Jewish people, much hatred and violence. No true form of Christianity whether Catholic or Protestant would be involved in the murderous bloodshed of people.

The source then of anti-Semitism in the Church is found not within the New Testament and the teaching of the Lord Jesus Christ, but rather within the hearts of men who were nothing but evil imposters and deceivers hiding their evil philosophies under the name of Christianity.

4. The Holocaust

The Holocaust of World War II is considered the culmination point of the history of anti-Semitism. It is estimated that four to six million Jews were killed during the years of German Nazism. Adolf Hitler, the German leader who led this campaign of murder, was able to bring about the allegiance of a predominantly nominal Christian nation in this anti-Semitic drive. German Christianity did not develop such an anti-Semitic idea, but the sin of doing nothing about this great crime lays squarely upon the shoulders of the German church. Because of the failure of the majority of the German Christians to react against and reject all such Jewish hatred, much blame is directed toward the Christian faith. However, it was not only the Christians of Germany who failed to act but those in the United States and Europe who knew of this atrocity and also did nothing.

Under the circumstances of the German dictatorship, the pleadings of helplessness and the obedience to the Scriptural command to submit to governmental powers were given by Christians. Yet the higher laws of God demanded a much different response and too few had the courage and conviction to obey God's Word, risk their lives and help stop the murdering of Jews.

What should Christians have done? This is a question that has been asked and will continue to deserve attention. There were Christians who responded and helped the Jewish people, such as the ten Boom family of Holland who hid Jews in their home against the laws of their country. But much, much more should have been done.[9] This question is one that each Christian must answer and then respond to help stamp out all forms of injustice and evil, whether it be directed toward Jews or Gentiles. Jewish believer Rachmiel Frydland who lived through the persecution of World War II, stated concerning the failure of Christians to protect the Jews,

> Maybe it is unfair and impetuous to condemn the majority of the German Christians who lived in Poland. Had I been born of German parents in Poland, I probably also would have followed the policies of my government, even if it included pillage, destruction and extermination of millions of people; especially if my government explained that it was done to save the world from 'Jewish Communism.' Only by the grace of God was I born a Jew, to be persecuted and not to have had the opportunity to persecute others. Who can know the heart of men, even my own heart? 'He that stands, let him watch lest he falls.'[10]

5. The Key to Understanding the Holocaust

The Holocaust demonstrates the fact that man's capacity for evil far outweighs human righteousness and goodness. Good people allow and commit evil actions, and no amount of human sincerity and desire can change that fact. The Holocaust demonstrates the world's great need of a Savior.

Governmental powers and educational and religious institutions cannot provide the answers to man's problems. Only God, the Creator of the world can change the inward, sinful nature and this is exactly the message of the Gospel (2 Corinthians 5:17; John 3:16-18). The following quotation is a fitting description of the sin of anti-Semitism;

An Associated Press article in 1945 written at Nuerenberg, October 26 states, 'Bull-necked, lugubrious Dr. Robert Lay, one-time luxury loving chief of Hitler's labor front, hanged himself in his cell last night at the Neurenberg jail, where he was awaiting trial as a war criminal. Col. John Harlan Amen, interrogation chief, disclosed today that Ley had left a document entitled, 'My Political Testimony,' which Amen said was a 'terrific apology for his anti-Semitism.' The message was directed to 'my German people.' Ley blamed anti-Semitism for Germany's downfall declaring: 'We have forsaken God, and therefore we were forsaken by God. We put human volition in the place of His Godly grace. In anti-Semitism, we violated a basic commandment of His creation. Anti-Semitism distorted our outlook, and we made grave errors. It is hard to admit mistakes, but the whole existence of our people is in question; we Nazis must have the courage to rid ourselves of anti-Semitism. We have to declare to the youth that it was a mistake.'[11]

Conclusion

Anti-Semitism is a major stumbling block between Jewish persons and the presentation of the Gospel. The Jewish sensitivity in this area is indeed understandable for much hate and evil has been directed toward the Jews. The material discussed in this chapter should prove helpful in understanding this problem.

The key in the Christian witness to the Jewish community is to demonstrate that the source of this problem is not found in the New Testament nor in the genuine Christian faith. Rather, it comes from the evil and sinful hearts of men who do not have the peace of God within them. All men, both Jew and Gentile have committed sinful, hateful acts and need the Savior, the Lord Jesus Christ. The Christian witness should emphasize that the Holocaust and similar events in Jewish history essentially point to man's great need of the Messiah of Israel. The Messiah's first appearance did not deal with political reformation, but rather it dealt with an inward reformation of the heart. If all the weapons of war were disarmed and destroyed, man would still invent ways of killing and committing violence. Real peace must start within man's heart and this is exactly what the Messiah came to bring. Genuine peace is only achieved when men repent of their sin and receive the forgiveness of sin by faith and trust in the Messiah, the Lord Jesus Christ. When He (the Prince of Peace) returns, His Kingdom of peace and righteousness will be founded upon this inward principle. The answer to anti-Semitism is not external change or improvement, but rather it is found in the inward change of man's heart that Jesus the Messiah alone can provide.

✆ ☙

Endnotes — Chapter 5

1.   *Webster's New World Dictionary* (New York: The World Publishing Co., 1967), p. 18.

2.   Henry J. Heydt, *Studies in Jewish Evangelism* (New York: American Board of Missions to the Jews, 1951), p. 68.

3.   Joshua Trachtenberg, *The Devil and the Jews* (New Haven, Conn: Yale Univ. Press, 1943), p. 126.

4.   *Ibid.*, p. 12.

5.   Jakob Jocz, *The Jewish People and Jesus Christ* (Grand Rapids: Baker Book House, 1979), pp. 93-94.

6.   Samuel Levine, *You Take Jesus, I'll Take God* (Los Angeles: Hamoroh Press, 1980), pp. 73-76.

7.   Pinchas Lapide, *Israelis, Jews and Jesus* (Garden City, New York: Doubleday and Company, 1979), p. 81.

8.   Samuel Sandmel, *A Jewish Understanding of the New Testament* (New York: KTAV Publishing House Inc., 1974), p. 10.

9.   My wife's grandmother, Janina Rabenda, who was a Polish Christian, helped and cared for Jewish people during World War II in their home city of Piotrkow Trybunalski, Poland.

10.   Rachmiel Frydland, *When Being Jewish was a Crime* (Nashville: Thomas Nelson Inc., 1978), p. 150.

11.   Heydt, op. cit., pp. 78-79.

CHAPTER 6

Jewish Polemics and
Christian Failures

The Jewish Argument

J ewish polemicists point out different areas of inconsistencies and failures on the part of Christianity as proof that the Christian faith is invalid. The first inconsistency is found within the realm of doctrines which are held by various forms of Christianity, yet contradict the teachings and principles of the New Testament. Isaac Troki relates concerning this:

> The majority of the followers of Christianity continue even at the present day to adore in their places of worship images of gold and silver, wood and stone, and many of them show divine reverence to the wafer, or sacramental bread by prostrating themselves before it. These practices they keep up in contradiction to the teachings of Jesus: who rigorously impressed upon his disciples and apostles to abstain from them, as well as the eating of sacrifices offered up to idols.[1]

A second Christian failure is stated by Isaac Mayer Wise:

> It [Christianity] cannot make us better men and better women, as it did not succeed in 16 centuries in civilizing and humanizing the nations under its sway ... Hence Christology is not the mother of these virtues, it can do us no good, it has done more harm than good to the nations of Europe.[2]

Gerald Sigal adds to this by saying,

> Christianity cannot be considered wholly good since so many wrongs have issued from its domination in many lands throughout extended periods in history. To argue, as many Christians missionary apologists do, that the evils resulting to the world in the wake of Christianity are not really of Christian origin is tantamount to claiming that the bad fruits growing on a tree were not produced by the tree. No amount of explaining can absolve Christianity from the innumerable wrongs stemming from the hegemony it has exercised over vast areas in the course of its tortuous history.[3]

The Christian Answer

Throughout the Jewish material referred to in this thesis, numerous arguments relating to these objections are mentioned. These seem to be the favorite polemic attacks used by Jewish polemicists.

The first argument raised by Mr. Troki concerning doctrinal inconsistency, is a very familiar one within Judaism. In response to this argument it must be affirmed that the defense of Christian doctrine is confined to the New Testament and the person and ministry of Jesus Christ, for that in essence is the Christian faith. The practices mentioned by Mr. Troki are not taught in the New Testament and should be rejected by all New Testament believers. The Roman Catholic Church, which is the form of Christianity being referred to here, has allowed much fallacious and horrendous [horrible] dogma into its teachings. This has basically transpired because it has strayed from the apostolic authority of the Scriptures. However, since these practices are not a part of the New Testament faith, they fail to apply to this presentation. God alone will be the Judge of the errors of the forms of Christianity which do not hold to the sole authority of the Scriptures.

The modern religious systems within Judaism itself are much divided in their application of the Hebrew Scriptures. But the Jewish failure to remain loyal to Biblical truth, by no means invalidates the Hebrew Scriptures or historic Biblical Judaism. In the same sense, the faults existing within aberrate forms of Christianity do not call into question the truthfulness of the New Testament. The New Testament warns concerning false teachers and deceivers, who add to and pervert the teachings of the New Testament (Matthew 7:15; 24:4-11; 2 Corinthians 11:1-5; Galatians 1:6-9; Jude 3). This is why such importance must be placed upon the appeal to the Scriptures alone as the basis of Biblical truth (2 Timothy 3:16-17).

The second objection referred to in this chapter deals with the problem of "Christianity's" sinful and evil actions. It is obvious that Jewish polemicists are unable to recognize that there is a difference between actions and events that have occurred under the name of Christianity and the New Testament faith. This problem has derived from the fact that the Jewish people have historically lived under some of the most corrupt representations of the Church. Evil actions such as immorality, wars, murders, and anti-Semitism have been blamed on Christ and His Church. There were periods of time in the Middle Ages when Christianity and the Gentile world at large were so inter-related that actions committed by Gentiles were considered by the Jewish community to be Christian. Other problems came through the powerful political realms in which Christianity became involved. But the historical happenings that have blackened the name of the Church did not find their source in the New Testament. Instead, misdirected Christians and imposters used Christianity as a banner to justify their evil deeds.

A modern example of this type of deception is found in the murderous and cultic practices of Jim Jones, who acted in the name of Christ, yet in no possible manner was related to the Lord Jesus and His Church. There are many other examples of falsifications that have occurred throughout history in which Christianity has become the cover for hideous and wicked crimes.

Mr. Sigal describes the bad fruits of Christianity and then asks how bad fruit growing on the tree can be said to not be a part of the tree? If Mr. Sigal had a proper understanding of Jesus' words in Matthew 7:15-23 and Luke 6:43-49, this problem would be cleared up. Jesus says,

> *"Wherefore by their fruits ye shall know them. Not everyone that saith unto me Lord, Lord, shall enter the kingdom of heaven; but he that doeth the will of my Father which is in heaven"* (Matthew 7:20-21).

Jesus is saying that bad fruit cannot be attributed to those who are doing the "will of my Father." If bad fruit is the result of their lives, then they are revealed to be "false prophets."

> *"Beware of false prophets, which come to you in sheep's clothing, but inwardly they are ravening wolves. Ye shall know them by their fruits"* (Matthew 7:15-16a).

It is true that Christians fail and sin at times, for the followers of the Lord Jesus have never been free from faults and failures. It is possible that sincere Christians may have been a part of wicked and immoral deeds, either unknowingly or foolishly. Yet the New Testament calls all such action sin and asserts that no genuine Christian can continue to practice such things and be considered a follower of Christ (1 John 3:6-10). Repentance, forgiveness and restoration are therefore necessary in such circumstances. The "will of my Father" mentioned by Jesus in Matthew 7:21, is to allow the bad tree and its fruit to be rooted up and the good tree of fellowship with Christ to be planted.

Conclusion

In defense of the Christian faith, the history of genuine Christianity reveals that it has been more of a power for good and blessing upon mankind than any other social or religious force. Education, hospitalization and support for the needy around the world has historically been provided, in the vast majority of cases, by the Christian Church.[4] On the continent of Africa alone, 85% of the schools and hospitals have been provided by Christian missionary movements.[5] Any examination today of causes to help the under-privileged and needy will reveal that Christianity is the leading force in these areas. To assert that the Christian faith has brought damage and hurt wherever it has been an influence is incorrect. The problems of Europe, the United States and the world, have not come from Christianity but rather from the sin, selfishness and rebellion of the human heart. Contrary to the claims of these Jewish polemicists, the Messiah, the Lord Jesus Christ, is the answer to man's needs and the testimony of thousands of changed lives can confirm this.

ED ED

ENDNOTES — CHAPTER 6

1. Isaac Troki, *Faith Strengthened* (New York: Hermon Press, 1970), p. 16.

2. Isaac Mayer Wise, *A Defense of Judaism Versus Proselytizing Christianity* (Cincinnati: The American Israelite, 1889), p. 127, cited in Walter Jacob, *Christianity Through Jewish Eyes* (Cincinnati: Hebrew Union College Press, 1974), p. 81.

3. Gerald Sigal, *The Jew and the Christian Missionary: The Jewish Response to Missionary Christianity* (New York: KTAV Publishing House, Inc., 1981), p. 203.

4. Statistics published by U.S. Center for World Missions—Frontier Fellowship, 1981 William Carey Library.

5. *"Penetrating the Last Frontiers"*—U.S. Center for World Missions, March/April, 1983, pp. 17-19.

CHAPTER 7

Jewish Polemics and Messianic Expectations

The Jewish Argument

Judaism sees the Messianic advent as a singular event in history, in which all of the Hebrew prophecy regarding the Messiah finds fulfillment. The Messiah will usher in the visible Davidic throne, and the nation of Israel will be pre-eminent among all the nations of the earth. This is the Jewish traditional expectation regarding the Messiah.

The argument that Jesus was not the Messiah because His coming failed to bring in the Messianic Kingdom is continually appealed to by Jewish polemicists. This objection has been examined earlier in this thesis, however, an analysis penetrating deeper into this argument should prove beneficial. Isaac Troki gives the essential elements of this argument;

> I was once asked by a Christian scholar, 'Why do you Jews refuse to believe that Jesus Christ was the Messiah, evidence concerning him having been given by the true prophets, in whose words you also believe?' ... A few of these arguments may be here introduced. He was not the Messiah is evident: lst, from his pedigree; 2ndly, from his acts; 3rdly, from the period in which he lived; and 4thly, from the fact that during his existence, the promises where not fulfilled, which are to be realized on the advent of the expected Messiah, whereas the fulfillment of the conditions alone can warrant a belief in the identity of the Messiah.[1]

He continues,

> As to the pedigree of Jesus, he was not a descendant of David, being merely affiliated to him through Joseph, as is testified in the Gospel ... As to the works of Jesus, we find that He says of himself, Matthew 10:34, 'Think not that I am come to make peace on earth; I came not to send peace but the sword.'

> On the other hand, we find Holy Writ attributing to the true and expected Messiah actions contrary to those of Jesus. ... Scripture says of the true and expected Messiah in Zechariah 9:10; 'And he shall speak peace unto the heathen ...'. And to the period of his existence, it is evident that he did not come at the time foretold by the prophets; for they predicted the advent of the Messiah to happen at the latter days, see Isaiah 11:2 ... Fourthly, we have to consider the promises contained in the words of the prophets.

> At the time of the King Messiah there is to be only one kingdom and one king, namely the true King Messiah. ... At the time of the King Messiah, there is to be in the world but one creed and one religion. ... At the time of the Messiah, the idolatrous images and their memorial, as also the false prophets and the spirit of profanity

are to vanish from the earth. ... At the time of the Messiah, there will be no sins and iniquities in the world. ... At the time of the King Messiah and after the war with Gog and Magog, there will be peace and tranquillity throughout the world, and men will no longer require any weapons of war ... At the time of the King Messiah there will be peace in the Holy Land between the ferocious and domestic animals. ... At the time of the Messiah there will be no troubles, cares, and anxieties ... At the time of the Messiah the Shechinah (effulgency of divine presence) shall return to Israel as in former days. ... the above indications pointed out by the prophets as indispensable attributes of the true Messiah, have not been fulfilled in Jesus the Nazarene.[2]

The Christian Answer

The four basic arguments listed by Troki are as follows: Jesus was not the Messiah based on 1) His pedigree. 2) His acts. 3) The time period in which He lived. 4) The promises were not fulfilled in Him .

To answer these objections, one must go to the New Testament and there the solutions to each of the arguments listed by Mr. Troki will be discovered.

1. *His Pedigree*

Concerning the first argument, Troki states that Jesus was not really the son of Joseph or a descendant of David because He was not the offspring of Joseph. Therefore, the genealogies which give Joseph's lineage recorded in Matthew 1:1-16 and Luke 3:23-38 do not apply to Jesus. He further points out so-called "discrepancies" between these two accounts which then invalidate them as trustworthy records.

Upon a careful examination of the New Testament the answer to this is found. Matthew 1:1-16 gives the genealogy of Jesus through Joseph, who was a descendant of David. Jesus, as Joseph's adopted son, became the legal heir and received the right to this father's inheritance. Matthew's genealogical records descend back from Joseph (through Solomon) to David and Abraham. This lineage establishes Jesus' right to the theocratic crown. Luke 3:23-38 on the other hand, records the genealogical line of Mary, through Nathan to David and then proceeds all the way back to Adam. Matthew refers to Joseph's lineage and Luke refers to Mary's lineage. On this basis, the obvious differences between the two accounts are explained. Why then does Luke 3:23 attribute his genealogy to Joseph, if it actually applies to Mary? Scholar J.W. Haley provides the answer; he states,

> Mary, since she had no brothers, was an heiress; therefore her husband, according to Jewish law, was reckoned among her father's family, as his son. So that Joseph was the actual son of Jacob, and the legal son of Heli ... The latter (Luke 3:23-38) employs Joseph's

name instead of Mary's in accordance with the Israelite law that 'genealogies must be reckoned by fathers not mothers.'[3]

From the book *A Harmony of the Gospels*, the following information regarding the lineage of Mary in Luke 3:23-38 is provided;

> The objection that Mary's name is not in Luke's version needs only the reply that women were rarely included in Jewish genealogies; though giving her descent, Luke conforms to custom by not mentioning her by name. The objection that Jews never gave the genealogy of women is met by the answer that this is a unique case; Luke is talking about a virgin birth. How else could the physical descent of one who had no human father be traced? Furthermore, Luke has already shown a creative departure from customary genealogical lists by starting with Jesus and ascending up the list of ancestors rather than starting at some point in the past and descending to Jesus.[4]

This understanding of Matthew's and Luke's genealogy of Jesus is supported by a number of early Church Fathers: Irenaeus, Justin Martyr, and Origen to name a few.[5] Jewish tradition also offers some evidence of this in the Talmud which refers to the pains of hell and states that, "Mary the daughter of Heli," was seen there. Haley relates regarding this,

> This statement illustrates not only the bitter animosity of the Jews toward the Christian religion, but also the fact that, according to received Jewish tradition, Mary was the daughter of Heli; hence, that it is her genealogy which we find in Luke.[6]

From this it is established that Jesus was a descendant of David legally through Joseph and actually, by physical descent, through His mother Mary. Mary's lineage through King David is also established in other New Testament references (Luke 1:32, 69; Acts 2:30; Romans 1:3).

2. His Acts

The second objection raised by Troki deals with the actions and works of Christ, which he feels are not in agreement with what the Hebrew Scriptures teach regarding the Messiah. Troki quotes Matthew 10:34 and Matthew 20:28 and cross-references these New Testament passages with portions of the Hebrew Scriptures such as Zechariah 9:10, Isaiah 2:4, Psalm 72:11 and Daniel 7:27 respectively. Matthew 10:34 states that Jesus came not to make peace, but to bring a sword. But Zechariah 9:10 and Isaiah 2:4 describe the coming of the Messiah to be that of the establishment of peace on the earth. In Matthew 20:28, Jesus said that He came not to be served, but rather to serve and give His life. Psalm 72:11 and Daniel 7:27 state that instead of serving others the Messiah will be served by all nations. These teachings of Jesus and the Messianic prophecies of the Hebrew Scriptures seem to be contradictory.

These objections are dealt with by looking at the context of both of these passages in Matthew. In the context of Matthew 10:30-42, Jesus is describing the cost of being His disciple, and He states that being His follower will result in a division between friends, family and the world in general. When a person accepts Jesus as Lord and Savior and sets out to obey and fulfill his Lord's commands, he will become different from those with whom he may associate. This brings about a separation and Jesus describes this by the term "sword." Jesus is not calling men to physical fighting and warfare in Matthew 10:34, but instead He calls men to total commitment to His Lordship, which will result in possible persecution and loss. The Hebrew Scriptures demonstrate this truth in the lives of men such as Abraham, Moses, David, Jeremiah, Elijah and others, who all suffered because they chose God's way rather than the accepted standards and ideas of their time period. This truth has also been realized in the lives of countless Jewish people who have received Jesus as their Messiah, only to be rejected by their family and friends. Others have faced persecution and even death because of this decision to follow Christ. In no way does this teaching of Jesus in Matthew 10:34 contradict the Messianic peace described in Zechariah 9:10 and Isaiah 2:4. Jesus declares throughout the New Testament that He is the Author of peace (John 14:27; 16:33; Matthew 5:21, 22, 43, 44), and that the full realization of His peace will take place at His Second Coming.

The second "contradictory" passage is also cleared up upon an examination of the context. In Matthew 20:20-28, Jesus discusses the purpose of His first mission and the principles of God's Kingdom. He is questioned concerning the establishment of the Messiah's throne and rulership. To this He replies in verses 22, 23, 26-28, that His coming is to fulfill a divinely intended purpose which is "to give His life a ransom [Greek 'lutron,' the redemptive price] for many"[7] (Matthew 20:28). This event which took place on the cross, fulfills the prophetic element of numerous Hebrew passages such as Isaiah 52:13-53:12, Isaiah 50:6, Psalm 22:1-18, Daniel 9:24, which state that the Messiah will die and bear the sin of mankind. In Matthew 20, Jesus establishes that His first coming is to culminate in His death and resurrection, but His Second Coming will bring in the full Messianic Kingdom and in that day all nations and people will pay homage to Him. By examining these passages it is evident that no conflict between the Hebrew Scriptures and the life of Jesus exists.

3. *The Time Period in Which He Lived*

Isaac Troki continues his objections by affirming that Isaiah 2:2 and Ezekiel 38:8 teach that the Messiah will appear in the latter days. While it is true that this is the time period of Messiah's coming, other Hebrew passages refer to Messiah's coming as being an earlier event (Daniel 9:24-27; Malachi 3:1-3; Genesis 49:10; Isaiah 11:1). As demonstrated in chapter 4, the time period to which these prophecies point is approximately AD 30-50. Therefore, the Hebrew Scriptures speak of two Messianic appearances. One at the midpoint of history, and the other at the end of time. Furthermore, the work and mission of the Messiah is also divided in the Hebrew Scriptures. The Messiah appears as the Suffering Messiah in Isaiah 52:13-53:12, Psalm 22:1-18, and as the Reigning Messiah in Isaiah 11, Zechariah 13-14.

The first time period and mission occurred in Jesus' first appearance as the Suffering Messiah (AD 30) and the latter will take place upon His return as the Reigning Messiah, at the culmination of time. This perfectly harmonizes the Messianic teachings of the Old Testament.

There is no passage in the entirety of the Hebrew Scriptures which asserts that the prophetic predictions concerning the Messiah will all be fulfilled in one Messianic appearance. Instead, there are numerous passages, such as those just cited, which describe two Messianic appearances and two Messianic ministries. There are also examples in the Hebrew Scriptures where men of God waited upon God for His timing. In Genesis 37-45, Joseph is rejected by his brethren, but many years later rescues and receives them again. In Exodus 1-15, Moses is delayed 40 years after his first attempt to deliver his people. In Samuel 17 through 2 Samuel 3, David waits eight years after he had been anointed king before he receives the throne of Israel. Many other passages of Scripture relate the importance of accepting God's salvation according to His timetable (Isaiah 8:17; Psalm 62:15; Daniel 12:12; Micah 7:7).

The coming of the Messiah and the salvation that He brings will transpire in agreement with God's purposes and plans, and not according to man's shortsightedness. God has simply chosen to provide His redemption through two Messianic appearances.

4. *The Promises were not Fulfilled in Him*

The fourth objection raised by Troki affirms that the Messianic promises were not fulfilled in Jesus. He mentions eight characteristics that will be a result of the Messianic Kingdom and the coming of the Messiah. First, he states that when Messiah comes, there will be one Kingdom and one King (Daniel 2:44). Obviously, since the time of Christ, there have been many kingdoms and Jesus is surely not a visible King. However, the New Testament teaches that Jesus claims to be the King-Messiah, whose rulership will one day be made fully visible (Matthew 25:34; 27:11; 12:28; 13:31-32; 15:31; Luke 1:32:33; 10:9; 22:29-30). Jesus' Kingdom, which is not an earthly Kingdom (John 18:36-37), is none the less, still a growing and ever expanding Kingdom (1 Corinthians 15:23-28; Ephesians 1:20-22). Millions have bowed before Him and recognized Him as the "King of Kings and

Lord of Lords" (Revelation 19:16). Jesus asserts in the New Testament that His Kingdom will fully manifest itself at His Second Coming, and at that time, all of the Messianic prophecies (Old Testament and New Testament) will find their completion in Him.

"When the Son of man shall come in his glory, and all the holy angels with him, then shall he sit upon the **throne of his glory***:*

"And before him shall be gathered all nations: and he shall separate them one from another ...

"Then shall the King say unto them on his right hand, Come, ye blessed of my Father ..." (Matthew 25:31, 32, 34).

This promise will most assuredly find completion and total fulfillment in Jesus.

Troki continues and lists seven more Messianic qualities that he states have not found fulfillment in Jesus. They are as follows. When the Messiah comes, all will worship the Lord God (Isaiah 66:23; Zechariah 14:16). All idolatry and false prophecy will vanish from the earth (Zechariah 13:2; Isaiah 2:18; Zephaniah 2:11). There will be no more sin and iniquity on the earth (Zephaniah 3:13; Jeremiah 3:13; Ezekiel 37:23). There will be peace and tranquility throughout the world (Isaiah 2:4; Ezekiel 39:9). There will be peace among all the animal life (Isaiah 11:6-9, 23-28). There will be no fear, problems or anxieties among those who dwell on the earth (Isaiah 65:16-22). And lastly, when Messiah comes, the Shechinah presence of God's glory will return to Israel (Ezekiel 38:26-28; 39:29; 43:7; 48:35; Joel 2:27; 3:17; Isaiah 11:9; Jeremiah 31:34).

The New Testament is in perfect agreement with all of the above citations. The New Testament teaches that at the return of the Messiah, all people and nations will bow and confess Him as Lord (Philippians 2:9-11; I Timothy 6:14-16). At Messiah's coming all idolatry and deception will be put away (Matthew 13:41; 2 Thessalonians 1:7-10). Messiah's coming will bring in the rulership of righteousness and justice and all evil and sin will be removed (Matthew 25:31-33; Jude 14,15). When Messiah comes, peace and goodness will prevail on the earth (2 Peter 3:10-13; Revelation 21:4-8). When Messiah comes, God's presence will uniquely reside among His people (Revelation 21:22-27; 22:3-6). In every detail mentioned by Troki, the New Testament supports the Hebrew Scriptures with remarkable agreement.

After all of the Jewish argumentation is presented, it basically boils down to one issue. Are the events recorded in the Gospel true? Is Jesus truly everything the Gospel writers say He is? In the New Testament Jesus claimed to be the Messiah, offered strong Biblical evidence from the Hebrew Scriptures for this assertion, and then stated He would bring the finalization of all the Messianic prophecy upon a second return. Jesus must become the center of discussion, not Jewish tradition. The focal point should then be the historicity of Jesus' life and His promise of returning to establish the Messianic Kingdom.

Even though the Jewish Messianic expectations may be correct in a future application, they *must* submit to the facts of history and Messiah's promise of a return. Jewish writers Dennis Prager and Joseph Telushkin explain the overall Jewish appraisal of this New Testament claim, regarding the Second Coming of Messiah;

> For Jews, however, this explanation is logically unsatisfactory and the idea of a second coming is nowhere to be found in the Bible. In fact, it appears likely that this idea was not even known to Jesus himself, for he told his followers that some of them would still be alive when all the messianic prophecies would materialize— Mark 9:1; 13:30. This idea of a second coming was apparently formulated by later Christians to explain Jesus' failure to fulfill the messianic prophecies.[8]

It has already been demonstrated in this chapter, that the Hebrew Scriptures *do* teach the concept of two Messianic appearances. In Daniel 7:13, the Messiah King is spoken of as coming in the clouds, with the power and authority of Jehovah. On the other hand, Zechariah 9:9 describes the Messiah's coming in humility, riding upon an ass. Two clear, separate, distinct pictures of the Messiah's appearances are demonstrated in the Hebrew Scriptures. As stated earlier, the two offices and functions of the Messiah are also pictured in the Hebrew Scriptures—the Suffering Servant and the Reigning Ruler. The objection stated here by Prager and Telushkin is therefore incorrect.

The second argument raised here by these two gentlemen, regarding the application of Jesus' words in Mark 9:1 and 13:30 is also erroneous. Jesus' statement in Mark 9:1 finds its fulfillment in verses 2-10 of the same chapter. In Mark 13:30, Jesus is referring to the generation that sees the events that He has been speaking of throughout that particular chapter. In no possible way did Jesus fail to teach the Second Coming. By simply examining Mark 13, Prager and Telushkin could discover this New Testament truth.

Lastly, it is interesting to note how many times the argument against the historical trustworthiness of the New Testament is brought up by Jewish polemicists. It is used concerning the claim of the Second Coming, for the simple reason that this approach quickly dismisses the subject matter and serves this useful purpose when no other objections can be offered against the evidence of the New Testament.

The New Testament teaching concerning Jesus' Second Coming cannot be brushed off as easily as Troki, Prager and Telushkin wish to think. The New Testament narrative was written by eyewitnesses. They accurately reported both the teachings and events of Jesus' life and ministry. *Early* in the historical records of the Gospel, Jesus affirmed that He would be put to death (Matthew 16:21; John 2:19-21) and that after three days He would rise again from the dead (Matthew 17:23; John 10:17,18). Both of these events transpired just as Jesus stated. Jesus also taught *early* in His ministry, that He would return to His Father and at a later time in history, come again in power and glory to establish God's visible Kingdom (Matthew 16:27; Mark 8:38; Luke 9:26; John 14:3). The apostles confirmed and preached this message with the greatest of intensity (Acts 3:20; 2 Thessalonians 4:15-17). The early Church also believed this and continuously upheld this as the great hope of the believer.

To suppose that the idea of the Second Coming of Jesus was put together as an effort to make the Messianic claims of Jesus look good does not meet the facts. It would not have taken much persecution and pressure for people to abandon such a concept, if the truthfulness of such an assertion as this could not be established by apostolic confirmation. If the apostles did not believe this or knew it to be false, they most certainly would not have died for such an ill-founded lie. Any examination of the apostles should prove that they were not men capable of developing an elaborately well conceived myth like this, and then promoting it with such persuasion as to convince the whole empire of Rome. The people and nations of the Roman world of the First Century were educated, skeptical and aware of the events around them. They were not isolated and gullible but instead had all the knowledge that transportation and communication could provide. The evidence of the Gospel of Jesus certainly convinced them as hundreds and thousands responded to the message of the early Church.

Had the events of Christ's life not been true, ample evidence could have been brought forth to erase this religious excessiveness. Yet nothing of this nature ever occurred. Why? Because the facts of the Gospels were true and beyond refutation.

Those who reject the New Testament affirmation of Jesus' death, resurrection and return seem to take no account of the impossibility of the Gospel information to be the result of a concerted cover-up by the early Church. If the narrative of the New Testament were formed by a collective conspiracy, it involved so many hundreds of people that perfect agreement and collaboration would be impossible. Evidence of any collusion is also totally absent from these writings. If fact, the testimonies of each of the Gospels appear at times to be contradictory. However, when a close cross-examination is undertaken, the material of each of the four writers harmonizes.

These writings deal with public events, places and dates, something that is notably absent in mythological and legendary writings. The writers stress the importance of truth and honesty and sternly rebuke all forms of lying and deception. To suppose that the information concerning the Second Coming of Jesus was a part of cover-up operation produced by the early Church to make the Messiahship of

Jesus agreeable with the Hebrew Scriptures totally ignores the plain evidence of history.

Conclusion

The Gospels are truthful, factual documents. They provide the details of the life and claims of Christ. When these documents are examined in the light of the Old Testament prophecies, the confirmation of Jesus and His Messianic credentials are enforced. Jesus claims to be the Messiah of Israel and states that His death will be the fulfillment of Scripture and the means by which all of mankind's sin against God will be atoned (Luke 24:44-48). He proves that these claims are true by rising from the dead and defeating man's greatest enemy—death (1 Corinthians 15:16-20, 54-57). He concludes by promising to return and fulfill the totality of the Messianic prophecies of the Hebrew Scriptures (Luke 21:25-28).

For those within Judaism who, for the sake of tradition, willingly ignore the events of the New Testament, no amount of evidence will convince them. But for those willing to believe, the Gospel offers more than enough basis for faith. The expectations of Judaism will be satisfied by the Messiah, Jesus of Nazareth, but for many it will be achieved at the expense of rejecting God's mercy and grace found only in the Savior of mankind, the Lord Jesus Christ.

ෂ ෴

ENDNOTES — CHAPTER 7

1. Isaac Troki, *Faith Strengthened* (New York: Hermon Press, 1970), p. 5.

2. *Ibid.,* pp. 6-14.

3. John W. Haley, *Alleged Discrepancies of the Bible* (Grand Rapids: Baker Book House, 1977), p. 326.

4. Robert L. Thomas and Stanley N. Gundry editors, *A Harmony of the Gospels* (Chicago: Moody Press, 1978), p. 317.

5. Haley, loc. cit.

6. *Ibid.*

7. W.E. Vine, *An Expository Dictionary of New Testament* Words (Nashville: Thomas Nelson Publishers, n.d.), p. 919.

8. Dennis Prager and Joseph Telushkin, *The Nine Questions People Ask About Judaism* (New York: Simon and Schuster Inc., 1975), p. 88.

CHAPTER 8

Jewish Polemics and New Testament Contradictions

The Jewish Argument

he argument that the New Testament contradicts the Hebrew Scriptures is a common Jewish objection to the Christian message. It is used with great regularity among most Jewish polemicists. Gerald Sigal raises this argument by saying,

> The missionary profession that the Hebrew Scriptures are the true word of God means that the New Testament can be true only if it agrees with the Hebrew Scriptures. This is demonstrably not the case. The disagreement between these two books is not due to the unbeliever's lack of spiritual insight. The disagreement between them lies in their intrinsically contradictory contents. There is a basic truth concerning the New Testament message that no claim to faith can ever eradicate: 'What is good is not new, and what is new is not good.'[1]

Isaac Mayer Wise, a Reform American Rabbi of the 19th Century, spoke concerning the unity of the Old and New Testament;

> The New Testament is the fulfillment and continuation of the Old, by the grace of the church and the book-binder.[2]

Isaac Troki stated regarding this,

> If our Christian brethren are sincerely anxious to separate truth from falsehood, they ought to examine the passages of the Old Testament quoted in the Gospels, and ascertain whether they are really applicable or not. A brief survey of such topics shows that the quotations in the Gospel can never be considered cogent or satisfactory.[3]

In his book *Hizzuk Emunah,* Troki proceeds to offer 75 to 80 examples of what he feels are clear contradictions and misquotations between the Hebrew Scriptures and the New Testament.

The examples of "contradictions" raised by Jewish sources are by no means exclusive to Judaism. The skeptical and atheistic opponents of the Christian faith have used these so called "discrepancies" for years in their objections to the message of the New Testament. Jewish polemicists should also know that these same sources attack the Hebrew Scriptures and point out an even greater number of "contradictions" and "errors" which supposedly invalidate the basis for Jewish faith. The Orthodox Christian community by *no* means accepts these assertions, but instead defends the entirety of the Bible (Old and New Testament) with great vigor. The vast majority of these "Biblical problems" have been solved by careful scholarship and answers can be found in numerous Christian books dealing with this subject matter. Even though these arguments are invalid, and for the most part defeated, they are still expressed by the opponents of Christianity.

Space does not permit a full investigation into this subject, but four examples of this argument will be examined. These examples are representative of a general type of "contradiction" pointed out by Jewish polemicists.

1. Acts 7:14-16

Gerald Sigal gives the first "contradictory" New Testament passage.

"Then sent Joseph, and called his father Jacob to him, and all his kindred, threescore and fifteen [75] souls.

So Jacob went down into Egypt, and died, he, and our fathers,

And were carried over into Sychem, and laid in the sepulchre that Abraham bought for a sum of money of the sons of Emmor, the father of Sychem" (Acts 7:14-16).

Sigal states regarding this;

There are several errors to be found in the above verses.[4]

He goes on to list six discrepancies between this passage and the Hebrew Scriptures. In this examination each objection will be listed individually along with the Christian answer.

a) ... and all his kindred, threescore and fifteen souls [75] (Acts 7:14b).

Sigal:

Jacob's family that came down to Egypt, inclusive of Joseph and his sons, numbered seventy persons, not seventy-five. (Genesis 46:27, Exodus 1:5, Deuteronomy 10:22).[5]

The answer to this is quite simple. Both figures (70 and 75) are correct, but they are calculated differently. The New Testament follows the Septuagint rendering of Exodus 1:5 which reads, "And all the souls from Jacob were seventy-five." John W. Haley gives the numerical calculation upon which the Septuagint and Acts 7:14b rests;

Jacob's children, grandchildren, and great-grandchildren amounted to sixty-six (Genesis 46:8-26). Adding Jacob himself, and Joseph with his two sons, we have seventy (Masoretic rendering of Exodus 1:5). If to the sixty-six we add the nine wives of Jacob's sons (Judah's and Simeon's wives were dead; Joseph could not be said to call himself, his own wife, or his two sons into Egypt; and Jacob is specified separately by Stephen), we have seventy-five persons, as in Acts.[6]

There is no discrepancy in these numbers; both figures are correct, based upon the different calculations used.

b) "So Jacob went down into Egypt, and died, he, and our fathers, And they were carried over into Sychem ..." (Acts 7:15-16a).

Sigal:

> Jacob was not buried in the city of Shechem, but in the cave of Machpelah, which is located in the city of Hebron (Genesis 23:19; 49:29-30; 50:13-14).[7]

The answer to this is that Jacob was of course, buried in the field of Machpelah (Genesis 50:13), and Luke (author of the Book of Acts, who is quoting Stephen) was well familiar with this. However in Acts 7:16a, Luke is referring to the *fathers* (sons of Jacob) in the statement regarding their place of burial. But Sigal goes on to state,

> The Hebrew Scriptures do not give any indication that the forefathers of the tribes of Israel were buried in Shechem. Only Joseph is said to have been buried there (Joshua 24:32).[8]

This objection is essentially an argument from silence. The Hebrew Scriptures and Rabbinic literature do not give any information regarding the burial place of the sons of Jacob, except for the mentioning of Joseph's burial in Shechem (Joshua 24:32). Dr. Adam Clarke gives a possible reason for this silence. He states,

> We have the uniform consent of the Jewish writers that all the patriarchs were brought out of Egypt, and buried in Canaan, but none, except Stephen, mentions their being buried in Sychem. As Sychem belongs to the Samaritans, probably the Jews thought it too great an honor for that people to possess the bones of the patriarchs, and therefore have carefully avoided making any mention of it.[9]

Along with this, the fact that Joseph, who was one of the sons of Jacob, was mentioned as being buried in Sychem, certainly makes it more than possible that the other sons were likewise buried in the same location.

c) "And were carried over into Sychem, and laid in the sepulchre that Abraham bought for a sum of money of the sons of Emmor the father of Sychem" (Acts 7:16).

Sigal culminates his argument by offering three related "contradictions."

First,

> Abraham did not buy a tomb in Shechem. He bought the cave of Machpelah, which he used as a burial place, and which, as previously stated is located in the city of Hebron (Genesis 23:19).[10]

Second,

> The cave of Machpelah was not bought from the sons of Hamor, but from Ephron the Hittite (Genesis 23:17-18; 50:13).[11]

And third,

It was Jacob, not Abraham, who purchased a piece of land near Shechem from the sons of Hamor. The author of Acts confused the two purchases (Genesis 33:19; Joshua 24:32).[12]

Regarding the first and third "contradictions" raised by Sigal, there is no question that Abraham bought the cave at Machpelah. However, there is good reason to believe that he also bought a parcel of land at Sychem. Haley says concerning this,

It is known that Sychem (Sechem) was the place where God first appeared to Abraham in the land of Canaan, and where the patriarch built an altar (Genesis 12:6-7). There is reason to believe that a man so scrupulous as was Abraham in respect to property would purchase the field where he built his altar.[13]

What about the passage in Joshua 24:32, which states that Jacob bought the burial ground in Shechem? Haley answers,

In the one-hundred and eighty-five years which intervened, the Shechemites may have reoccupied the location, and Jacob may have renewed the purchase made by his grandfather. Of this consecrated field, a portion may have been set by Jacob as a burial place.[14]

Christian scholar Gleason Archer agrees with this explanation and offers further evidence to support it. He says,

Quite similar is the case of the well of Beersheba. Originally that well was dug by Abraham's workmen, and he paid for the rights of the property by offering seven lambs to Abimelech, king of Gerar (Genesis 21:27-30). But later on, owing to the nomadic habits of Abraham and his family, the property rights he had legally acquired became ignored, and the tract on which the well was located fell back into the possession of the local inhabitants. It was not until many years later that Isaac, having reopened the well to care for his livestock, found it expedient to secure the ownership by paying for it once more, rather than to assert his legal title to it by means of a range war.[15]

Stephen (quoted by Luke) was probably aware of this information by reliable oral tradition, and therefore stated these facts even though they were not recorded in the Old Testament.

Another problem between Joshua 24:32 and Acts 7:16 is that both accounts state that the land was bought from "the sons of Emmor [*Hamor*] the father of Shechem." If Acts 7:16 refers to Abraham as the purchaser and Joshua 24:32 refers to Jacob, the time period difference makes it impossible that they both purchased the land from the same people. Haley says concerning this problem,

According to the usage of the New Testament Greek (in Acts 7:14-16), we should read 'of the sons of Emmor the son of Sychem.' We are thus carried back to a Shechem and Hamor antecedent to Abraham, and quite different from those of whose sons Jacob made the purchase, Genesis 33: 18-20. The way is thus cleared. Abraham made the original purchase, and Jacob renewed and confirmed the transaction.[16]

From this explanation, the first and third "contradictions" raised by Sigal are dealt with and solved.

Sigal states concerning the second "contradiction,"

> The cave of Machpelah was not bought from the sons of Hamor, but from Ephron the Hittite.[17]

The answer to this is very simple. Acts 7:14-16 is not referring to the cave at Machpelah, but rather to the parcel of land at Shechem. Therefore, no contradiction occurs.

2. *Mark 2:25-26*

A second problem raised by Jewish sources between the New Testament and the Hebrew Scriptures is stated by Mr. Sigal; he refers to Mark 2:25-26.

> *"And he said unto them, Have ye never read what David did, when he had need, and was an hungered, he, and they that were with him?*
>
> *"How he went into the house of God in the days of Abiathar the high priest, and did eat the shewbread, which is not lawful to eat but for the priests, and gave also to them which were with him?"* (Mark 2:25-26).

Regarding this Sigal states,

> Although Mark does not specifically say that David's companions also ate the holy bread, Matthew and Luke both state that they did eat it (Matthew 12:4, Luke 6:4). However, from the question put to David by the high priest, Ahimelech: 'Why are you alone, and no man with you?' (1 Samuel 21:2), it is obvious that David came alone to the high priest. Moreover, as just indicated, it was not Abiathar who was high priest at the time this incident took place, but Abiathar's father, Ahimelech. Abiathar was the sole survivor of the slaughter of the priests at Nob, who were killed for having fed David. Matthew and Luke, in repeating this story, do not mention the name of the high priest (Matthew 12:3, 4; Luke 6:2, 3). We are faced with the question of determining whether Jesus or the evangelists was the source of this misreading of Scriptures.[18]

Mr. Sigal's first point asserts that David was alone with the high priest, according to 1 Samuel 21:1, 2, but all three of the Gospel accounts state that he was accompanied by other men. From this, a contradiction between the Hebrew Scriptures and the New Testament is declared to exist. The answer to this is extremely simple and would not even need to be dealt with if Mr. Sigal would read the rest of the context of 1 Samuel 21:1-7. When David approached Ahimelech, the high priest was fearful and asked; "Why art thou alone, and no man with thee?" Ahimelech knew David to be King Saul's son-in-law, and as an individual who was continually accompanied by special attendants. Therefore he was fearful, not meeting David in the customary manner. Ahimelech had no knowledge of the division and sharp difference that had taken place between David and Saul. However, was David really alone? By examining verses three through six, the fact that David was accompanied by other men is plainly obvious. In verses four and five, he twice refers to the young men who accompanied himself with this group of men by using the word "us." Verse four also implies that the young men along with David ate of the bread. Mr. Sigal's argument therefore has no basis.

The second point of this objection asserts that Jesus gave the wrong name to the high priest. Jesus says in Mark 2:25-26 that the high priest's name was Abiathar, yet 1 Samuel 21:1, 2 states that his name was Ahimelech. Christian scholar Gleason Archer states concerning this apparent discrepancy,

> Did Jesus err when he referred to the wrong high priest? A careful examination of Mark 2:26 reveals that Christ did not actually imply that Abiathar was already high priest at the time of David's visit. He simply said, 'Epi Abiathar archieroîs,' which means 'in the time of Abiathar the high priest'. As things turned out, bloody King Saul soon had Ahimelech and the entire priestly community of Nob massacred by Doeg the Edomite (1 Samuel 22:18,19) and Abiathar the son of Ahimelech was the only one fortunate enough to escape. He fled to join David (v. 20) and served as his priest all through David's years of wandering and exile. Naturally he was appointed high priest by David after David became king, and he shared the high priesthood with Zadek, Saul's appointee, until David's death. Under these circumstances it was perfectly proper to refer to Abiathar as the high priest—even though his appointment as such came somewhat later, after the incident at Nob—just as it would be proper to introduce an anecdote by saying, 'Now when King David was a shepherd boy,' even though David was not actually a king at the time he was a shepherd boy.
>
> According to W.F. Arndt and F.W. Gingrich (*A Greek-English Lexicon of the New Testament*; Chicago: University of Chicago 1957; p. 286) 'epi' with the genitive simply means 'in the time of'; and that is the meaning that applies in Mark 2:26 (the same construction as Acts 11:28 'in the time of Claudius' and Hebrews 1:2 'in the time of the last of these days') (*ep'eschatou ton hemeron touton*). The episode did happen 'in the time of' Abiathar; he was not only alive but actually present when the event took place, and he very shortly afterward became high priest as a result of Saul's murdering his father, Ahimelech. If Jesus' words are interpreted in the way He meant them there is absolutely no variance with historical fact.[19]

Did Jesus give the wrong name and make a mistake by citing Abiathar instead of Ahimelech? No. Abiathar, who by association with King David was much more famous in Jewish history than was his father Ahimelech, is cited to place the event in the "time of" the one far better known.

3. *Galatians 4:4*

The third contradictory argument is given by Mr. Sigal. He says,

> In Galatians 4:4, Paul claims that 'God sent forth His Son, born of a woman, born under law'. If we presume a birth without a man's assistance, we still have the problem that Jesus was not born in accordance with the Law. His birth, according to the New Testament, violates the laws of the Torah which specify what constitutes adultery. Mary, according to the New Testament, did not conceive by her betrothed, Joseph. Therefore, she committed adultery "under law" (Deuteronomy 22:23-24). As a result, the Christian missionary claim that Jesus was born of a woman engaged to a man, yet had God as his father, must be considered to refer to an illegitimate birth. God's law does not allow for Him to seduce a maiden, even through the medium of the Holy Spirit. What would be the worth of a moral code that is violated by God Himself? The seduction of a female by a god fits, at best, in the realm of pagan mythology. Such a statement made in reference to God of Israel is an abomination.[20]

Mr. Sigal asserts that Galatians 4:4 and the entire Gospel claim of virgin birth of Jesus is contradictory to the Torah and was derived from pagan mythology. In examining the Torah and Deuteronomy 22:23-24, in particular, no possible application between adultery and the virgin birth of Christ can be found. Adultery "under law" is limited to human relationships, and can be committed only by sexual intercourse. Deuteronomy 22:23-24 has absolutely no link with what is taught concerning the birth of Christ. Deuteronomy 22:23 states,

> *"If a damsel that is a virgin be betrothed unto an husband, and a man find her in the city, and lie with her;"*

The Torah makes it clear that adultery is committed by the uniting of a man and a woman only. The union described in Matthew 1:23-25, and Luke 1:31-38 has nothing at all to do with sexual intercourse. The virgin birth was totally and completely miraculous and stands outside of any human analogy or explanation. To even suggest immorality on the part of God shows a lack of understanding the miraculous nature of the virgin birth. Early Church Father, Justin Martyr (AD 100-165) stated regarding this,

> The phrase 'Behold a virgin shall conceive' (Isaiah 7:14), means, certainly, that the virgin shall conceive without intercourse. For if she had had intercourse with anyone at all, she would not be a virgin. But the power of God, coming upon the Virgin, overshadowed her, and caused her, while yet a virgin, to conceive.[21]

The fact that the New Testament explicitly states that Mary was a virgin when she gave birth to Jesus, clarifies the total supernatural element of this event. The description by Sigal of a god seducing a female and then applying this to the virgin birth of Christ most certainly is an abomination, and his statement regarding it shows a genuine misunderstanding. The claim of the New Testament is that Jesus is God (John 1:1-14), and if God were to become a man, this type of miraculous entrance is required. This is exactly the mode of entrance that the Hebrew Scriptures spoke of concerning the Messiah (Genesis 3:15; Isaiah 7:14).

Regarding Mr. Sigal's assertion that the virgin birth of Jesus was derived from pagan mythology, Christian scholar J.G. Machen in his work *The Virgin Birth of Christ,* totally and completely annihilates all such theories.[22] The historicity and truthfulness of the virgin birth is an established fact, and points to the miraculous intervention of God in the affairs of men.

4. *Matthew 23:35*

The last Jewish claim concerning a supposed New Testament contradiction covered here is Matthew 23:35. This verse reads,

> *"That upon you may come all the righteous blood shed upon the earth, from the blood of righteous Abel unto the blood of Zacharias son of Barachias, whom ye slew between the temple and the altar"* (Matthew 23:35).

Sigal says regarding this verse,

> Matthew's Jesus made an egregious [gross] error which illustrates the inaccuracy of the evangelical account. The Hebrew Scriptures inform us that it was Zechariah, the son of Jehoiada the priest, who was slain by the altar (2 Chronicles 24:20-21). Any attempt to reconcile this discrepancy by which Zechariah, the son of Jehoiada the priest, and Zechariah, the son of Berechiah (Zechariah 1:1), are to be viewed as identical, is completely without foundation. Zechariah, the son of Jehoiada, was slain in the days of Joash, king of Judah (ca. 840 BCE), while the prophet Zechariah, the son of Berechiah, did not prophesy until the second year of Darius (ca. 520 BCE), which followed the return from the Babylonian captivity. There is absolutely no reason to believe that Zechariah, the son of Berechiah, the son of Iddo, died in the manner described. The Scriptures do not indicate when, where or how Zechariah, the son of Berechiah, died. However, it is obvious that the death described by Matthew was suffered by another person, Zechariah, the son of Jehoiada.[23]

Mr. Sigal asserts that Jesus referred to the wrong Zechariah in Matthew 23:35 (also Luke 11:51), thereby demonstrating the inaccurate and nontrustworthy nature of the New Testament. In carefully examining this passage, no contradiction is found. Matthew does give an accurate and correct report of Jesus' words in verse 35. Dr. Gleason Archer says regarding this account in Matthew,

... we discover that the Zechariah He [Jesus] was referring to was indeed the son of Berachiah [not Jehoiada] and that he was indeed the last of the Old Testament martyrs mentioned in the Hebrew Scriptures. In other words, Christ is recalling to His audience the circumstances of the death of the prophet Zechariah, son of Berachiah (Zechariah 1:1) whose ministry began around 520 and ended a bit later than 480 BC. The Old Testament contains no record of events during the first few decades of the fifth century BC, until about 457, the date of Ezra's return to Jerusalem. But it may very well have been that sometime between 580 and 570 Zechariah the prophet was martyred by a mob in much the same way Zechariah the son of Jehoiada was some three centuries earlier. Since Jesus referred to Zechariah as the last of the Old Testament martyrs, there can be no legitimate doubt that it was the eleventh of the twelve minor prophets He had in mind. Therefore we can only conclude that the later Zechariah died in much the same way the earlier one did, as a victim of popular resentment against his rebuke of their sins.

Since there are about twenty-seven different individuals mentioned in the Old Testament bearing the name Zechariah, it is not surprising if two of them happened to suffer a similar fate. In other words if we take Matthew 23:35 just as it stands, it makes perfect sense in its context: and it offers no contradiction to any known established facts of history.[24]

The narrative of Matthew 23:35 does not contradict any historical fact, but instead gives additional information on the death of Zechariah, the son of Barachias that is not found within the Old Testament. If this fact was found in the writings of Josephus or any other historical source, it would be accepted by Jewish sources as truthful. But because it is stated in the Gospel accounts of the life of Jesus, it is considered false. This indeed is a biased methodology, for the historical truthfulness and reliability of the New Testament is impressive. Matthew has given here a true account of the death of Zechariah, the son of Barachias, and the claim of a Biblical misapplication in Jesus' words is unfounded.

Conclusion

The New Testament is in no possible manner contradictory in nature. The events, dates, places and persons referred to in the New Testament are accurate and trustworthy. There are other contradictory claims made by Jewish polemicists concerning the New Testament, but a careful examination of these reveals that no such problem exists. There may be some difficulties that are not easily and readily answered; nevertheless, time and further research will bring the necessary light needed to clear up these difficulties. The New Testament is historically and archaeologically reliable.

✍ ❧
ENDNOTES — CHAPTER 8

1. Gerald Sigal, *The Jew and the Christian Missionary: The Jewish Response to Missionary Christianity* (New York: KTAV Publishing House Inc., 1981), p. 292.

2. Isaac Mayer Wise, *A Defense of Judaism Versus Proselytizing Christianity* (Cincinnati: The American Israelite, 1839), p. 106, cited in Walter Jacob, *Christianity Through Jewish Eyes* (Cincinnati: Hebrew Union College Press, 1974), p. 87.

3. Isaac Troki, *Faith Strengthened* (New York: Hermon Press, 1970), p. 209.

4. Sigal, op. cit., p. 269.

5. Ibid.

6. John W. Halev, *Alleged Discrepancies of the Bible* (Grand Rapids: Baker Book House, 1977), p. 389.

7. Sigal, loc. cit.

8. Ibid.

9. Adam Clarke, *Clarke's Commentary, Vol. V* (New York: Abingdon Cokesbury Press, n.d.), p. 729.

10. Sigal, loc. cit.

11. Ibid.

12. Ibid., p. 270.

13. Haley, op. cit., p. 357.

14. Ibid.

15. Gleason Archer, *Encyclopedia of Bible Difficulties* (Grand Rapids: Zondervan Publishing House, 1981), p. 378.

16. Haley, loc. cit.

17. Sigal, op. cit., p. 269.

18. Ibid., p. 254.

19. Archer, op. cit., p. 362.

20. Sigal, op. cit., p. 283.

21. William Jurgens, "St. Justin the Martyr" in *The Faith of the Early Fathers, Vol. I* (Collegeville, Minn.: The Liturgical Press, 1970), p. 53.

22. This work provides a complete analysis of this subject matter. J. Gresham Machen, *The Virgin Birth of Christ* (New York: Harper and Brothers Pub., 1930).

23. Sigal, op. cit., p. 220.

24. Archer, op. cit., p. 338.

CHAPTER 9

Jewish Polemics and the Apostle Paul

The Jewish Argument

he Apostle Paul is cited as the chief problem-maker in causing the division between the Hebrew Scriptures and the New Testament in the area of law and works versus grace and faith. Jewish scholastic circles make a further distinction between the doctrine of Paul and the teaching of the Lord Jesus. Jesus is looked upon as a rabbi who made no attempt to sway from Judaism, but instead remained within the doctrinal boundaries of His Jewish background. Paul, on the other hand, is viewed as the founder of Christianity, who theologically separated the two faiths. Samuel Levine says concerning this,

> How could Paul overrule Jesus? ... you will see that Jesus never advocated disobedience of Torah law. Paul however changed all this.[1]

He concludes and says,

> Thus Paul said that believers in Jesus need not obey Torah law, and Jesus said you must obey Torah law. And the Christians follow Paul not Jesus! Isn't that ridiculous?[2]

A Comparison

Are the teachings of the New Testament inconsistent with the Hebrew Scriptures? Was Paul the founder of a faith-type message, which contradicted the Hebrew Scriptures and Jesus Himself? The following chart is provided to answer these questions.

HEBREW SCRIPTURES
The Law
Oh how I love thy law! it is my meditation all the day.

(Psalm 119:97)

The Law's Purpose
Thy word is a lamp unto my feet and a light unto my path.

(Psalm 119:105)

The Duration of the Law
Behold the days come, saith the Lord, that I will make a covenant with the house of Israel and with the house of Judah:

Not according to the covenant that I made with their fathers ...

But this shall be the covenant that I will make with the house of Israel; ... I will put my law in their inward parts, and write it in their hearts ...

... for I will forgive their iniquity, and I will remember their sin no more.
(Jeremiah 31:31-34)

JESUS
The Law
Think not that I am come to destroy the law or the prophets: I am not come to destroy, but to fulfill.

(Matthew 5:17)

The Law's Purpose
... all things must be fulfilled 'which are written in the law of Moses, and in the prophets and in the psalms concerning me.
(Luke 24:44)

Search the Scriptures; for in them, ye think ye have eternal life: they are they which testify of me.

(John 5:39)

The Duration of the Law
The law and the prophets were until John: since that time the kingdom of God is preached, and every man presseth into it.

(Luke 16:16)

PAUL
The Law
Wherefore, the law is holy and commandment holy and just and good.
(Romans 7:12)

Do we then make void the law through faith? God forbid: yea we establish the law.
(Romans 3:31)

But we know that the law is good, if a man use it lawfully.

(1 Timothy 1:8)

The Law's Purpose
Wherefore, the law was our schoolmaster to bring us to Christ, that we might be justified by faith.

(Galatians 3:24)

Duration of the Law
But after faith is come, we are no longer under a schoolmaster (the law).
(Galatians 3:25)

HEBREW SCRIPTURES

The Fact of Man's Sin

For there is not a just man upon the earth, that sinneth not.

(Ecclesiastes 7:20)

... all our righteousness are as filthy rags

...

(Isaiah 64:6)

The Source of Salvation

He that is our God is the God of salvation

...

(Psalm 68:20a)

... salvation is of the Lord.

(Jonah 2:9c)

Salvation belongeth unto the Lord ...

(Psalm 3:8)

The Atonement

for it is the blood that maketh atonement for the soul.

(Leviticus 17:11)

The Relationship Between Faith and Righteousness

And he [Abraham] believed in the Lord; and He counted it to him for righteousness.

(Genesis 15:6)

...the just shall live by faith.

(Habakkuk 2:4b)

JESUS

The Fact of Man's Sin

And this is the condemnation, that light is come into the world, and men loved darkness rather than light, because their deeds were evil.

(John 3:19)

The Source of Salvation

For God so loved the world, that He gave His only begotten Son that whosoever believeth in Him should not perish, but have everlasting life.

(John 3:16)

The Atonement

For this is my blood of the new testament which is shed for many for the remission of sins.

(Matthew 26:28)

The Relationship Between Faith and Righteousness

I said therefore unto you, that ye shall die in your sins; for if ye believe not that I am he, ye shall die in your sins.

(John 8:24)

PAUL

The Fact of Man's Sin

For all have sinned and come short of the glory of God.

(Romans 3:23)

The Source of Salvation

For by grace are ye saved through faith; and that not of yourselves: it is gift of God:

Not of works, lest any man should boast.

(Ephesians 2:8-9)

The Atonement

[Jesus] "In whom we have redemption through his blood, even the forgiveness of sins. (Colossians 1:14)

The Relationship Between Faith and Righteousness

Therefore being justified by faith, we have peace with God, through our Lord Jesus Christ"

(Romans 5:1)

Conclusion

The position taken by some within Judaism that the Apostle Paul was the dividing force between Judaism and the Christian faith does not agree with the facts. Neither is there any Scriptural evidence that the Apostle Paul and the Lord Jesus laid doctrine down for the Church that was contradictory in nature. When the Scriptures are compared on the whole, no such distinctions can be found. Any honest examination of the New Testament will indicate that the Apostle Paul's teachings were an extension of what the Lord Jesus had already established earlier.

∅ ঽ

ENDNOTES — CHAPTER 9

1. Samuel Levine, *You Take Jesus, I'll Take God* (Los Angeles: Hamoroh Press, 1980), pp. 79-80.
2. *Ibid.*, p. 80.

CHAPTER 10

Jewish Polemics and the Mosaic Law

The Jewish Argument

T he argument that Christianity violates the Law of Moses is appealed to by numerous Jewish polemicists. Isaac Troki describes this argument.

> Many Christians oppose us with the opinion that the Mosaic law had not been established for a permanent, but only for a limited period, and was totally abrogated by Jesus, who bequeathed to his disciples and followers a new law which dispensed them from conforming to the ancient statutes and ordinances laid down in the Mosaic code.[1]

He continues by affirming;

> The immutability of the law is pronounced in Deuteronomy 27: 1, 'And thou shalt listen to the voice of the Lord, and do all His commandments which I command you this day.' The same is repeated in a subsequent passage, it being said, 'If thou wilt but listen to the voice of the Lord thy God to observe His commandments which are written in the book of this law.' This manifestly proves that the gracious promises and assurances will only be realized provided we rigidly follow the precepts prescribed in the book of Moses.[2]

The Christian Answer

The fallacy of this objection is found in the fact that nowhere in the New Testament is it taught that Jesus came to abolish the Mosaic Law and then establish a New Law. Instead, the New Testament teaches that Jesus came to fulfill and complete the Mosaic Law. Jesus said,

> *"Think not that I am come to destroy the law, or the prophets: I am not come to destroy, but to fulfill.*
>
> *For verily I say unto you, Till heaven and earth pass, one jot or one tittle shall in no wise pass from the law, till all be fulfilled"* (Matthew 5:17-18).

Jesus stated in verse 18, *"Till heaven and earth pass, one jot or one tittle shall in no wise pass from the law, **till all be fulfilled.**"* According to Matthew 5:17 and many other New Testament references, this fulfillment occurred in Jesus and His ministry. In numerous instances, Jesus taught that the Law and the Scriptures pointed to and found fulfillment in Himself.

"Search the scriptures; for in them ye think ye have eternal life: and they are they which testify of me" (John 5:39).

*"And he said unto them, These are the words which I spake unto you, while I was yet with you, that all things must be **fulfilled**, which were written in the law of Moses, and in the prophets, and in the psalms concerning me"* (Luke 24:44).

Jesus taught that His coming was to fulfill and complete the purpose and plan of God revealed in the Old Testament.

*"Jesus saith unto them, My meat is to do the will of him that sent me, and to **finish** his work"* (John 4:34).

*"But I have a greater witness than that of John: For the works which the Father hath given me to **finish**, the same works I do"* (John 5:36).

The summation of this fulfillment took place in Jesus' work on the cross.

*"I have glorified thee on the earth: I have **finished** the work that thou gavest me to do"* (John 17:4).

*"When Jesus therefore had received the vinegar, he said, **It is finished:** and he bowed his head, and gave up the ghost"* (John 19:30).

The Greek word for "finish" used in these passages is "teleo" and it means "to end," "to complete," ["fulfill"].[3] These passages are affirming that Jesus finished and completed God's purposes spoken of by Him in Matthew 5:17-18.

The New Testament further teaches,

"Jesus, when he had cried with a loud voice, yielded up the ghost.

And, behold, the veil of the temple was rent from the the top to the bottom; and the earth did quake, and the rocks rent; ..." (Matthew 27:50-51).

This passage teaches that when the Crucifixion event was completed, the Law of Moses and the Old Covenant was fulfilled and satisfied (Hebrews 8:1-13; 10:1-22) and a New Covenant was established (Matthew 26:28; Hebrews 8:7-13).

The Hebrew Scriptures also teach that God would make this New Covenant with Israel (Jeremiah 31:31-34) and that this Covenant (not Law) would be expanded to include the Gentiles (Isaiah 60:3).

"Behold, the days come, saith the Lord, that I will make a new covenant with the house of Israel, and with the house of Judah:

Not according to the covenant that I made with their fathers in the day that I took them by the hand to bring them out of the land of Egypt; which covenant they brake, although I was an husband unto them, saith the Lord:

But this shall be the covenant that I will make with the house of Israel; After those days, saith the Lord, I will put my law in their inward parts, and write it in their hearts; and will be their God, and they shall be my people.

And they shall no more teach every man his neighbor, and every man his brother, saying. Know the Lord: for they shall all know me, from the least of them unto the greatest of them, saith the Lord: for I will forgive their iniquity, and I will remember their sin no more" (Jeremiah 31:31-34).

This Covenant spoken of in Jeremiah 31:31-34, is contrasted to the Old Covenant established through Moses. Therefore, the argument that this New Covenant is something less than a Covenant of equal status with that which was given by God to Israel at Sinai, is to be rejected.

Jeremiah points out three results of this New Covenant, all of which were consummated in the New Testament. First, verses 31-34 state that when this Covenant is established, the true purpose and meaning of the Law will be completed in the hearts of men. The Lord says, "I will put my law in their inward parts, and write it in their hearts; and will be their God, and they shall be my people" (Jeremiah 31:33c). In other words, the New Covenant will bring a far better observance of the Law than before, not by outward ceremonies, but by an inward obedience from the heart. Jeremiah does not state in this passage that the substance of the Law would change, but rather that the manner of observance would be far different.

Second, Jeremiah says that this Covenant will bring a new relationship with God,

"And they shall teach no more every man his neighbor, and every man his brother, saying, Know the Lord: for they shall all know me, from the least of them unto the greatest of them" (Jeremiah 31:34a).

Lastly, Jeremiah says that the relationship with God will not be based on human works or merit, but rather on the forgiveness of sin.

"For I will forgive their iniquity, and I will remember their sin no more" (Jeremiah 31:34c).

These are exactly the results of the Covenant relationship that the Messiah established (Matthew 26:28; Mark 12:24; Luke 22:30). Throughout the Hebrew Scriptures, God points out that His goals and purposes for mankind are to make men holier and more like Himself. For example,

"And it shall come to pass, when ye be multiplied and increased in the land, in those days, saith the Lord, they shall say no more, The ark of the covenant of the Lord: neither shall it come to mind: neither shall they remember it; neither shall they visit it; neither shall that be done any more.

At that time they shall call Jerusalem the throne of the Lord; and all the nations shall be gathered unto it, to the name of the Lord, to Jerusalem: neither shall they walk any more after the imagination of their evil heart" (Jeremiah 3:16-17).

This passage is speaking of the time in the future, at the return of the Messiah, when God's Kingdom will visibly reside on the earth. It shows that the goal and purpose of God does not remain within the externals of the Mosaic Law, but rather it extends into a relationship with Him out of a clean heart. This is the progressive purpose of the New Covenant (Jeremiah 31:31-34) which will be consummated in the return of the Messiah.

Conclusion

To summarize the Christian response to the argument concerning the duration of the Law, the New Testament too teaches the permanence of the Law. But this permanence is found only in the fact that it is now fulfilled and consummated in the New Covenant. The purpose and true meaning of the Law is found in the finished work of the Messiah on the cross.

Scholar A. Lukyn Williams relates,

> The many laws of Moses press heavily. But heavier still is the moral claim of the Law of Moses as a whole. Heaviest of all is the moral claim of the life of Jesus, as a revelation of what man can be. Yes, sinners we are when tested by the laws of Moses; greater sinners when tested by the Law as a whole; greater sinners still when tested by the life of Jesus. Yet from all this pressure and weight did Christ set us free, because by faith we are united to Him the Risen and Ascended Lord. Is this to destroy the Law? Is it not rather to bring it into full power and effect? St. Paul was right when he said (Romans 3:31), 'Do we make the law of none effect through faith? God forbid: nay, we establish the law.' 'The Gospel,' says a writer of growing reputation, 'is the power to fulfill the Law,' by the royal law of nearness to Christ and union with Him. This is the 'Law of Christ.'[4]

ENDNOTES — CHAPTER 10

1. Isaac Troki, *Faith Strengthened* (New York: Hermon Press, 1970), p. 87.

2. *Ibid.*, p. 92.

3. W.E. Vine, *An Expository Dictionary of the New Testament Words* (Nashville: Thomas Nelson Publishers, n.d.), p. 431.

4. A. Lukyn Williams, *Christian Evidences for Jewish People, Vol. I* (Cambridge: W. Heffer and Sons Limited, 1910), p. 145.

CHAPTER 11

Jewish Polemics and Atonement for Sin

The Jewish Argument

The Old Testament system of sacrifice has not been in effect within Judaism since the destruction of the Temple in AD 70. Because of this long span of time without this Old Testament provision, Judaism sees a lack of significance in sacrifice for sin and substitutionary atonement. Samuel Levine argues,

> Blood is not essential; Jesus is not essential, because God will always accept a broken, repentant spirit ... (Psalm 51:17). The obvious answer is that in Leviticus, God is simply saying that He gave us the option of using blood, not that blood is essential.[1]

Gerald Sigal relates,

> While sacrifices were a valid manifestation of repentance when the Temple was in existence, subsequent to its destruction, the door was not closed to the sinner, as he can still approach God in contrite prayer and ask for atonement.[2]

Both Levine and Sigal go on to point out that there are numerous means by which God forgives sin, such as prayer, genuine repentance and a humble and contrite spirit. All of this brings forgiveness that is "achieved" by the offering of the heart."[3]

The Christian Answer

Contrary to these statements, the Hebrew Scriptures teach the absolute necessity for substitutionary atonement and sacrifice. In Leviticus, the Lord states the central importance of the sacrifice for sin;

> *"For the life of the flesh is in the blood: and I have given it to you upon the altar to make an atonement for your souls: for it is the blood that maketh an atonement for the soul"* (Leviticus 17:11).

The point is made clear in the passage, "for it is the blood that maketh an atonement for the soul." No option is given. Remission of sin is based on the shedding of blood (Exodus 29:36; Leviticus 1:1-4; 4:13-36; 9:7; 10:17; 14:12-32; 16:6-34; 19:22; Numbers 15:22-28). Salvation and forgiveness of sin is provided solely by God's provision (Psalm 3:8; 68:20; Jonah 2:9). No human endeavor or merit can ever gain this. This is the teaching of the Hebrew Scriptures, and nowhere in the Old Testament is it taught that obedience to the Torah Law, repentance or good works will make one righteous before God. Instead, God provided the sacrifice system of atonement, which was a part of Israel's Covenant with Him.

The Hebrew Scriptures further teach that an acknowledgment of sin, a repentant heart, and a obedient, humble spirit must be the response of man to God's provision for sin in the sacrifice atonement (Psalm 51:17; 32:5; 69:31-32; 1 Samuel 15:72; 1 Kings 8:44-52; Hosea 14:2). These qualities and actions, which were mentioned by Levine and Sigal, are not a means of attaining forgiveness, but rather are man's response to God's salvation. God is never interested in an external offering or commitment without the internal cry of the heart. Bible scholar T.C. Hammond says regarding this,

> The animal sacrifices, if accompanied by faith in the offerer, made a covering for sin, that is, sin was covered from God's sight so that it no longer invited the reaction of His wrath. Both Old Testament and New Testament state plainly that God had no pleasure in animal sacrifice, except in so far as they were to the penitent sinner who brought them a true symbol of his faith in the pardoning love of God. It must be considered that the prophets who spoke so much against a mere external observance of sacrifice were themselves observers of the customary ritual.[4]

The New Testament teaches that the animal sacrifices of the Old Testament were temporary pictures and illustrations of the one true sacrifice for sin that was provided by the Messiah on the cross (Hebrews 7:1-28; 8:1-13; 9:1-28; 10:1-12). The Hebrew Scriptures also teach this as passages such as Isaiah 53 and Psalm 22 refer to the suffering and death of the Messiah who provides atonement for sin by his death (Isaiah 53:6). The Messiah's sacrifice was offered once for all the sins of mankind, past, present, and future. On this basis, the righteous men and women of the Old Testament who lived by faith in God and trusted in His provision for sin found their salvation in the completion of the Old Testament sacrifices, Jesus, the Lamb of God (John 1:29; Hebrews 10:1-12).[5]

Conclusion

Judaism fails to see the central importance of the Biblical teaching of atonement for sin. The Hebrew Scriptures teach this essential principle and no amount of denying can change this truth. The Christian answer to Judaism should emphasize this Biblical doctrine and demonstrate that Jesus is the fulfillment of this system. The Old Testament sacrifices were incomplete and had to be offered year after year (Leviticus 16-17). Jesus however, "once suffered for sins, the just for the unjust, that he might bring us to God ..." (1 Peter 3:18).

The New Testament asserts,

> *"And almost all things are by the law purged with blood; and without the shedding of blood is no remission.*
>
> *It was therefore necessary that the pattern of things in the heavens should be purified with these; but the heavenly things themselves with better sacrifices than these.*

For Christ is not entered into the holy places made with hands, which are the figures of the true; but into heaven itself, now to appear in the presence of God for us:

Nor yet that he should offer himself often, as the high priest entereth into the holy place every year with the blood of others;

For then must he often have suffered since the foundation of the world: but now once in the end of the world hath he appeared to put away sin by the sacrifice of himself.

And it is appointed unto men once to die, but after this the judgment:

So Christ was once offered to bear the sins of many; and unto them that look for him shall he appear the second time without sin unto salvation" (Hebrews 9:22-28).

Jesus is the summation and fulfillment of the Old Testament sacrifice system, and He alone can provide forgiveness of sin. Good works, repentance, and service to God will not earn salvation or atonement. Only by receiving the finished work of Christ on the cross and trusting in Him as Savior is cleansing and right standing before God obtained (Romans 5:1; 10: 1-13; Ephesians 2:8-9).

∅ ∂

ENDNOTES — CHAPTER 11

1. Samuel Levine, *You Take Jesus, I'll Take God* (Los Angeles: Hamoroh Press, 1980), p. 46.

2. Gerald Sigal, *The Jew and the Christian Missionary: The Jewish Response to Missionary Christianity* (New York: KTAV Publishing House Inc., 1981), pp. 276-277.

3. *Ibid.*, p.13.

4. T.C. Hammond, *In Understanding Be Men* (Revised ed.; Downers Grove: Inter-Varsity Press, 1968), p. 118.

5. The destruction of the Temple in AD 70 and the subsequent loss of the sacrifice system is further historical evidence that this God-given method of sin atonement was completed and no longer necessary due to its fulfillment in the Messiah's sacrificial death on the cross in AD 33.

CHAPTER 12

Jewish Polemics and the "Pagan Origins" of Christian Doctrine

The Jewish Argument

T̲he Christian teaching regarding the virgin birth, the deity and resurrection of Christ and the triune nature of God are criticized by Jewish polemicists to be absurd, irrational ideas, contrary to man's reason. This criticism continues by asserting that these Christian doctrines were actually derived from pagan mythology, not from the teaching of Christ and the apostles. Reform Jewish scholar Isaac Mayer Wise gives an example of the first part of this argument;

> Christianity can never become the religion of all mankind, because its teachings are contrary to the common sense of man.[1]

The next step taken by Jewish polemicists asserts that the origins of these teachings came from pagan sources. Hugh J. Schonfield argues concerning this,

> Christianity, as a religion in its own right, is in serious trouble. Its difficulty has arisen because of its fundamental belief in the deity of Jesus as God incarnate, which caused those responsible for the crucifixion—in the Church's view—to be denounced as deicides. But now it is being increasingly recognized by eminent Christian theologians, notably in a recent book, *The Myth of God Incarnate*, that there is adequate evidence to establish that Jesus, a Jew, made no claim to be divine, and that the doctrine was a paganized interpretation of the early church's conviction that he was the Messiah (Christ). The final step was taken with the definition of the Godhead as a Trinity, composed of God the Father, God the Son, and God the Holy Spirit, a step of metaphysical character that transferred the native habitat of Jesus from the Holy land to Heaven.[2]

This examination will look at four of the doctrines which are attacked most frequently. These are the virgin birth, the deity and resurrection of Christ and the triune nature of God. These four doctrines are all uniquely tied together and form an inseparable unit of truth. They must either be totally accepted or totally denied in order to remain consistent with the teachings of the New Testament. The four doctrines are, of course, all equally attacked by Jewish polemicists.

1. The Virgin Birth

The argument that the virgin birth of Christ is derived from pagan mythology is stated by Gerald Sigal;

> In diluting Judaism so that it could meet the beliefs of the pagan world, the evangelists adopted a number of grotesque distortions of

biblical belief. One of these is that a virgin has become pregnant, not by man, but of the 'Holy Spirit,' and she has given birth to the Messiah.[3]

2. The Deity and Resurrection of Christ

Mr. Sigal relates the Jewish argument against the deity of Christ;

Christianity has been misled into deifying Jesus because of its confusion concerning the meaning of the unity of God. This confusion is the result of the influence of the pagan religions on Church doctrine and practice. In the Hellenized Egyptian cult of Isis, her consort Sarapis, and their child Horus formed a sacred trinity. Roman emperors were usually deified during their lifetime. The postmortem deification of world rulers and their ascension to heaven, as well as salvation through identification with risen saviors, were established teachings among the pagan religions of the Roman Empire.[4]

Samuel Levine continues this argument and says concerning the resurrection of Christ,

The resurrection story is a fabricated hoax; it never happened. However, those early followers just could not believe that their savior simply died and was no more. They wanted to make Jesus into a god; they needed to make Jesus a god. ... Once the Christians made a god out of Jesus, they had to create a story that would be befitting a god. ... They therefore, took the pagan myths that were prevalent in the area, saw that the theme of resurrection was appropriate, and then claimed that Jesus also must have resurrected himself. They were in enough control of their imagination, however, to limit their story to unverifiable statements, so that their report could not be tested and proven to be untrue.[5]

3. The Triune Nature of God

Mr. Sigal proposes the argument against the Trinity and the influence of pagan religions on the Church's view of God;

It is a basic belief among most Christians that God is three beings in one: God the Father, God the Son, and God the Holy Spirit. This belief, called the Trinity, is not only diametrically opposed to Jewish belief, but is the very antithesis of the teachings of the Torah, the Prophets, and the Writings concerning the oneness of God ... The title 'Épiphanes' (the God made manifest) conferred on Eastern kings, described their divine nature as manifestations of the glory of the pagan god. Thus, it was not difficult to advance the idea of a triune god in the early Christian Church of the pagan world. The erroneous Christian interpretation of the nature of God as a triune being, with its roots lying deep in paganism, found its expression in the Nicene Creed, which later became the foundation for both Catholic and later Protestant beliefs on the subject of the Trinity.[6]

The Christian Answer

In refuting these Jewish claims, three areas of evidence will be examined. First, Hebrew Scriptural support; second, historical evidence; third, the fallacy of the "myth argument."

1. Hebrew Scriptural Support

a) The Virgin Birth

In the Old Testament there are two passages which teach the concept of the virgin birth. In Genesis 3:15, God speaks to the serpent (Devil) and states,

> "And I will put enmity between thee and the woman, and between thy seed and her seed; it shall bruise thy head, and thou shalt bruise his heel" (Genesis 3:15).

This prophecy has traditionally been considered to have a Messianic application. *The Jerusalem Targum* states that the designation of "heels of the Messiah" was probably derived from this verse. It also applies this verse to the "days of the Messiah," putting it into a Messianic framework.[7] In short, this passage states that the Deliverer Messiah would come by means of the woman's seed, not the man's, and it points to a virgin conception for the Deliverer referred to in Genesis 3.

A second Old Testament reference is found in Isaiah 7:14;

> "Therefore the Lord himself shall give you a sign; Behold, a virgin shall conceive, and bear a son, and shall call his name Immanuel" (Isaiah 7:14).

Much discussion has centered around the Hebrew word "almah" and the translation of it as "virgin." Earlier, this passage was dealt with and the objections concerning this translation were answered. The case for the translation of "almah" as "virgin" is grammatically solid and this passage does prove to be a clear prophetic indication of the virgin birth of the Messiah.

b) The Deity and Resurrection of Christ

There are numerous passages in the Old Testament which point to the divine character of the Messiah. Psalm 2:1-7 and Proverbs 30:4, assert that the Messiah will be the Son of God—Deity. Isaiah 7:14 states that this coming "son" would be called "Immanuel," which is translated, "God with us." Isaiah 9:6, 7 describes this "son" (relating back to Isaiah 7:14) as having divine qualities and attributes. Micah 5:2 says that the Messiah's "coming forth" will be from eternity. Malachi 3:1 and Isaiah 40:3 state that the Messianic messenger and forerunner will be actually preparing the way for Jehovah Himself.[8] Jeremiah 23:5-6 states that the name of the Messiah will be "The Lord Our Righteousness," implying His deity. Daniel 7:13-14 describes the Messiah as coming with the authority of Jehovah in the clouds of heaven and receiving everlasting dominion over all the nations of the earth. In Zechariah 12:10, Jehovah speaks of the Messiah who was "pierced" and refers to this person as Himself. Other passages can be cited and then joined to New Testament verses to substantiate the deity of Jesus:

Isaiah 40:28 .... John 1:1-14; Colossians 1:16-17
Isaiah 40:11 .... Luke 2:11
Isaiah 43:14-15 .... Luke 1:35
Isaiah 45:23 .... Philippians 2:11
Isaiah 60:19-20 .... John 8:12
Psalm 18:2 .... 1 Peter 2:6-8, Ephesians 2:20-22
Hosea 13:14 .... Titus 2:10-13
Exodus 3:14 .... John 8:58
Jeremiah 31:34 .... Mark 2:7-10
Joel 2:32 .... Romans 10:9-13

By examining the Old Testament Scriptures, a solid basis for the deity of the Messiah is found.

Regarding the resurrection of the Messiah, passages such as Isaiah 53:8-10, Psalm 22:19-21 and Daniel 9:26 state that the Messiah is to die. Psalm 30:3, 41:10, Hosea 6:2, coupled with Psalm 16:10, assert that the Messiah will rise again from the dead, thereby conquering man's greatest enemy—death. The Psalmist David states,

"For thou wilt not leave my soul in hell; neither wilt thou suffer thine Holy One to see corruption" (Psalm 16:10).

The Apostle Peter in Acts 2:22-36 relates that this prophecy has found fulfillment in the Lord Jesus Christ and His resurrection. The Jewish argument that this verse applies to King David has no basis, as the Apostle Peter pointed out long ago;

"Men and brethren, let me freely speak unto you of the patriarch David, that he is both dead and buried, and his sepulchre is with us unto this day" (Acts 2:29).

In other words, David's body has indeed seen "corruption" through the grave, but the "Holy One" that David referred to, the Lord Jesus, never experienced the corruption and decay of His body for He rose from the dead never to die again (1 Corinthians 15:19-20).

c) *The Triune Nature of God*

There is much Jewish confusion on the issue of the Trinity and most of it is derived from a complete lack of understanding regarding the New Testament teaching on the nature of God. The New Testament teaches that the essence of God is a mystery (1 Timothy 3:16), and beyond man's ability to grasp or fully understand. However, many things about Him can be known from the Scriptures. Both the Old and New Testament state that God is one Being (monotheism). Because of the limitations of the human language, definitions and descriptions that fully convey God's nature are unsatisfactory. But they do prove helpful in providing a framework for a proper understanding of Biblical truth. The New Testament definitional teaching regarding the Trinity, states that *the infinite God is one Being, and within His unity of nature there are three distinct persons or personalities who are co-equal.* This definition is beyond the laws of finite mathematics or logic, yet man's distorted reason is not the judge of divine truth and revelation. Instead, the evidence of God's Word is the basis for the determination of truth. The Biblical evidence for the plural nature of God is remarkably sound. There are numerous Old Testament passages which convey this concept. The Hebrew word "Elohim," which is a plural noun, is used over 2,000 times and implies the God over all creation, who alone is the supreme Deity.[9] It is used to also describe false gods (Exodus 20:3; Deuteronomy 13:3), angels (Exodus 22:8) and even men (1 Samuel 28:13). However, on the whole it is basically a word describing the plural nature of God. This in itself does not prove the Trinity, but it does present evidence that leads into this great Biblical truth.

The word "Elohim" is not the only Hebrew noun form that could have been employed to describe God. The singular form of Elohim— "Eloah" occurs about 250 times in the Old Testament, to indicate both false gods and Jehovah Himself.[10] Why then did the Hebrew Scriptures use the plural noun when a singular noun could have been used to describe the one, true, living God? The answer seems to point to the fact that within the oneness of God, there also exists a plurality of distinctions (persons or personalities) and the word "Elohim" was used to convey this truth.

Jewish sources continuously point to the "Shema" (Deuteronomy 6:4), as the basis for the teaching of the absolute unity of God. "Hear, O Israel, the Lord our God is one Lord." The emphasis of this passage establishes the oneness of God. Yet even within this verse there are indications that this oneness includes a plurality. Two Hebrew words are used in the Scriptures that are translated "one"—"yachid" and "echad". In Deuteronomy 6:4, the word "echad" is used. This word refers to a compound one. There are many examples in the Hebrew Scriptures where this word is used in the sense of "many making one."[11]

"... And the evening and the morning were the first [echad] [evening and morning] (Genesis 1:5b).

"Therefore shall a man leave his father and mother, and shall cleave unto his wife: and they shall be one [echad] *flesh"* [two people] (Genesis 2:24)

"... a branch with one [echad] *cluster of grapes ..."* [many grapes] (Numbers 13:23).

"The whole congregation together [echad] *was forty and two thousand three hundred and threescore"* [many people] (Ezra 2:64).

"And join them one to another into one [echad] *stick;"* [two sticks] (Ezekiel 37:17).

These examples make it clear that the Hebrew word "echad" does not always refer to an absolute one, but also to a compound or plurality of one.

The word "yachid" on the other hand means "only one," and would be the appropriate word to use in teaching the absolute oneness of God.[12] Instead, the word "echad" was used in Deuteronomy 6:4, which implies that the oneness of God can be a plurality, as the teaching of the Trinity asserts. This, coupled with the fact that God— "Elohim" (plural noun), is used in this verse strengthens the case that Deuteronomy 6:4 perfectly agrees with the New Testament concept of God's triune unity. There are cases in the Old Testament where God uses plural pronouns when He speaks of Himself—Genesis 1:26: "And God [Elohim] said, Let *us* make man in *our* image, after *our* likeness." Genesis 3:22: "And the Lord God [Elohim] said, Behold, the man is become as one of *us* ..." Genesis 11:7: "Go to, let *us* [Elohim] go down, and there confound their language, that they may not understand one another's speech ...". Isaiah 6:8: "Also I heard the voice of the Lord saying, Whom shall I send, and who will go for *us?*"

God is also described with plural adjectives: Joshua 24:19: Holy God (Holy Gods). ..." Psalm 148:2: "Let Israel rejoice in him that made him ..." (makers). Ecclesiastes 12:1: "Remember now thy Creator (Creators) ..." From the basis of these Hebrew plural nouns, pronouns and adjectives, the plurality of God's oneness can be seen.

There are also numerous passages in the Scriptures where God is spoken of as two personalities (Hosea 1:7; Psalm 45:7-8; Genesis 19:24; Zechariah 2:12-13; Psalm 50:1; Joshua 22:22; Psalm 110:1). The Hebrew Scriptures further demonstrate three personalities in the same passage in reference to God. In Isaiah 48:12-16, the Lord, Jehovah and His Spirit are mentioned. In Isaiah 63:7-10, Jehovah, the Angel of His presence (face), and the Holy Spirit are mentioned together. Throughout the Old Testament, three distinct personalities are considered Divine.

1. The Lord Jehovah—Genesis 15:2; 11 Samuel 7:29; Isaiah 7:7; Joshua 7:7; Psalm 69:6.
2. The Angel of Jehovah—(Jehovah Himself) Numbers 11:29; Judges 3:10.
3. The Spirit of God—Genesis 1:2; Psalm 51:11; Isaiah 11:2; 40:13; Isaiah 59:19.

In Genesis 18-19, the Lord appears before Abraham numerous times as the angel of the Lord (Jehovah) and is cited to be Jehovah Himself. Other passages also indicate this: Genesis 16:7, 13; Genesis 22:11-12; Genesis 31:11, 13; Exodus 3:2, 4; Exodus 23:20-23.

The Hebrew Scriptures teach the absolute and perfect unity of God, yet they also reveal that there exists a plurality in the oneness of the Godhead. The first personage (Jehovah) sends and commissions the second person of the Godhead, called the Angel or Messenger of Jehovah. The third person, referred to as the Holy Spirit or Spirit of Jehovah, is also sent by the first personage and closely relates to the ministry and function of the second person. This of course finds perfect agreement with the New Testament, which describes Jehovah as God the Father, God the Son, and God the Holy Spirit.

There is evidence from various Jewish traditional sources that reveal the concept of the plurality of God within Judaism. The *Zohar*, a compilation of Jewish mystical writings comments on Deuteronomy 6:4 and discusses the plurality of persons within the oneness of God.

Hear, O Israel, YHVH Elohenu YHVH is one! These three are one. How can the three Names be one? Only through the perception of Faith: in the vision of the Holy Spirit: in the beholding of the hidden eyes alone. The mystery of the audible voice is similar to this, for though it is one yet it consists of three elements—fire, air and water, which have, however, become one in the mystery of the voice. Even so it is with the mystery of the threefold Divine manifestations designated by YHVH Elohenu YHVH—three modes which yet form one unity.[13]

Within the Jewish Passover, there is also an interesting observance. Jewish-Christian, Rachmiel Frydland stated concerning the Jewish traditional Passover and the Trinity;

Many Christians today realize the deep significance of the Passover, from which is taken the Lord's supper. It was only many years later that I began to see that the three matzos represented the Trinity, and that it was the middle one, the Son, which was broken for us. I watched my father solemnly wrap it in white linen, bury it, and then bring it out again—resurrected, at the time of the third cup of wine. Truly, the Lord had said that this piece of pure, unleavened, and broken bread was His body. We all partook of it at the Passover table along with the third cup, which we called the 'cup of Redemption.'[14]

From this and other sources that could be referred to, it is evident that the concept of God's plurality was not foreign to Jewish tradition or Scriptural exegesis. The Jewish polemicists may reject the teaching of God's plural nature and accuse the Christian faith of borrowing from pagan religions; however, if this be true, then the Hebrew Scriptures must also be likewise accused, for this doctrine is embedded in the *Law,* the *Prophets* and the *Writings.* Dr. John Warwick Montgomery summarizes the Biblical evidence for God's triune nature;

The doctrine of the Trinity is not 'irrational'; what is irrational is to suppress the biblical evidence for Trinity in favor of unity, or the evidence for unity in favor of Trinity.[15]

The Bible teaches the Triune nature of God and the evidence from the Scriptures must be the basis upon which this truth stands.

2. Historical Evidence

a) Virgin Birth

The New Testament states that Jesus was born by means of a virgin birth (Matthew 1:18-25; Luke 1:27-35; John 1:14; 3:16). The Gospel writers appeal to this birth as an historical event indicating that Jesus was indeed God incarnate (John 1:1-14). Along with this New Testament basis, the early Church Fathers give support to the factual nature of the virgin birth of Christ by referring to it in many of their writings. Christian scholar Robert Gromacki states concerning this,

Ignatius of Antioch in Syria (c. 110) defended the virgin birth in his volumes: *To the Ephesians*; *To the Smyrnaeans*; *To the Magnesians*; and *To the Trallians* ... Aristides (c. 125) defended the doctrine in his *Apology for the Christians to the Roman Emperor*. Justin Martyr (c. 150) wrote two such defenses: *Apology* and *Dialogue with Trypho* ... Tatian contributed his *Diatessaron* and *Address to the Greeks*. Melito of Sardis referred to his belief in the virgin birth in three volumes: *Discourse on the Cross; Discourse on the Soul and Body ;* and *From Melito the Bishop, on Faith*. Irenaeus (c. 175) wrote *Against Heresies*. Clement of Alexandria used *The Instructor and Miscellanies* in his defense. Hippolytus composed: *Refutation of All Heresies*; *Treatise on Christ and Anti-Christ*; *On Proverbs XXIV* and *Against Beron and Helix*. Tertullian referred to the doctrine in: *On the Flesh of Christ*; *The Prescription Against Heretics*; *Against Praxeas*; and *Against Marcion*. Origen, in the first half of the third century, defended the virgin birth in his famous volume *Against Celsus*.[16]

Gromacki continues,

The Apostle's Creed, produced in Gaul about the fifth or sixth century, was based upon an old Roman baptismal confession, dated as early as AD 200. Both Tertullian and Irenaeus used the latter in the middle of the second century. The key text read: 'Born of the Holy Ghost and the Virgin Mary.' The convert, before his baptism, had to include that in his confession of faith. That shows that the doctrine of the virgin birth was so firmly entrenched in the life of the early church that it was deemed to be one of the fundamental doctrines. No one would be admitted into a Christian assembly nor recognized as a genuine believer without faith in it.[17]

From this information, it is evident that belief in the virgin birth was accepted throughout the early Church in the early part of the Second Century. J.G. Machen stated concerning this,

At about AD 110, belief in the virgin birth was no new thing; it was not a thing that had to be established by argument, but had its roots deep in the life of the Church.[18]

The argument that the virgin birth was a mythological addition which slipped into the Christian faith many years after the death of the apostles and eyewitnesses of Christ's life, is clearly erroneous. Belief in the virgin birth was an established doctrine for one reason: it was an historical fact, attested to by the eyewitnesses of the life of Christ (Luke 1:1-3; 2 Peter 1:16).

b) The Deity and Resurrection of Christ

Throughout the Gospels, Jesus makes the claim of being God incarnate (John 5:17-18, 20, 24; 8:58; 8:19; 14:1; 10:30-35). He forgives sin (Mark 2:5; Matthew 9:2), receives worship (John 20:28-29; Matthew 28:9), and exhibits power and authority that belongs only to God (John 10:17-18; Matthew 5:21-22; John 5:27). The Jewish rulers understood the claims of Jesus.

> *"Therefore the Jews sought the more to kill him, because he not only had broken the Sabbath, but said that God was his Father, making himself equal with God"* (John 5:18).

> *"The Jews answered him, saying, For a good work we stone thee not; but for blasphemy; and because that thou, being a man, makest thyself God"* (John 10:33).

The apostles continue this declaration, leaving no question that Jesus claimed the status of Deity (John 1:1-14; Colossians 1:13-19; 2:6-9; Titus 2:13; 3:4; Hebrews 1:1-14). William Biederwolf sums up the message of the New Testament;

> A man who can read the New Testament and not see that Christ claims to be more than a man, can look all over the sky at high noon on a cloudless day and not see the sun.[19]

The early Church Father's writings also demonstrate the widely held belief in the deity of Jesus. Ignatius of Antioch (AD 70-110) gives possibly the clearest declaration concerning the early Church's belief in the deity of Christ. In his *Letter to the Ephesians,* he states,

> There is one Physician, who is both flesh and spirit, born and not born, who is God in man, true life in death, both from Mary and from God, first able to suffer and then unable to suffer, Jesus Christ our Lord.[20]

He continues,

> For our God, Jesus Christ, was conceived by Mary in accord with God's plan.[21]

In his *Letter to the Romans*, he says,

> ... to the Church beloved and enlightened after the love of Jesus Christ, our God ...[22]

Justin Martyr (AD 100-165) in his *First Apology* states,

> And again, hear how Isaiah expressly foretold that He was to be born of a virgin. He stated the following; 'Behold, a virgin shall conceive and bear a son; and for his name they shall say 'God with us.'[23]

He states further in his writing,

> These words, then have become the proof that Jesus Christ is the Son and Apostle of God, being of old the Word, appearing at one time in the guise of fire and at another time as an incorporeal image. And now, by the will of God and for the sake of the human race, He has become man ...[24]

Other early Church Fathers such as Clement of Rome (AD 80-101), Clement of Alexandria (AD 150-211), Irenaeus (AD 140-202), Tertullian (AD 155-220) and Origen (AD 185-253) all taught the deity of the Lord Jesus Christ.[25]

The doctrine of the resurrection of Jesus is another of the cornerstone teachings of the Christian faith. Throughout the New Testament, the Resurrection is asserted to be an historical fact (Matthew 28:1-20; Mark 16:1-20; Luke 24:1-53; John 20, 21; Acts 1:1-10). The Apostle Paul wrote the Book of 1 Corinthians in AD 56, only 20 to 25 years after the life of Christ. He stated,

> *"For I delivered unto you first of all that which I also received, how that Christ died for our sins according to the scriptures;*
>
> *And that he was buried, and that he rose again the third day according to the scriptures:*
>
> *And that he was seen of Cephas, then of the twelve:*
>
> *After that, he was seen of above five hundred brethren at once; of whom the greater part remain unto this present, but some are fallen asleep.*
>
> *After that, he was seen of James; then of all the apostles"* (1 Corinthians 15:3-7).

An examination of the witness of the early Church Fathers concerning the resurrection of Christ finds total support for the truthfulness of this event. Polycarp (AD 69-155) states,

> May He set your lot and portion among His saints—and ourselves along with you, and all others under heaven who in the future will believe in our Lord Jesus Christ and in His Father, who raised Him from the dead.[26]

It should be pointed out that Polycarp was a student of the apostles, and is noted to have been particularly a pupil under the Apostle John. Irenaeus said concerning Polycarp in *Against Heresies,*

> Polycarp, however, was instructed not only by the Apostles, and conversed with many who had seen Christ, but was also appointed bishop of the Church in Smyrna, by the Apostles in Asia. I saw him in my early youth; for he tarried a long time, and when quite old he departed this life in a glorious and most noble martyrdom. He always taught those things which he had learned from the Apostles ...[27]

Ignatius stated concerning the resurrection of Jesus,

> He underwent all these sufferings for us, so that we might be saved; and He truly suffered, just as He truly raised Himself, not as some unbelievers contend, when they say that His passion was merely in appearance ... I know and believe that He was in the flesh even after the resurrection. And when He came to those with Peter He said unto them: 'Here, now, touch Me, and see that I am not a bodiless ghost.' Immediately they touched Him and, because of the merging of His flesh and spirit, they believed. For the same reason they despised death and in fact were proven superior to death. After His resurrection He ate and drank with them as a being of flesh, although He was united in spirit to the Father.[28]

Ignatius who was the bishop of Antioch and died as a martyr, was, like Polycarp, a companion of the apostles. Both of these men could appeal directly back to eyewitness sources concerning the resurrection of Jesus. Their appeal, along with that of all of the early Church Fathers, was that Jesus did indeed rise again from the dead.

c) *The Triune Nature of God*

The Christian faith is clearly monotheistic and agrees with the Hebrew "Shema" that God is One. The God of Israel is repeatedly affirmed in the New Testament to be the only God and Creator of the universe (John 17:3; Mark 12:28-29; 1 Corinthians 8:1-6). The New Testament continues from this basis and teaches the doctrine of the triune nature of God:

God, the Father— 1 Corinthians 8:6; Galatians 1:1; Ephesians 1:2; Romans 1:7.

God the Son— John 1:1-3, 14; (Isaiah 43:10; 44:8; 43:5):John 8:58 (Exodus 3:14) Revelation 1:16-18; (Isaiah 41:4; 44:6; 48:12); Colossians 1:13-17, Hebrews 1:1-14.

God the Holy Ghost— Acts 28:25-26; (Isaiah 6:8-9); 2 Corinthians 3:17; Acts 5:3-4; Hebrews 10:15; (Jeremiah 31:31-34); John 3:6, 1 John 5:4; 1 Corinthians 3:16-17; 2 Corinthians 6:16.

The New Testament asserts that the Father is *God* (Matthew 11:25; Ephesians 4:6); the Son is *God* (John 1:1-4, 14; Romans 9:5) and the Holy Spirit is *God* (Acts 5:3, 4). The Father is *Lord* (Matthew 22:37, the Son (Jesus) is *Lord* (John 20:28; Philippians 2:10,11) and the Holy Spirit is *Lord* (2 Corinthians 3:16). The doctrine of God's triune nature is affirmed in the Gospel of Matthew;

> *"Go ye therefore, and teach all nations, baptizing them in the name* [singular] *of the Father, and of the Son, and of the Holy Ghost"* (Matthew 28:19).

In this passage, Jesus commands His followers to make disciples in all the nations of the earth, baptizing them in the name (singular) of Father, Son, Holy Spirit–one name, three persons.

Other passages indicate the oneness of the Godhead (2 Corinthians 13:14; John 10:30; 14:10-11, 17-23; 1 Peter 1:2). The New Testament teaches both the unity of God and triune nature of God. In no way does His oneness detract from His plurality, nor His plurality from His oneness.

The doctrine of the Trinity was subject to much controversy in the early Church. Some of the early Church theologians, such as Origen, Lucian of Antioch, Sabellius and Arius, taught un-Biblical views of the triune nature of God. However, the teaching of the Trinity was accepted on the whole, throughout the early Church only to be challenged by men such as those listed here. Because of this challenge, a systematic doctrine regarding the Trinity was finally established in the Council of Nicea (AD 325). The Council of Nicea did by no means arbitrarily endorse this doctrine, but rather recognized and systematized what the early Church had clearly believed and what the apostles and prophets had always taught. Early Church Fathers, such as Clement of Rome, Ignatius, Justin Martyr, Irenaeus, and Tertullian, describe in their writings the apostolic teaching regarding the triune nature of God.[29]

Clement of Rome:

> Do we not have one God, one Christ, and Spirit of Grace poured out upon us? For as God lives, and as the Lord Jesus lives, and the Holy Spirit ...[30]

Ignatius:

> You are like stones for a temple of the Father, prepared for the edifice of God the Father, hoisted to the heights by the crane of Jesus Christ, which is the cross, using for a rope the Holy Spirit.[31]

Justin Martyr:

> We will prove that we worship Him reasonably; for we have learned that He is the Son of the True God Himself, that He holds a second place, and that the Spirit of Prophecy a third.[32]

Irenaeus:

> It was not angels, then who made us nor who formed us, nor did angels have the power to make an image of God. It was not some power existing far from the Father of the universe, nor was it anyone else, other than the Word of the Lord. God had no need of others to make what He had already determined of Himself to make, as if He had not His own hands. For with Him always are the Word and the Wisdom, the Son and the Spirit, through whom and in whom He made all things freely and spontaneously; and to whom He spoke, saying: 'Let us make man in our image and likeness.'[33]

The teaching regarding God's triune nature was not a Third and Fourth Century pagan development as Jewish polemicists would like to believe. Instead, the New Testament teaches this most important doctrine throughout its pages. The early Church Fathers of the Second

Century, also provide supportive evidence indicating that they recognized the New Testament teaching regarding God's triune nature.

3. The Fallacy of the Myth Argument

The myth argument asserts that the fundamental truths of the Christian faith were borrowed from pagan mythology. In refuting this Jewish thesis, four areas of evidence will be examined. a) The violation of logic. b) The differences between the Gospel accounts and mythology. c) The time period of the composition of the Gospels. d) The character and nature of the apostolic Church.

a) The Violation of Logic

Jewish polemicists point out various similarities and parallels between mythology and the Gospel. Greek and Roman mythology includes many legends concerning "savior gods," "virgin births," "god-men," and "resurrected heroes."[34] When this information is compared to the Gospel narratives, some obvious similarities can be seen. Upon this basis, they argue that the Gospel writers borrowed from pagan sources in their composition concerning Christ's life. However, there is no logical necessity for assuming that later documents borrowed from earlier documents because of some noted similarities between them. This is an example of the logical fallacy of *post hoc ergo propter hoc* ("after this, therefore, because of this").[35] Everything in life consists of parallels and if an event or experience must be without similarity to be true, then all reality would be held in question. To assert that a later idea or event was caused by a similar one previous to it, just because the first idea or event was earlier is extremely faulty reasoning. Pagan accounts of mythological gods, etc., may have been earlier in date, but it does not follow that the Gospel writers therefore copied from these sources.

b) The Differences Between the Gospel Accounts and Mythology

When a careful and thorough examination is made between the Gospels and mythology, the differences between them demonstrate that the borrowing from mythology could not have been undertaken by the Gospel writers. R.G. Gromacki states concerning the virgin birth,

> ... the pagan authors did not set their stories against a legitimate historical background, whereas the Gospel narratives are inseparably connected to the historical circumstances of the first century (cf. Luke 2:1-2). The pagan birth narratives contain records of sons born who were half god and half man. The child began to exist at his conception. However, the New Testament claimed that Jesus Christ always existed and that He acquired a human nature only in his incarnation. ... The incarnation of Christ was bathed in holiness. He was conceived in order to die redemptively for the sinful condition of men. The pagan birth stories revealed the greed and the sexual lust of the gods toward mortal women. After the conception,

Jesus experienced normal human development (Luke 2:52). In the pagan birth account of the birth of Pallas Athena who had no mother, he sprang out of the head of Zeus, full grown and in full armor. The place of Christ's birth was inconspicuous, a lowly manger in the presence of a carpenter and shepherds. The pagan accounts were recorded against a background of gross polytheism, whereas the virgin birth of Christ was written against the culture of a tenacious Jewish monotheism.[36]

The resurrection of Christ is also unlike the mythological stories of resurrected gods. The Gospel writers appealed to this event as an historical event, open to the examination of public scrutiny. The Greek and Roman legends were placed beyond the realm of historical verifiability and were applied to non-historical characters in mystical and other worldly realms.[37]

The teaching of the Trinity is also acutely different from the polytheistic concepts found in mythology. The polytheistic ideas of triads and tritheisms consist of three separate gods or goddesses, whereas the Trinity is unique and describes God as one Being, revealing Himself in three personalities (or persons)—the Father, the Son, and the Holy Ghost.

c) *The Time Period of the Composition of the Gospels*

The Gospel narratives were written within 30 to 50 years of the earthly ministry of Christ (AD 40-80). W.F. Albright, an eminent Biblical archaeologist affirms concerning the date and authorship of the New Testament books,

> In my opinion, every book of the New Testament was written by a baptized Jew between the forties and the eighties of the first century AD.[38]

Even liberal scholars, such as John A.T. Robinson conclude that the evidence for the early authorship of the New Testament is much earlier than the dates held by many liberal theologians. In his book *Redating the New Testament,* Dr. Robinson affirms that the entire New Testament was written before AD 70.

Dr. John Warwick Montgomery states regarding the dating of the books of the New Testament,

> Specifically, present-day scholars date the more important New Testament materials as follows: the Pauline letters, AD 51-62; Mark's Gospel, 64-70; the Gospels according to Matthew and Luke, 80-85; Acts, shortly after Luke, which is really 'Part One' of the two-part work; John's Gospel, no later than 100.[39]

For the Gospel narrative to have been mythological in nature, far greater amount of time would have been required in order for such development to have existed. Myths and legends require many years to develop and become a part of a society. Robert H. Gundry relates regarding this,

The single generation between Jesus and the writing of the gospels did not allow enough time for extensive proliferation of tradition about Jesus. Mythologies normally do not develop in less than half a century.[40]

The writing of the facts concerning Christ were completed in such close proximity to His life and ministry, that no legendary tradition could possibly have been allowed to continue. Eyewitnesses, both believer and hostile, would still have been alive and able to correct any such tendency.

d) *The Character and Nature of the Apostolic Church*

The apostles, who were the writers of the New Testament, were Jewish, not Greek or Roman. They had no personal link between the things which they had witnessed of Christ's life and mythology. They knew the difference between a myth and reality. The Apostle Peter said regarding the life of Christ,

> *"For we have not followed cunningly devised fables* [myths or legends], *when we made known unto you the power and the coming of our Lord Jesus Christ, but were eyewitnesses of His majesty"* (2 Peter 1:16).

The argument that these apostles, such as Paul, created a mythological framework from which the Gospel was preached is totally lacking in evidence and does not agree with the facts. To assume that eleven of the 12 disciples of the Lord died for the sake of the propagating of myths is certainly unreasonable. No one dies for something he knows to be false. Throughout the writings of the New Testament, mythology, foolish stories and empty or vain fables are strongly condemned (Colossians 2:6-8; 1 Timothy 1:4; 4:7; 2 Timothy 4:4). Yet honesty and factual truth is stated as an absolute necessity on the part of Christians (Mark 10:19; 11 Corinthians 8:21; Philippians 4:8; Hebrews 13:18; Ephesians 4:25; Colossians 3:9).

To suppose that the apostolic Church, with its strong appeal to truthfulness, would allow such erroneous material to continue goes against common sense. No such legendary material would have been tolerated.

Conclusion

In every detail, the Gospel records prove to be historical rather than mythological. The differences between mythology and the New Testament narrative is plainly obvious. C.S. Lewis, a professor of Medieval and Renaissance literature of Cambridge University and an expert in the study of mythology, stated,

> I have been reading poems, romances, vision—literature, legends, myths all my life. I know what they are like. I know that no one of them is like this [referring to the Gospel accounts of Christ's life].[41]

The evidence clearly goes against the theory that the doctrines of the Christian faith are derived from pagan mythology. The facts of the virgin birth, the deity and resurrection of Christ, and the triune nature of God, have been taught and stressed within Christianity for one basic reason—they are true!

ᛃ ᛃ

ENDNOTES — CHAPTER 12

1. Isaac Mayer Wise, *A Defense of Judaism Versus Proselytizing Christianity* (Cincinnati: The American Israelite, 1839), p. 127, cited in Walter Jacob, *Christianity Through Jewish Eyes* (Cincinnati: Hebrew Union College Press, 1974), p. 81.
2. Hugh J. Schonfield, *After the Cross* (London, England: A.S. Barnes and Company, 1981), preface, VII.
3. Gerald Sigal, *The Jew and the Christian Missionary: The Jewish Response to Missionary Christianity* (New York: KTAV Publishing House Inc., 1981), p. 20.
4. *Ibid.*, p. 125.
5. Samuel Levine, *You Take Jesus, I'll Take God* (Los Angeles: Hamoroh Press, 1980), p. 71
6. Sigal, loc. cit.
7. Alfred Edersheim, *The Life and Times of Jesus the Messiah* (3d. ed.); Grand Rapids: Wm. B. Eerdmans Pub. Co., 1971), p. 711.
8. Jewish scholar, Ben Zion Bokser states concerning this passage and its implications (Isaiah 40:3). "The original Hebrew, as well as the Septuagint translation, make it clear that 'Lord' is here used as a synonym for God, since the second half of the verse calls specifically to make straight the 'paths of God' ..." This scholar then asserts that this passage could not refer to the Messiah, because the Messiah will not be Jehovah." [Ben Zion Bokser, *Judaism and the Christian Predicament* (New York: Alfred A. Knopf Inc., 1967), p. 257.]
9. Robert Young, *Young's Analytical Concordance to the Bible* (Revised ed.; Grand Rapids: Wm. B. Eerdmans Pub. Co., 1973), p. 412.
10. *Ibid.*, p. 411
11. *Ibid.*, p. 716.
12. *Ibid.*, p. 719.
13. *Zohar.*, Vol. III, Exodus 43b.
14. Rachmiel Frydland, *When Being Jewish was a Crime* (Nashville: Thomas Nelson Inc., 1974), pp. 83-84.
15. John Warwick Montgomery, *How Do We Know There is a God?* (Minneapolis: Bethany Fellowship, 1972), p. 14.
16. R.G. Gromacki, *The Virgin Birth: Doctrine of Deity* (Nashville: Thomas Nelson Inc., 1974), pp. 83-84.
17. *Ibid.*, p. 84.
18. J. Gresham Machen, *The Virgin Birth of Christ* (New York: Harper and Brothers Pub., 1930), p. 7.
19. William E. Biederwolf, quoted in *Encyclopedia of Religious Quotations,* ed. Frank Mead (Westwood: Fleming H. Revell, n.d.), p. 50.

20. William Jurgens, "Ignatius, Letter to the Ephesians," in *The Faith of the Early Fathers,* Vol. I (Collegeville, Minn: The Liturgical Press, 1970), p. 18.

21. *Ibid.*

22. *Ibid.*, p. 21.

23. Justin Martyr, "First Apology," in *The Faith of the Early Fathers,* op. cit., p. 53.

24. *Ibid.*, p. 54.

25. Citations by these church fathers can be found in William Jurgens, *The Faith of the Early Fathers,* op. cit., pp. 5-214.

26. Polycarp, "Letter to the Philippians," in *The Faith of the Early Fathers,* op. cit., p. 29.

27. Irenaeus, "Against Heresies" in *The Faith of the Early Fathers,* op. cit., p. 90.

28. Ignatius, "Letter to the Smyrnaeans," in *The Faith of the Early Fathers,* op. cit., p. 24.

29. Jurgen's op. cit., pp. 5-214.

30. Clement, "Letter to the Corinthians," in *The Faith of the Early Fathers,* op. cit., pp. 11-12.

31. Ignatius, "Letter to the Ephesians," in *The Faith of the Early Fathers,* op. cit., p. 18.

32. Justin Martyr, "First Apology," in *The Faith of the Early Fathers,* op. cit., p. 52.

33. Irenaeus, "Against Heresies," in *The Faith of the Early Fathers,* op. cit., p. 96.

34. Sigal, op. cit., p. 20.

35. Gromacki, op. cit., p. 179.

36. *Ibid.*

37. Some historical personages, such as Plato, Alexander the Great, Buddha, etc., had god-derived birth claims made concerning them. These stories, however, were fitted into the mythological framework of their respective cultures. No historical documentation is made concerning these legends, and their mystical, nonhistorical nature is plainly evident. For more information on this issue, see J. Gresham-Machen, *The Virgin Birth of Christ* (New York: Harper and Brothers Pub., 1930), pp. 326-332.

38. William F. Albright, quoted in *Christianity Today, Vol. 7,* Jan. 18, 1963, p. 3.

39. John Warwick Montgomery, *History and Christianity* (San Bernardino Here's Life Publishers Inc., 1983), pp. 34-35.

40. Robert H. Gundry, *A Survey of the New Testament* (Grand Rapids: Zondervan Publishing House, 1970), p. 71.

41. C.S. Lewis, "Faulting the Bible Critics," *Christianity Today,* June 9, 1967, p. 7.

CHAPTER 13

Jewish Polemics and the Historical Reliability of the New Testament

The Jewish Argument

he majority of Jewish arguments appeal to exegetical and rationalistic type dialogue. However, there are also attacks made on the historical reliability of the New Testament. Samuel Sandmel, a Jewish scholar, relates this argument.

> We cannot be precise about Jesus. We can know what the Gospels say, but we cannot know Jesus. If our objective is an accurate history of Jesus, then we are more apt to find that the Gospels obscure than reveal him. The acute differences in the Gospels rise to impede a merely literary appreciation of them.[1]

In Mr. Sandmel's book, *A Jewish Understanding of the New Testament,* he reveals that his position against the historical reliability of the New Testament is directly influenced by the Form Critical theories formulated by liberal Christian theologians. These theories simply state that the Gospels are narratives formed out of the faith needs of the early Church. They are not historical or factual documents, but rather are based on the traditional ideas within the Church. The accounts of Jesus' life are simply legendary in nature and have no historical value. Only small portions of the Gospels may contain material that is factual and authentic. Mr. Sandmel explains this by saying,

> Since many of the claims of the church rested neither on pure logic nor on ordinary historical attestation, the desire to prove them led to the searching of the Old Testament for passages which could be construed to support the church contentions. This was especially the case with the claims about Jesus. It is likely that very early in the history of the church, passages from the Old Testament, usable as proof-texts, were assembled into a collection.

> Folk legends about appealing heroes became Christian by the device of inserting Jesus in the place of the traditional subject. The cure of the sick, the healing of the infirm, and indeed the exorcism of demons out of swine were readily usable when once the hero of such incidents became Jesus. Legends of a general character, too, were often found useful to preachers by the device of retelling them about Jesus.[2]

According to these theories, the "words" and "deeds" of Jesus, along with the legends about Him, existed in oral form, in separate small units called "pericopes." From this basis, the written narratives of the Gospels were formed. Sandmel continues,

Jesus is mentioned in the rabbinic literature, but the passages are rather late retorts to post-New Testament Christian claims. They are of no value for the history of Jesus. A mention of Jesus in Josephus is regarded by most scholars as an interpolation; and the handful of conservatives who do not declare in favor of the interpolation concede that the passage is so reworked as to be of no historical value. Jesus is not mentioned in Greek or Latin histories of the period ... The Gospels then, are our only real source. But, as we have said, they came at least two or three generations after Jesus; not from Palestine, but from the Diaspora; and they were written in Greek, not Aramaic. Some pericopes, we have said, were shaped by the church, while others were created by it. Within almost every pericope the hand of the growing church can be discerned. It is only within the narrowest limits that one can discern readily separable layers of traditions.

The Gospels do not in reality tell us about Jesus; they tell us about the faith, the problems, and the interests of the church which created them.[3]

In another source he concludes by saying,

What Schweitzer said almost sixty years ago is just as true now, that the Jesus of history is beyond recovery ...[4]

Another argument is cited by Isaac Troki. He makes the amazing statement that the New Testament "was composed many years after Jesus."[5] He implies that it was in the time period of Constantine, 300 years after Christ, that the final portions of the New Testament were written.

Gerald Sigal continues on this same theme,

A major difficulty facing a study of the alleged resurrection of Jesus is that all the information concerning it comes from the New Testament, a book which contains many inaccuracies. The accounts of what occurred in the days following the crucifixion form some of the most dubious chapters in the entire New Testament. This is due, in part, to the fact that the authors of the New Testament and especially the evangelists, wrote many years after the death and burial of Jesus ... Belief in the resurrection of Jesus, so crucial to the theology of missionary Christianity, is based on unsubstantiated evidence. The Gospel accounts of the resurrection are not the result of objective observation by trustworthy eyewitnesses. As a result, the veracity of the resurrection accounts is highly questionable.[6]

The Jewish argument is then established, that the Gospel accounts of Christ's life and ministry are unreliable and untrustworthy. They are built upon legendary materials attributed to Jesus by the early Church which authored these writings. This argument is by no means original with Judaism. It is rather a byproduct of the Enlightenment and the Historical Critical Methodology of Johann Semler (1725-1791). It has proceeded to take many varying forms, yet the assertions are all the same: the Gospels are not truthful, factual accounts of the life of Jesus of Nazareth. It is interesting to note how unbelief borrows from unbelief, and in the Jewish case, it is one of borrowing from so-called "Christian" sources. The problem with this argument is that it is totally fallacious in the whole and in the part, and the evidence against this position is astounding.

The Christian Answer

Since the Christian faith is firmly grounded in the historical reliability of the Gospel documents, an examination of the historicity of the Gospels and the New Testament as a whole is very important. The proceeding examination will look at five areas of evidence which will demonstrate the weakness of this Jewish argument.

1. The Fallacious Nature of Form Criticism.
2. The Historical Verification Methods Applied to the New Testament.
3. The Early Authorship of the Gospels.
4. Archaeology and the New Testament.
5. The Laws of Legal Evidence and the Gospels.

1. The Fallacious Nature of Form Criticism

The main thrust for the Jewish argument against the historical reliability of the Gospels finds its source in the Form Critical approach to the Gospels. In the following section, three areas of evidence will be presented which reveal the fallacious nature of this discipline. This will be followed by a summarization of the Orthodox Christian position regarding Form Criticism.

a) Presuppositions

Form Criticism is based on a number of presuppositions (assumptions). The first major presupposition asserts *that miracles do not occur.* Any account within the New Testament literature that contains the miraculous is then promptly rejected. Dr. John Warwick Montgomery, a lawyer, historian and theologian reveals the problem behind this type of reasoning,

> The only way we can know whether an event can occur is to see whether in fact it has occurred. The problem of 'miracles,' then, must be solved in the realm of historical investigation, not the realm of philosophical speculation. And note that a historian in facing alleged 'miracle,' is really facing nothing new.

> All historical events are unique, and the test of their factual character can be only the accepted documentary approach that we have followed here. No historian has a right to a closed system of natural causation ...[7]

C.S. Lewis, a great Christian author and apologist continues along this theme and states,

Now of course we must agree with Hume that if there is absolutely 'uniform experience' against miracles, if in other words they have never happened, why then they never have. Unfortunately, we know the experience against them to be uniform only if we know that all reports of them are false. And we can know all the reports to be false only if we know already that miracles have never occurred. In fact, we are arguing in a circle.[8]

The observance and study of history must examine facts and draw its conclusions on this basis. Form Criticism appeals to philosophical theory rather than evidence, and because of this approach proves to be faulty in its view of history.

A second presupposition of Form Criticism affirms that the early Church was illiterate. In examining the New Testament a number of educated men appear in the early Church. Luke the evangelist was a physician, which required a high level of education (Colossians 4:14). Matthew was a Roman tax-collector which demanded the skills of math and writing (Matthew 9:9; 10:3). Paul was educated under the great Jewish teacher, Gamaliel (Acts 22: 3). Apollos, an early preacher in the Church, was a highly skilled orator (Acts 18:24-28). Other men such as Stephen, Philip, Barnabas, Mark and James, were men of leadership and learning, not men plagued with illiteracy. The large quantity of written literature coming from the early Church period also denies such an assumption. The evidence of the New Testament refutes this theory of Form Criticism.

A third presupposition argues that the nature of the *oral tradition of the early Church was unsound.* This again does not agree with the facts. The Jewish people in the New Testament period were, on the whole, well trained in remembering oral tradition. In the Jewish religion, it was customary to memorize the teachings of the rabbis. In the Mishna, Aboth II, 8 it is stated,

A good pupil was like a plastered cistern that loses not a drop.[9]

The early Church was made up mainly of Jewish people and this type of respect for oral teaching was maintained throughout the early stages of the Church.

A number of other factors combined to insure a reliable transmission process for the oral teaching in the early Church period. The presence of eyewitnesses during the time when the oral tradition was formed served to establish a corrective element against nonfactual material being incorporated into the Gospel narratives. The fact that written Gospels were composed within 30 years of the time of Christ, leaves no time for error to develop in the oral transmission process. In examining the New Testament, a clear distinction between the sayings of Jesus and the writer's own narrative was maintained (1 Corinthians 7:10, 12, 25; 13:23; 15:3). The early Church had deep convictions concerning the teaching authority of Jesus and this served to insure the accurate and reliable transmission of His words. When all of these factors are combined, the presuppositions of Form Criticism are demonstrated to be incorrect.

b) Literary Criticism

Another problem with the formulations of Form Criticism is that the literary criteria used to substantiate their theories are faulty. C.S. Lewis, professor of Medieval and Renaissance Literature at Cambridge University and an expert in the field of literary criticism stated,

> The reconstruction of the history of a text, when the text is ancient sounds very convincing. But one is sailing by dead reckoning; the results cannot be checked by facts ... The 'assured results' of modern scholarship as to the way in which an old book was written are 'assured,' we may conclude, only because the men who knew the facts are dead and can't blow the gaft ... The Biblical critics, whatever reconstructions they devise, can never be crudely proved wrong. St. Mark is dead. When they meet St. Peter there will be more pressing matters to discuss.[10]

Regarding the literary criticism applied to his own writings, he had this to say,

> Until you come to be reviewed yourself you would never believe how little of an ordinary review is taken up by criticism in the strict sense: by evaluation, praise or censure of the book actually written. Most of it is taken up with imaginary histories of the process by which you wrote it.[11]

He concludes by saying,

> Now I must record my impression; then, distinct from it, what I can say with certainty. My impression is that in the whole of my experience not one of these guesses has on any one point been right, that the method shows a record of 100% failure. You would expect that by mere chance they would hit as often as they miss. But it is my impression that they do no such thing. I can't remember a single hit.[12]

c) Oral Tradition Process

Form Criticism affirms that the Gospels were composed from individual sayings of Jesus which were retained through oral transmission. These narratives were later collected by editors who composed the Gospel accounts.

Much nonfactual material is stated to have been put into these writings as a result of this. According to form critics, the oral tradition process went from simple sayings and narratives about Jesus to more complex traditions.

There are two problems with this theory. First, the New Testament documents deny that the Gospels were the end result of an oral tradition process. Passages such as Luke 1:1-3, John 19:35, Acts 2:22,

26:24-26, 2 Peter 1:16, 1 John 1:1-3 assert that the Gospel narratives were built upon eyewitness testimony. Therefore, this theory is to be rejected. Secondly, the premise that oral transmission goes from simple to complex traditions is also incorrect. The following information denies such reasoning.

E.B. Abel states,

> Contrary to the conclusions derived from Form Criticism, studies of rumor transmission indicate that as information is transmitted, the general form or outline of a story remains intact, but fewer words and fewer original details are preserved. [13]

W.S. Taylor observes,

> With frequent reproduction, omission of details, simplification of events and structure ... may go on almost indefinitely.[14]

Studies of memory and rumor transmission indicate that rather than going from simple to complex, the opposite occurs, and simplification of information over a period of time takes place. This evidence, of course, directly opposes the premises of Form Criticism.

d) *The Orthodox Christian Position Regarding Form Criticism*

In summary, the following nine points represent the position of Orthodox Christianity in its rejection of the "assured results" of Form Criticism.

(1) Oral tradition in the New Testament time period as sound. The Jewish people were well-trained in remembering oral teaching.

(2) The internal evidence of the Gospels reveal that the accounts of Christ's life and ministry were not written by editors in the Church, but by eyewitnesses or writers who appealed to eyewitness sources.

(3) The time period between the death and resurrection of Christ and the writing of the Gospels was too short to allow erroneous material to enter the New Testament message.

(4) Eyewitnesses of Christ's life, both believer and hostile, were present within the time period of the composition of the Gospels, and provided a corrective influence to error.

(5) Archaeology and historical testing methods confirm the historicity of the Gospels.

(6) Form Criticism relies on assumed factors (presuppositions) and appeals to theory rather than evidence.

(7) The methods of Form Criticism prove to be erroneous when applied to other areas of research and study.

(8) The principles of Form Criticism do not agree with the basic laws of tradition. Studies in oral transmission indicate that as information is transmitted, the general outline remains, and details are omitted rather than added.

(9) The theoretical nature of Form Criticism violates the legal principles of evidence upon which truth and false issues are determined in our Judicial systems. It (Form Criticism) would be rejected in a court of law.

2. *The Historical Verification Methods Applied to the New Testament*

It can be demonstrated that by testing the New Testament documents according to the general principles of literary criticism, they prove to be an excellent source of reliable history. Chauncey Sanders, a military historian, established a testing methodology which represents the general means employed in testing historical records. The test covers three basic areas which are classified as the bibliographical, the internal and the external tests.

a) *Bibliographical Test*

A definition of this test is as follows.

> The Bibliographical test is an examination of the textual transmission by which documents reach us. In other words, since we do not have the original documents, how reliable are the copies we have in regard to the number of manuscripts (MSS) and the time interval between the original and extant copy.[15]

This test asks two questions. First, how many copies still exist that represent the originals? Secondly, what is the time interval between the autographs (original documents) and the earliest copies?

The answer to the first question is that the New Testament has an overwhelming number of Greek copies and early versions which number about 24,633. When this number is compared with other historical works dating from the same time period as the New Testament, the magnitude of the textual attestation of the New Testament is evident.[16]

Author	Written	Earliest Copy	Time Span	# of Copies
Caesar	100-44 BC	900 AD	1,000 years	10
Livy	59 BC-17 AD			20
Plato (Tetralogies)	427-347 BC	900 AD	1,200 years	7
Tacitus (Annals)	100 AD	1100 AD	1,000 years	20(-)
" (Minor Works)	100 AD	1000 AD	900 years	1
Pliny the Younger	61-113 AD	850 AD	750 years	7
Thucydides (History)	460-400 BC	900 AD	1,300 years	8
Suetonius	75-160 AD	950 AD	800 years	8
Herodotus	480-425 BC	900 AD	1,300 years	8
Horace			900 years	
Sophocles	496-406 BC	1000 AD	1,400 years	193
Lucretius	Died in 55 or 53 BC		1,100 years	2
Catullus	54 BC	1550 AD	1,600 years	3
Euripides	480-406 BC	1100 AD	1,500 years	9
Demosthenes	383-322 BC	1100 AD	1,300 years	200
Aristotle	384-322 BC	1100 AD	1,400 years	49
Aristophanes	450-385 BC	900 AD	1,200 years	10
Homer	900 BC	400 BC	500 years	643
New Testament	40-100 AD	125 AD	25 years	over 24,000

Along with this already tremendous amount of textual material, there is further evidence that helps to establish the text of the New Testament. This is provided in quotations of the New Testament by the early Church Fathers. J.H. Greenlee states that these quotations:

are so extensive that the New Testament could virtually be reconstructed from them without the use of New Testament manuscripts.[17]

The writings of the Fathers have been well preserved and have been open to the careful investigation of Biblical scholars. Sir David Dalrymple conducted research in this area and his conclusion was the following,

Suppose that the New Testament had been destroyed, and every copy of it lost by the end of the third century, could it have been collected together again from the writings of the Fathers of the second and third centuries?[18]

His answer was a most definite, yes.

Look at those books. You remember the question about the New Testament and the Fathers? That question roused my curiosity, and as I possessed all the existing works of the Fathers of the second and third centuries, I commenced to search, and up to this time I have found the entire New Testament, except eleven verses.[19]

The manuscript verifiability of the New Testament indeed stands on a firm foundation. S.E. Peters states that

... on the basis of manuscript tradition alone, the works that made up the Christian's New Testament were the most frequently copied and widely circulated books of antiquity.[20]

The second area of this test deals with the time interval between the writing of the originals (autographs) and the earliest extant copy. The dates for the writing of the Gospels and the New Testament books are accepted by almost all Biblical scholars to be before AD 100. With AD 100 as the starting date, how many years of separation are there between the writing of the autographs and the earliest extant copies? The following time list will provide the necessary facts concerning this.[21]

AD 100	Completion of the New Testament books.
AD 120-130	*John Rylands Manuscript.* A papyri fragment containing a small portion of the Gospel of John found in Egypt.
AD 150-200	*Bodmer Papyrus II.* A fragment containing most of the Gospel of John.
AD 200	*Chester Beatty Papyri.* A collection of papyrus codices containing most of the New Testament.
AD 300-350	*Codex Vaticanus.* A codex containing the entire New Testament.
AD 350	*Codex Sinaiticus.* A codex containing the entire New Testament.

AD 340-350 *Codex Ephraemi Rescriptus*. A codex containing the entire New Testament.

AD 425-450 *Codex Alexandrinus*. A codex containing the entire New Testament.

This list shows that the time gap between the date of the completion of the New Testament books and the earliest extant copies, starts within 200 years and is then bridged by other dates to come within 30 years. Compare this to the material found in the chart on page 247. There is no question that the New Testament documents have the shortest time span between the writing of the originals and the earliest copies of any of the historical records listed. Sir Frederick Kenyon, former principal librarian of the British Museum and one of the greatest authorities in the field of textual criticism, stated that the New Testament is,

> ... far better attested than that of any other work of ancient literature.[22]

F.F. Bruce, who was Ryland's professor of Biblical Criticism and Exegesis at the University of Manchester, stated concerning the New Testament,

> There is no body of ancient literature in the world which enjoys such a wealth of good textual attestation as the New Testament.[23]

b) *The Internal Test*

This test asks one basic question: What do the documents say? Is it hearsay, tradition or first-hand testimony? This test proceeds from the simple, fundamental principle that literary criticism should always follow Aristotle's dictum that,

> the benefit of the doubt is to be given to the document itself, not arrogated by the critic to himself. This means that one must listen to the claims of the document under analysis, and not assume fraud of error unless the author disqualifies himself by contradictions or known factual inaccuracies.[24]

Concerning this test, the New Testament documents state the following,

> *"Forasmuch as many have taken in hand to set forth in order a declaration of those things which are most surely believed among us,*
>
> *Even as they delivered them unto us, which from the beginning were eyewitnesses, and ministers of the word;*
>
> *It seemed good to me also, having had perfect understanding of all things from the very first, to write unto thee in order, most excellent Theophilus,*
>
> *That thou mightest know the certainty of those things, wherein thou hast been instructed"* (Luke 1:1-4).
>
> *"And he that saw it bare record, and his record is true: and he knoweth that he saith true, that ye might believe"* (John 19:35).

"But Peter and John answered and said unto them, Whether it be right in the sight of God to hearken unto you more than unto God, judge ye.

For we cannot but speak the things which we have seen and heard" (Acts 4:19-20).

"For we have not followed cunningly devised fables when we made known unto you the power and coming of our Lord Jesus Christ, but were eyewitnesses of his majesty" (2 Peter 1:16).

"That which we have seen and heard declare we unto you" (1 John 1:3a).

Throughout the New Testament, the writers claim to be recording *firsthand, eyewitness information.* This information must be accepted and then examined not from the position of assuming guilt, but rather from that of unbiased respect. When difficulties or apparent contradictions arise within the text, the following methodology should be employed.

Think for a moment what needs to be demonstrated concerning a difficulty in order to transfer it into the category of a valid argument against doctrine. First, we must be certain that we have correctly understood the passage, the sense in which it uses words or numbers. Second, that we possess all available knowledge in this matter. Third, that no further light can possibly be thrown on it by advancing knowledge, textual research, archaeology ... Unsolved problems are not of necessity errors. This is not to minimize the area of difficulty; it is to see it in perspective. Difficulties are to be grappled with and problems are to drive us to seek clearer light; but until such time as we have total and final light on any issue we are in no position to affirm, 'Here is a proven error ...' It is common knowledge that countless objections have been fully resolved since this century began.[25]

It can be strongly supported by Biblical scholars, that the Gospels are harmonious and fully noncontradictory in nature. The seeming "contradictions" are actually evidence of each writer's unique perspective, demonstrating that collaboration and collusion on the part of the Gospel writers did not occur. When the total picture of the Gospels is examined, so-called discrepancies and errors can one by one be explained and harmonized. The narrative of the New Testament must be accepted if a genuine inquiry regarding historicity is desired. The New Testament most certainly fulfills the requirements of this test.

c)   *The External Test*

The third test sets forth to determine if other historical sources confirm or deny the internal claims of the documents under examination. Do other sources substantiate the authenticity and the truthfulness of the New Testament documents?

There are a number of historical sources which confirm that the eyewitness authors of the Gospel narratives wrote of these events within 30-50 years of the life of Christ. The early Church Fathers provide ample proof of this assertion.

Papias (AD 130-140), who was a disciple of the Apostle John, stated that Mark obtained his information from the Apostle Peter;

> The Elder [Apostle John] used to say this also: Mark having been the interpreter of Peter, wrote down accurately all that he [Peter] mentioned, whether sayings or doings of Christ; not, however, in order.[26]

Papias also confirmed the authorship of the Gospel of Matthew.

Irenaeus (AD 140-202), who was a disciple of Polycarp, who in turn was a disciple of the Apostle John stated,

> Matthew also issued a written Gospel among the Hebrews in their own dialect, while Peter and Paul were preaching at Rome, and laying the foundations of the Church. After their departure, Mark, the disciple and interpreter of Peter, did also hand down to us in writing what had been preached by Peter. Luke also, the companion of Paul, recorded in a book the Gospel preached by him. Afterwards, John, the disciple of the Lord, who also had leaned upon his breast, did himself publish a Gospel during his residence at Ephesus in Asia.[27]

Justin Martyr (AD 100-165), indicated that the apostles did indeed write and record accounts of the life of Christ. He stated,

> ... on the day called Sunday, all who live in cities or in the country gather together in one place, and the memoirs of the apostles are read, as long as time permits.[28]

All four of the Gospel writers are confirmed to be the actual recorders of the New Testament accounts of Christ's life by the testimony of the early Church Fathers. Through the chain-authority of the apostles to the early Church Fathers, the reliability of the authorship of the Gospels is demonstrated.

Along with this evidence, the early dating of the Gospels is also confirmed by other early Church sources. There is a large amount of early Church material which alludes to and makes quotations from the New Testament writings. These sources, which are all early Second Century, help to confirm the First Century authorship of the Gospels.

The Epistle of Pseudo-Barnabas (AD 70-130), refers to the contents of the Gospel of Matthew.[29]

Clement of Rome (AD 80-101), in his epistle *Corinthians,* quotes from all three synoptic Gospels. Clement himself had contact with the apostles and called himself "a disciple of the apostles."[30]

Ignatius (AD 70-110) mentioned in his writings the Gospel of Matthew and the Gospel of John along with numerous references to Paul's letters.[31]

Polycarp (AD 69-155) cited the Gospel of Mathew and the Gospel of Mark along with the Book of Acts and other New Testament books. Men such as Justin Martyr (AD 100-165), Origen (AD 183-253), Tertullian (AD 155-220), Hippolytus (AD 170-236) also confirm the early date of the New Testament writings by referring to the New Testament books throughout their writings.[32] With men and literature dating into the First Century which quote from the New Testament books, the Second Century authorship of the documents is shown to be totally impossible. This points to the early, apostolic character of the New Testament narrative.

Irenaeus gives an accurate summation of the role of the early Church Father's testimony concerning the apostolic authenticity of the New Testament;

> For the Lord of all gave the power of the Gospels to his apostles, through whom we have come to know the truth, that is, the teaching of the Son of God ... This Gospel they first preached. Afterwards, by the will of God, they handed it down to us in the Scriptures to be the pillar and ground of our faith.[33]

The New Testament and its early authorship is confirmed by numerous historical sources so that any question regarding its apostolic origin is to be rejected.

3. The Early Authorship of the Gospels

Another source of information which points to the early authorship of all four Gospels comes from an investigation of history. Reliable Church history affirms that both the Apostle Peter and the Apostle Paul died in the persecution of Nero in AD 64. Eusebius speaks concerning Paul and Peter and their martyrdom during the time of Nero's persecution,

> It is related that in his (Nero's] time, Paul was beheaded in Rome itself, and that Peter was likewise crucified. ...[34]

Biblical scholarship states that the Gospel of Luke was written, together with the Book of Acts by Luke the physician.[35] The conclusion of the Book of Acts, in which Paul's life is a major theme, does not mention his death. It may be reasonably determined from this that Paul had not died yet. This puts the authorship of both the Gospel of Luke and the Book of Acts before AD 64. The Gospel of Mark is generally conceded by Biblical scholars to have been written before Luke which then similarly dates it before AD 64. The Gospel of Matthew includes an account of Jesus' prediction of the destruction of the Temple in Jerusalem in Matthew 24. Matthew does not mention the fulfillment of this which took place in AD 70 under the Roman leader Titus, whose armies destroyed Jerusalem and the Temple. The absence of this information is probably because the fulfillment had not taken place during the composition of the Gospel of Matthew. This information then dates Matthew before AD 70.

A fragment of John's Gospel, *The John Rylands Manuscript*, which is dated AD 120-130, has been discovered in Egypt, hundreds of miles away from Ephesus, in Asia, where it was composed.[36] The amount of time for a manuscript to travel that far requires more than a couple of decades, which probably places the date for the authorship of John's Gospel around AD 85-90. When all of this information is examined, there is good historical evidence that all of the Gospel accounts and the Book of Acts were written before AD 90 and for Matthew, Mark, and Luke as early as AD 55, only 25 years after Christ. This indeed is an excellent source of evidence for the early First Century authorship of the Gospels and the apostolic origin of the New Testament.

4. Archaeology and the New Testament

Archaeology has confirmed many events, places and customs dealt with in the New Testament. The following are a few of the discoveries of archaeology that confirm the historical trustworthiness of the material found in the New Testament.[37]

The Census—Luke 2:1-3; Critics have long argued that this census never took place and that Quirinius was not the governor at the time mentioned by Luke. Archaeological discoveries now confirm both the Roman census, which took place every 14 years starting in 23-22 BC, and the governorship of Quirinius which occurred around 7-6 BC.[38]

Lystra and Derbe—Acts 14:6; Some have supposed that the account given by Luke, that Lystra and Derbe were located in Lycaonia and Iconium was incorrect. However, discoveries made by Sir William Ramsey in 1910 confirmed Luke as correct in his geographical identification of these cities.[39]

Lysanias the Tetrarch of Abilene—Luke 3:1; Ancient historians only spoke of one Lysanias who was killed in 36 BC. An inscription found near Damascus dating between AD 14-29, mentions "Freedman of Lysanias the Tetrarch."[40]

Erastus, the city treasurer of Corinth—Romans 16:23; The Apostle Paul mentions Erastus. A discovery at Corinth produced an inscription which translates, "Erastus, curator of public buildings, laid this pavement at his own expense."[41]

Synagogue of the Hebrews—Acts 18:4-7; A fragmented inscription appears to bear these very words, found in Corinth.[42]

The Journeys of Paul—Archaeological discoveries identify most of the ancient cities to which the Apostle Paul traveled. His journeys can be accurately examined because of numerous archaeological findings.[43]

Part or District of Macedonia—Acts 10:12; Luke's usage of the Greek word "meris" to refer to a part or a district of Macedonia proves to be correct. Excavations have found this very word "meris" used to describe a district or division of a city or area.[44]

No Gentiles in the Temple—Acts 21:28; Luke mentions a riot which took place in Jerusalem because the Apostle Paul brought a Gentile into the Temple. Inscriptions have been found stating; "No foreigner may enter within the barrier which surrounds the Temple and enclosure. Anyone caught doing so will be responsible for ensuing death."[45]

The Pavement—John 19:13; There is no other known record of this court outside of the New Testament. Discoveries have been made which conclusively prove the existence and location of the site within Jerusalem.[46]

The Pool of Bethesda—John 5:2; A fairly sound identification of this pool has been discovered in the northeast section of Old Jerusalem.[47]

Sir William Ramsay, one of the world's greatest archaeologists, started his career as a non-believer, convinced that the New Testament was by no means a reliable set of historical documents. However, after examining archaeological evidence and comparing it to the narrative in the New Testament, he changed his mind. He states,

Great historians are the rarest writers ... The fire which consumes the second-rate historian only leaves the real master brighter and stronger and more evidently supreme.[48]

After 30 years of investigation he stated,

Luke is a historian of the first rank; not merely are his statements of fact trustworthy ... this author should be placed along with the very greatest of historians.[49]

He also adds,

Luke's history is unsurpassed in respect of its trustworthiness.[50]

W.F. Albright, another great archaeologist, states,

As critical study of the Bible is more and more influenced by the rich new material from the ancient Near East, we shall see a steady rise in respect for the historical significance of now neglected or despised passages and details in the Old and New Testament.[51]

He also relates,

... the New Testament proves to be in fact what it was formerly believed to be: the teaching of Christ and his immediate followers between AD 25-80.[52]

Yale archaeologist, Millar Burrows summarizes the benefit of archaeology in relationship to the New Testament;

... archaeological work has unquestionably strengthened the confidence in the reliability of the Scriptural record.[53]

There are numerous archaeological discoveries which confirm the accurate historical knowledge of the New Testament writers. There is no question that archaeology supports the historical reliability of the New Testament.

5. *The Laws of Legal Evidence and the Gospels*

Legal systems attempt to provide reasonable and reliable means for testing the truth or falsehood of given situations. When the canons of legal evidence are applied to the Gospels, the results prove to be very significant. Dr. John Warwick Montgomery covers four fundamental principles of the laws of evidence as applied to the Gospels.

> The ancient documents rule: ancient documents will be received as competent evidence if they are 'fair on the face' (i.e., offer no internal evidence of tampering) and have been maintained in 'reasonable custody' (i.e., their preservation has been consistent with their content). Applied to the Gospel records, and reinforced by responsible lower (textual criticism), this rule would establish their competency in any court of law.[54]

Simon Greenleaf, who was possibly the world's greatest authority in legal evidence, verbalized this rule:

> Every document, apparently ancient, coming from the proper repository or custody, and bearing on its face no evident marks of forgery, the law presumes to be genuine, and devolves on the opposing party the burden of proving it to be otherwise.[55]

When applied to the Gospels, Simon Greenleaf states,

> They are found in familiar use in all the churches of Christendom, as the sacred books to which all denominations of Christians refer, as the standard of their faith. There is no pretense that they were engraven on plates of gold and discovered in a cave, nor that they were brought from heaven by angels; but they are received as the plain narratives and writings of the men whose names they respectively bear, made public at the time they were written; and though there are some slight discrepancies among the copies subsequently made, there is no pretense that the originals were anywhere corrupted.[56]

Dr. Montgomery continues to relate concerning these principles.

> The 'patrol evidence' rule: external, oral testimony or tradition will not be received in evidence to add to, subtract from, vary, or contradict an executed written instrument such as a Will. Applied to the biblical documents, which expressly claim to be 'executed' and complete (Revelation 22:18-19), this rule insists that the Scripture be allowed to 'interpret itself' and not be twisted by external, extra-biblical data (comparative New Eastern religious texts and practices, *Sitz im Leben* interpretations, 'historical-critical method,' 'New Hermeneutic,' etc.[57]

The New Testament asserts its completeness and execution throughout its pages, demonstrating, the correct application of this legal rule, Jude 3, Hebrews 1:1-3, Galatians 1:6-9. Dr. Montgomery continues,

> The 'hearsay rule' ... a witness must testify of his own knowledge, not on the basis of what has come to him indirectly from others. Applied to the New Testament documents, this demand for primary-source evidence is fully vindicated by the constant asseverations of their authors to be setting forth 'that which we have heard, which we have seen with our own eyes, which we have looked upon, and our hands have handled, the Word of life' (John 1:1).[58]

The last rule affirms,

> The related 'cross-examination' principle: All trials proceed upon the idea that some confidence is due to human testimony, and that this confidence grows and becomes more stedfast in proportion as the witness has been subjected to a close and searching cross-examination (Justine Ruffin, in State v. Morriss, 84 N.C. 764). Applied to the apostolic proclamation, this rule underscores the reliability of testimony to Christ's resurrection which was presented contemporaneously in the synagogues—in the very teeth of opposition, among hostile cross-examiners who would certainly have destroyed the case for Christianity had the facts been otherwise. [59]

The New Testament writers preach and declare events that were common knowledge to those living in Jerusalem and the surrounding areas of Palestine.

> *"Ye men of Israel, hear these words; Jesus of Nazareth, a man approved by God among you by miracles and signs, which God did by him in the midst of you, as ye yourselves also know:*
>
> *Him, being delivered by the determinate counsel and foreknowledge of God, ye have taken, and by wicked hands have crucified and slain:"* (Acts 2:22-23).
>
> *"For the king knoweth of these things, before whom also I speak freely: for I am persuaded that none of these things are hidden from him; for this thing was not done in a corner.*
>
> *King Agrippa, believest thou the prophets? I know that thou believest.*
>
> *Then Agrippa said unto Paul, Almost thou persuadest me to be a Christian"* (Acts 26:26-28).

F.F. Bruce states regarding this cross-examination principle,

> The earliest preachers of the gospel knew the value of first-hand testimony, and appealed to it time and time again, 'We are the witnesses of these things' was there constant and confident assertion. And it can have been by no means so easy as some writers seem to think to invent words and deeds of Jesus in those early years, when so many of His disciples were about, who could remember what had and had not happened. ... And it was not only friendly

eyewitnesses that the early preachers had to reckon with; there were others less well disposed who were also conversant with the main facts of the ministry and death of Jesus ... Had there been any tendency to depart from the facts in any material sense, the possible presence of hostile eyewitnesses in the audience would have served as a further corrective.[60]

In determining the reliability and credibility of testimony, Simon Greenleaf gives five areas by which courts of law can determine whether the testimony of a witness is acceptable or not;

The credit due to the testimony of witnesses depends upon, firstly, their honesty; secondly, their ability; thirdly, their number and the consistency of their testimony; fourthly, the conformity of their testimony with experience; and fifthly, the coincidence of their testimony with collateral circumstances.[61]

Greenleaf takes each of these tests and tries the testimony of the Gospel witnesses. He states,

And first, as to their honesty. Here they are entitled to the benefit of the general course of human experience, that men ordinarily speak the truth, when they have no prevailing motive or inducement to the contrary. This presumption, to which we have alluded, is applied in courts of justice, even to witnesses whose integrity is not wholly free from suspicion: Much more is applicable to the evangelists, whose testimony went against all their worldly interests. The great truths which the apostles declared, were that Christ had risen from the dead, and that only through repentance from sin, and faith in him, could men hope for salvation. This doctrine they asserted with one voice, everywhere, not only under the greatest discouragement, but in the face of the most appalling terrors that can be presented to the mind of men. ... Yet this faith they zealously did propagate; and all these miseries they endured undismayed, nay, rejoicing. As one after another was put to a miserable death, the survivors only prosecuted their work with increased vigor and resolution. ... It was therefore impossible that they could have persisted in affirming the truths they have narrated, had not Jesus actually risen from the dead, and had they not known this fact as certainly as they knew any other fact.[62]

The honesty of the evangelists is well established upon these facts. Concerning the second test, Greenleaf says,

In the second place, as to their ability ... the ability of a witness to speak the truth, depends on the opportunities which he has had for observing the fact, the accuracy of his powers of discerning, and the faithfulness of his memory in retaining the facts, once observed and known. ... It is always to be presumed that men are honest, and of sound mind, and of the average and ordinary degree of intelligence. ... This is sufficient for our purpose, in regard to these witnesses. But more than this is evident, from the minuteness of their narratives, and from their history. Matthew was trained, by his calling, to habits of severe investigation and suspicious scrutiny;

and Luke's profession demanded an exactness of observation equally close and searching. The other two evangelists, it has been well remarked, were as much too unlearned to forge the story of their Master's life, as these were too learned and acute to be deceived by any imposture.[63]

The evangelists, who provide eyewitness testimony, clearly meet the criteria of evidence both in their ability of observing and understanding the facts and in the faithfulness of their memory.

The third test deals with the number of witnesses (which in this case are four) and the consistency and agreement of their reports. Greenleaf relates,

> In the third place, as to their number and the consistency of their testimony. ... There is enough of discrepancy to show that there could have been no previous concert among them; and at the same time such substantial agreement as to show that they all were independent narrators of the same great transaction, as the events actually occurred. ... The discrepancies between the narratives of the several evangelists, when carefully examined, will not be found sufficient to invalidate their testimony. Many seeming contradictions will prove, upon closer scrutiny, to be in substantial agreement; and it may be confidently asserted that there are none that will not yield, under fair and just criticism. If these different accounts of the same transactions were in strict verbal conformity with each other, the argument against their credibility would be much stronger. All that is asked for these witnesses is, that their testimony may be regarded as we regard the testimony of men in the ordinary affairs of life.[64]

The fourth test examines the area of the conformity of the evangelists testimony with experience. Regarding this fourth test Greenleaf states,

> The title of the evangelists to full credit for veracity would be readily conceded by the objector if the facts they relate were such as ordinarily occur in human experience, and on this circumstance an argument is founded against their credibility. Miracles, say the objectors, are impossible; and therefore the evangelists were either deceivers or deceived; and in either case their narratives are unworthy of belief. ... Without stopping to examine the correctness of this doctrine, as a fundamental principle in the law of evidence, it is sufficient in this place to remark, that it contains this fallacy: it excludes all knowledge derived by inference or deduction from facts, confining us to what we derive from experience alone, and thus depriving us of any knowledge, or even rational belief, or the existence or character of God.[65]

He continues,

> Thus much, however, may here be remarked; that in almost every miracle related by the evangelists, the facts, separately taken, were plain, intelligible, transpiring in public, and about which no person of ordinary observation would be likely to mistake ... If they

were separately testified to by different witnesses of ordinary intelligence and integrity in any court of justice, the jury would be bound to believe them; and a verdict, rendered contrary to the uncontradicted testimony of credible witnesses to any of these plain facts, separately taken, would be liable to be set aside, as a verdict against evidence.[66]

The argument against the miraculous, which is presuppositional in nature, does not stand up in the investigation of the law of evidence. Again, the credibility of the Gospel record is maintained.

The final test applied to the testimony of the witnesses deals with "the coincidence of their testimony with collateral and contemporaneous facts and circumstances."[67]

After a witness is dead, and his moral character is forgotten, we can ascertain it only by a close inspection of his narrative, comparing its details with each other, and with contemporary accounts and collateral facts. ... it is not possible for the wit of man to invent a story, which, if closely compared with the actual occurrences of the same time and place, may not be shown to be false. Hence it is, that a false witness will not willingly detail any circumstances, in which his testimony will be open to contradiction, nor multiply them where there is danger of being detected by a comparison of them with other accounts, equally circumstantial. He will rather deal in general statements and broad assertions; and if he finds it necessary for his purpose to employ names and particular circumstances in his story, he will endeavor to invent such as shall be out of the reach of all opposing proof; and he will be the most forward and minute in details, where he knows that any danger of contradiction is least to be apprehended.[68]

This test is actually the same as the external test that was examined previously. Here one discovers that history and archaeology do confirm many of the facts related in the Gospels, thereby again confirming the credibility and trustworthiness of the evangelists. Greenleaf concludes his examination of the evangelists by saying,

Either the men of Galilee [the evangelists] were men of superlative wisdom, and extensive knowledge and experience, and of deeper skills in the arts of deception than any and all others, before or after them, or they have truly stated the astonishing things which they saw and heard.[69]

From this evidence, it is clear that a court of law would accept the facts of Christ's life and ministry as truthful, reliable evidence. The testimony of the Gospel writers is firsthand, eyewitness information and can be trusted.

Conclusion

The New Testament provides the historical basis for information on the events of Christ's life and the doctrines held by the Christian faith. Therefore, the historical reliability of these documents is extremely important in verifying the truthfulness of the Gospel message. When the evidence for the historical reliability of the New Testament is examined, no argument espoused by the Jewish polemicists stands firm. None of the arguments verbalized by Samuel Sandmel, Gerald Sigal and Isaac Troki, find substantial, evidential support, but rather consist only of conjecture and theory. It is very simple to use terms such as "folk legends," "myths," "proof texting," "hero stories" and "pericopes," but all of this talk must be silenced when evidence is called for. When the Gospels are examined, not on the basis of theory or presupposition, but on the basis of evidence, their historical reliability and genuineness is impeccable. To refuse the historicity of the Gospels and the New Testament is sheer, biased skepticism.

∅ ∅

ENDNOTES — CHAPTER 13

1. Samuel Sandmel, *We Jews and Jesus* (New York: Oxford University Press, 1980), p. 124.
2. Samuel Sandmel, *A Jewish Understanding of the New Testament* (New York: KTAV Publishing House Inc., 1974), p. 109.
3. *Ibid.*, pp. 194-195.
4. Sandmel, *We Jews and Jesus*, op. cit., p. 107.
5. Isaac Troki, *Faith Strengthened* (New York: Hermon Press, 1970), p. 227.
6. Gerald Sigal, *The Jew and the Christian Missionary: The Jewish Response to Missionary Christianity* (New York: KTAV Publishing House Inc., 1981), p. 238.
7. John Warwick Montgomery, *History and Christianity* (San Bernardino: Here's Life Publishers Inc., 1983), p. 75.
8. C.S. Lewis, *Miracles* (New York: Macmillan Pub. Co., 1975), p. 105.
9. Montgomery, *History and Christianity,* op. cit., pp. 37-38.
10. C.S. Lewis, *Christian Reflections* (Grand Rapids: Wm. B. Eerdmans Pub. Co., 1967), pp. 160-161.
11. *Ibid.*, p. 159.
12. *Ibid.*, p. 160.
13. E.L. Abel, "Psychology of Memory and Rumor Transmission and their Bearing on Theories of Oral Transmission in Early Christianity," *Journal of Religion, Vol. 51*, October, 1971, pp. 375-376.
14. W.S. Taylor, "Memory and Gospel Tradition," *Theology Today,* Vol. 15, Jan. 1959, p. 473.
15. Josh McDowell, *Evidence That Demands a Verdict* (San Bernardino, Ca.: Here's Life Publishers, 1979), P. 39.
16. *Ibid.*, pp. 42-43
17. Harold J. Greenlee, *Introduction to New Testament Textual Criticism* (Grand Rapids: Wm. B. Eerdmans Pub. Co., 1964), p. 54.

18. Charles Leach, *Our Bible, How We Got It* (Chicago: Moody Press, 1898), p. 35.

19. *Ibid.*, pp. 35-36.

20. S.E. Peters, *The Harvest of Hellenism* (New York: Simon and Schuster, 1971), p. 50.

21. Norman L. Geisler and William E. Nix, *A General Introduction to the Bible* (Chicago: Moody Press, 1968), pp. 268-275.

22. Frederick G. Kenyon, *Recent Developments in the Textual Criticism of the Greek Bible* (London, England: Macmillan and Company, 1933), p. 74.

23. F.F. Bruce, *The Books and the Parchments* (Revised ed.; Westwood: Fleming H. Revell Co., 1963), p. 178.

24. Montgomery, *History and Christianity*, op. cit., p. 29.

25. Robert M. Horn, *The Book That Speaks For Itself* (Downers Grove: Inter-Varsity Press, 1970), pp. 86-87.

26. Eusebius. *Historia Ecclesiastica III.* p. 39.

27. Irenaeus. *Adversus Haereses III.* p. 1.

28. Justin Martyr. *Apology I.* p. 67.

29. Geisler and Nix, op. cit., p. 99.

30. McDowell, op. cit., p. 51.

31. Geisler and Nix, op. cit., p. 100.

32. *Ibid.*, pp. 100-101.

33. Irenaeus. *Adversus Haereses.* V. 67.

34. Eusebius. *Historia Ecclesiastica* 11. 25.

35. Montgomery, *History and Christianity,* op. cit., p. 35.

36. Geisler and Nix, op. cit., p. 268.

37. McDowell, op. cit., pp. 65-74.

38. John Elder, *Prophets, Idols and Diggers* (New York: Bobbs-Merrill, 1960), pp. 159-160.

39. Joseph Free, *Archaeology and Bible History* (Wheaton: Scripture Press Publications, 1969), p. 317.

40. F.F. Bruce, "Archaeological Confirmation of the New Testament," in *Revelation and the Bible,* ed. Carl Henry (Grand Rapids: Baker Book House, 1969), p. 321.

41. F.F. Bruce, *The New Testament Documents: Are They Reliable?* (Downers Grove: Inter-Varsity Press, 1964), p. 95.

42. *Ibid.*

43. William F. Albright, *Recent Discoveries in Bible Lands* (New York: Funk and Wagnells, 1955), p. 118.

44. Free, op. cit., p. 320.

45. Bruce, in *Revelation and the Bible,* op. cit., p. 326.

46. William F. Albright, *The Archaeology of Palestine* (Revised ed. Harmondsworth, Middlesex: Pelican Books, 1960), p. 141.

47. Bruce, *Revelation and the Bible,* op. cit., p. 329.

48. William M. Ramsay, *St. Paul the Traveller and Roman Citizen* (Reprint ed.; Grand Rapids: Baker Book House, 1979), p. 3.

49. William M. Ramsay, *The Bearing of Recent Discovery on the Trustworthiness of the New Testament* (Grand Rapids: Baker Book House, 1953), p. 222.

50. *Ibid.*, p. 81

51. William F. Albright, *From Stone Age to Christianity* (Baltimore: John Hopkins Press, 1946), p. 81.

52. *Ibid.*, p. 23

53. Millar Burrows, *What Mean These Stones?* (New York: Meridian Books, 1956), p. 1.

54. John Warwick Montgomery, *The Law Above the Law* (Minneapolis: Dimension Books, Bethany Fellowship Inc., 1975), p. 87.

55. Simon Greenleaf, *The Testimony of the Evangelists,* p. 98, in John Warwick Montgomery, *The Law Above the Law* (Minneapolis: Dimension Books, Bethany Fellowship Inc., 1975).

56. Greenleaf, op. cit., p. 99.

57. Montgomery, *The Law Above the Law,* op. cit., pp. 87-88.

58. *Ibid.*, pp. 88-89.

59. *Ibid.*

60. Bruce, *The New Testament Documents: Are They Reliable?* op. cit. pp. 33, 44-46.

61. Greenleaf, op. cit., p. 118.

62. *Ibid.,* pp. 118-119.

63. *Ibid.*, pp. 121-122.

64. *Ibid.*, pp, 122-123.

65. *Ibid.*, pp. 125-126.

66. *Ibid.*, p. 127.

67. *Ibid.*, p. 128.

68. *Ibid.*, pp. 128-129.

69. *Ibid.*, p. 140.

CHAPTER 14

The Christian Apologetic

A description in one word for the Christian faith is *facts*. The Christian message rests firmly upon the facts recorded in the New Testament documents. A description in one word for Judaism is *tradition*. Whether one is speaking of Judaism in light of the Reform, Conservative, or Orthodox traditions, the very core of Judaism will still be tradition.

The Christian appeal to Judaism asks that the facts of Jesus' life and ministry be examined and not refused for the sake of this tradition. Is the Gospel true? Is Jesus the Messiah spoken of in the Hebrew Scriptures? Did Jesus rise from the dead? These questions must be answered honestly and without traditional bias by the genuine seeker of truth.

There are three steps that should be employed in an apologetic approach to Judaism. First, the historicity of the Gospels must be established. Second, the Messianic prophecies that have found fulfillment in Jesus should be presented. And third, the factual truthfulness of the resurrection of Jesus should be demonstrated.

The Historicity of the Gospels

Judaism reacts to the New Testament with traditional unbelief and skepticism. The unbelieving Jew refuses the historicity of the New Testament and upon this basis rejects the Messiahship of Jesus and the application of the Hebrew prophecies in relationship to Him. The Christian, on the other hand, responds to the New Testament with believing faith. He then interprets the Hebrew prophecies concerning the Messiah through the light of the New Testament facts. Receiving Jesus as Savior and Lord requires believing the facts concerning Him found in the New Testament. The Christian apologetic to Judaism must therefore start by establishing the historicity of the New Testament documents. In Chapter 13, material is provided which attempts to demonstrate that the New Testament is a reliable and trustworthy historical document, fully supported by archaeological and historical data. If the historicity of the New Testament is rejected, one must likewise reject all of ancient history as well, for the New Testament has as great a support for its historicity as that of any historical document of equal date.

Messianic Prophecies

The next step in the apologetic approach is to demonstrate that the Hebrew prophecies did indeed find fulfillment in Jesus and were not the result of proof-texting or manipulating of Scripture. The Old Testament prophecies found fulfillment in Jesus because the facts of Jesus' life were predicted by the Hebrew prophets. In this thesis, a number of Hebrew Scriptural passages applied to Jesus in the New Testament are examined. The Christian exegesis of these Messianic passages is both explained and defended and also supported by ancient Rabbinical interpretation. In no manner is the Christian interpretation fallacious historically or contextually. When the Christian exegesis of the Hebrew prophecies is coupled with the historical reliability of the New Testament, the verification of Scriptural fulfillment in Jesus is strengthened. The fulfillment of the Messianic prophecies in the person of Jesus of Nazareth is, on this basis, well established.

The Resurrection of Christ

The last step in this Christian apologetic approach is to present the resurrection of Jesus. This is essentially the key to this evidential presentation; therefore, it will be covered in some detail.

The New Testament claims that Jesus rose from the dead and the writers of the Gospels serve as the eyewitness sources for this event (John 20:24-31; Acts 1:1-3; 1 John 1:1-3). As demonstrated earlier, the early Church Fathers also attest to the truthfulness of the Resurrection.

The evidence of the origin and growth of the Church points to the factual nature of the Resurrection. The Church began about AD 33, in the city of Jerusalem and survived amidst persecution and hostile attitudes.[1] If the Resurrection event were not true, the declarations regarding its truthfulness in the very city of the alleged happening, within only a few days of the actual occurrence, would have been quickly diffused and dismissed. But instead, 3,000 people believed after hearing the Gospel message given by the Apostle Peter (Acts 2:41), and 5,000 more believed a few days later (Acts 4:4). The Book of Acts reports that multitudes of people within and around Jerusalem believed the truthfulness regarding the Resurrection (Acts 5:12-16; 6:7-8). If the Resurrection were not true, hostile eyewitnesses, with the support of the Roman and Jewish leadership, most certainly would have presented evidence of this deception, such as finding and presenting the body of Jesus. However, no such action took place.

Historical evidence, such as the worship by Christians on the first day of the week (the day of Christ's resurrection) also indicates the importance and general belief by the early Church of the Resurrection event. The early Christians were Jews, who rigidly held to the observance of the Sabbath. Nevertheless, they were willing to change their day of worship from Saturday (Sabbath) to Sunday, despite their long-held tradition, for one reason: to honor Christ on the day that He rose from the dead.

The ordinances of baptism and communion (which identify with Christ's death and resurrection) date back into the early Church, before the establishment of the New Testament Canon of Scripture.[2] The reason these ordinances originated and survived is because they found their meaning in the historical fact of Christ's death and resurrection.

The lives of the disciples were also drastically changed by the Resurrection. During the days surrounding the crucifixion, the disciples were fearful and lacked the courage to follow their Master. But after the Resurrection, nothing could stop their bold proclamation of Christ. Reliable Church history reveals that eleven of the twelve apostles went on to die for the faith that they proclaimed.[3]

The conversion of skeptical men as Thomas, Saul (Paul), and James, also points to the fact that the evidence for the Resurrection fully persuaded unbelievers.

A final evidence for the Resurrection is the changed and transformed lives of thousands of people who have trusted and believed in the living Messiah as their resurrected Savior and Lord.

When all of this evidence is examined, the conclusion is that the Resurrection did take place, and that it verifies that Jesus is the Messiah, the Son of God.

Pinchas Lapide, an Orthodox Jewish scholar agrees with the evidence presented here and asserts that Jesus did rise again from the dead. He believes that Judaism and Christianity are two roads which both lead to God. He has written a book in which he relates that Jesus became, through His death and resurrection, the Messiah and Savior of the Gentiles.[4] He says,

> Without the resurrection of Jesus, after Golgotha, there would not have been any Christianity.[5]
>
> ... Thus, according to my opinion, the resurrection belongs to the category of the truly real and effective occurrences, for without a fact of history, there is no act of true faith. In other words: Without the Sinai experience—no Judaism; without the Easter experience—no Christianity. Both were Jewish faith experiences whose radiating power, in a different way, was meant for the world of nations. For inscrutable reasons, the resurrection faith of Golgotha was necessary in order to carry the message of Sinai into the world.[6]

He continues and says,

> Jesus, therefore, without doubt, belongs to the praeparatio messianica of the full salvation which is still in the future. He was a 'paver of the way for the King Messiah' as Maimonides calls him, but this does not mean that his resurrection makes him the Messiah for the Jewish people.[7]

Lapide says concerning the return of Jesus as the Messiah of Israel,

I cannot imagine that even a single Jew who believes in God would have the least thing against that ... Should the coming one be Jesus, he would be precisely as welcome to us as any other person whom God would designate as the redeemer of the world. If he would only come.[8]

It is refreshing to see an Orthodox Jewish scholar who has faced the evidence for the Resurrection and recognized that is is indeed an historical fact. The only problem with Mr. Lapide's appraisal of the Resurrection is that he fails to see this event in the full force that God demands for it to have. The resurrection of the Lord Jesus is unlike any resurrection experience recorded in the Holy Scriptures. Jesus predicted His death (Matthew 16:21; 17:23; 20:19; John 2:19-21; 10:17-18; 13:7) and then claimed that He had the power to raise Himself from the dead, defeating man's greatest enemy, death (John 19:17-18). He pointed to the Resurrection as the God-given sign that He was who He claimed to be, the Messiah, the Son of God, Deity (Matthew 12:39-40; Romans 1:4).

The New Testament goes on to declare that the resurrection of the Messiah has brought about the assurance of everlasting salvation (Acts 17:31; Romans 4:25; 1 Corinthians 15:17), the promise of eternal life (John 11:25-26) and a future bodily resurrection for all believers (John 6:39; 2 Corinthians 4:14; Romans 8:11).

If one rejects the evidence for the Resurrection and the verification that it provides concerning the Messiahship of Jesus, it must be done blindly. Thomas Arnold, a historian and former holder of the chair of modern history at Oxford University, stated concerning the historical evidence for the resurrection of Jesus,

I have been, for many years, used to study the histories of other times, and to examine and weigh the evidence of those who have written about them, and I know of no one fact in the history of mankind which is proved by better and fuller evidence of every sort, to the understanding of a fair inquirer, than the great sign which God hath given us that Christ died and rose again from the dead.[9]

One of the greatest legal minds in the history of Great Britain, John Singleton Copley, stated,

I know pretty well what evidence is; and I tell you, such evidence as that for the resurrection has never broken down yet.[10]

The Resurrection is an established fact of history and it provides the key to the Christian apologetic proclamation not only to the Jewish people, but to all who have not responded to the Messiah, the Lord Jesus.

Conclusion

The Christian apologetic to Judaism is based on evidence and facts. The greatest form of Jewish opposition to this approach lies basically in tradition. The Christian goal is not to remove tradition from Judaism, for this is essentially what Judaism is. Some of these traditions are Biblical; others are not. Instead, the Christian apologetic appeal must demonstrate that truthful tradition must submit to facts. Good tradition will always be supported by facts, but tradition that resists and opposes historical facts is fallacious and must be forsaken.

∅ ૭

ENDNOTES — CHAPTER 14

1. B.K. Kuiper, *The Church in History* (Grand Rapids: Wm. B. Eerdmans Pub. Co., 1951), p. 31.

2. Henry M. Morris, *Many Infallible Proofs* (San Diego: Creation Life Publishers, 1974), p. 32.

3. *Ibid.*, p. 29.

4. Pinchas, Lapide, *The Resurrection of Jesus*, trans. Wilhelm C. Linss (Minneapolis: Augsburg Publishing House, 1983).

5. *Ibid.*, p. 149.

6. *Ibid.*, p. 92.

7. *Ibid.*, p. 152.

8. *Ibid.*, pp. 20-21

9. Thomas Arnold, *Sermons on the Christian Life—Its Hopes, Its Fears and Its Close* (6th ed.; London: n.n., 1859), p. 324.

10. Wilbur Smith, *Therefore Stand* (Boston: W.A. Wilde Co., 1945), p. 425.

CHAPTER 15

How to Witness to a Jewish Person

Introduction

 he purpose of Christian apologetics truly finds its fulfillment in the preaching of the Gospel. The Scriptures command,

"Go ye therefore and teach [make disciples of] *all nations, baptizing them in the name of the Father and of the Son and of the Holy Ghost:*

Teaching them to observe all things whatsoever I have commanded you: and lo, I am with you alway, even unto the end of the world" (Matthew 28:19-20).

This evangelistic command, given by the Lord Jesus Himself, applies to all Christians. United with this evangelistic command is the apologetic exhortation of the Apostle Paul,

"But sanctify [set apart] *the Lord God in your hearts: and be ready always to give to every man that asketh you a reason of the hope that is in you with meekness and fear"* (1 Peter 3:15).

Again, this command applies to all Christians.

The starting point of evangelism is always the preaching of the Gospel, which centers in proclaiming Jesus as Savior and Lord. Following this proclamation, the defending of the Faith may be called upon. However, in both instances the goal is to lead people to the Savior—the Lord Jesus Christ. It is therefore, the Gospel first, and apologetics second.

In a thesis dealing with the Christian apologetic to Judaism, it would only be appropriate to give the ultimate conclusion to this matter by stressing the great importance of Jewish evangelism.

The Apostle Paul gives the significance of Jewish evangelism in a number of New Testament references.

"For I am not ashamed of the gospel of Christ: for it is the power of God unto salvation to every one that believeth; to the Jew first and also to the Greek [Gentile]*"* (Romans 1:16).

"I say the truth in Christ, I lie not, my conscience also bearing me witness in the Holy Ghost,

That I have great heaviness and continual sorrow in my heart.

For I could wish that myself were accursed from Christ for my brethren, my kinsmen according to the flesh:" (Romans 9:1-3).

"Brethren, my heart's desire and prayer to God for Israel is, that they might be saved" (Romans 10:1).

The Apostle Paul's desire and burden for Israel should still remain as a vital part of the present Church body. The responsibility of Jewish evangelism is laid squarely upon all those who profess Jesus as Savior and Lord.

All evangelism, including that accomplished among Jewish people, can never be reduced to human procedures and techniques. Only as the Holy Spirit deals with people, convicting them of sin and showing them their need of the Savior, will people be brought to a saving knowledge of Christ (Zechariah 4:6; John 16:8-14; 1 Corinthians 2:12-14). This is absolutely fundamental to evangelism. Still, however, correct missionary methods and procedures combined with each evangelist's personality play important roles in bringing people to Christ.

Basic Principles

The following principles of the Gospel message to the Jewish community must be clearly understood.

1. Know the Gospel

The Gospel is not based on the peculiar denominational structures or doctrines that can be found among many Protestant organizations. Instead, the Gospel is grounded firmly upon the person of Jesus and His accomplished work on the cross. The Scriptures state clearly what the Gospel is.

"Moreover, brethren, I declare unto you the gospel which I preached unto you, which also you have received and wherein ye stand.

By which also ye are saved, if ye keep in memory what I preached unto you, unless ye have believed in vain.

For I delivered unto you first of all that which I also received, how that Christ died for our sins according to the scriptures;

And that he was buried, and that he rose again the third day according to the scriptures:" (1 Corinthians 15:1-4)

In relating the Gospel, a simple outline such as the following one will state the essence of the Gospel.

The Message—*Jesus*

a) *Who is He?*
He is truly God—John 5:18; 8:58; 10:30; 14:9.
He is truly a man—John 4:6; 11:35.
He is truly the Messiah—John 1:41; 4:25-26; Matthew 16:15-17.

b) *His diagnosis of the human nature*

In Mark 7:1-23, Jesus says that sin is the basic problem of man. Sin defiles, captures hearts, and cuts men off from God and His love and plan for their lives. Sin simply defined is the disease of rebellion against God, of going one's own way and ignoring the laws and purposes of God. The results of sin are boredom, loneliness, moral weakness, lack of purpose and direction, hate, war, murder, as well as spiritual and physical death.

c) *The Fact and Meaning of His Crucifixion*

In Matthew 26:28, Jesus said that His death on the cross was for the forgiveness and remission or removal of sin. The disciples of Jesus also assert this (1 Peter 3:18; Romans 5:1; 1 John 1:1-10).

d) *The Fact and Meaning of His Resurrection*

Jesus died for man's sin. He experienced physical death and separation from God. However, He rose from the dead and He provides the power to remove the sin problem (Luke 24:36-48; John 20:24-31). Through the Resurrection, God gave visible witness of the acceptance and effectiveness of the Messiah's death and the payment for sin.

e) *How Does One Receive the Work of the Cross by the Messiah and Become One of His Followers?*

Recognize—I am a sinner (Jeremiah 17:9; Ecclesiastes 7:20; Romans 3:23).

Repent—Turn from my sin, change my mind (Proverbs 28:13; Matthew 4:17).

Believe—Jesus died and rose again to pay the price for my sin and rebellion (John 3:16).

Receive—Jesus as my Messiah and Savior (John 1:12; Romans 10:8-13).

Become—A member of God's family (John 1:12; Hebrews 10:25; 1 John 5:11-13).

2. *Know the Background of the Person with Whom You are Sharing a Gospel Witness*

In reference to the Jewish people, a knowledge of the traditions of Judaism, the sensitive areas between Christianity and Judaism and the general beliefs of each division within Judaism is important. Jewish persons belonging to Reform Judaism tend to view the Scriptures in a liberal and rationalistic manner. Emphasizing the trustworthiness of the Scriptures, the personality of the Messiah along with the Gospel proclamation should be the general Christian approach. Jewish people in the Conservative and Orthodox ranks basically adhere to the truthfulness of the Hebrew Scriptures and the Christian witness can build upon this foundation in sharing Christ. However, each Jewish person must be treated as an individual and not simply filed into a neat category. A knowledge of the material covered in this thesis will certainly help equip the Christian witness for the purpose described here.

3. Develop a Good, Basic Knowledge of the Bible

An understanding of Messianic prophecies fulfilled in Jesus, of Biblical salvation principles, and of apologetic skills will prove very helpful in Jewish evangelism. The use of apologetic skills which establish the reliability of the New Testament documents as well as historical evidence for the resurrection of Christ will also be valuable. In some cases, setting forth the validity of miracles may be necessary as some Jewish people, especially those from the Reform tradition, hold to an anti-supernatural view of the Bible. Demonstrating the general reliability of the Bible, including the Old Testament (Hebrew Bible) as well as the New Testament, may also be necessary when witnessing to skeptical Jewish persons. Among the Jewish community there are many agnostics and those who doubt the existence or the possibility of knowing God. Here, an understanding of the theistic proofs would prove helpful. All of this requires doing some homework, but it will result in fruitfulness in evangelizing among Jewish people.

4. Apply Good Evangelistic Methods

In Jewish evangelism, there are a number of important points that need to be considered. The following 10 points are necessary facts of knowledge in witnessing to Jewish people.

a) Be a real friend to a Jewish person and earn his confidence and trust. The best form of Jewish evangelism is friendship evangelism.

b) Encourage conversations of issues and problems relating to life in general. Attempt to get your friend into a study of the Bible as it relates to these subjects. Remember, good witnessing should always be a dialogue.

c) Recognize the sensitivities and objections of Jewish people. These areas will be presented later in this section.

d) Show respect for Jewish tradition relating to Jesus and do not become critical of Jewish blindness concerning Him, such as the rabbinical rejection of the Gospel and the New Testament. Avoid all critical comments and arguments; however, *never* hedge on Biblical truth.

e) Understand that formulas will not provide the necessary means for bringing Jewish people to Jesus. The real key to success in Jewish evangelism is twofold: "a willing spirit and much patience."[1] It takes dedication and hard work to bring Jewish people to Jesus.

f) Prayer is a vital key. There are intellectual, moral and spiritual problems relating to the reception of the Gospel. Intercessory prayer is very important in evangelism because God chooses to act in significant ways resulting from prayer. The spiritual dimension of man necessitates spiritual warfare and this battleground is directly affected through prayer (Ephesians 6:11-18; 2 Corinthians 10:3-5).

g) Offer to pray for the needs of your Jewish friend. Many times the verbal proclamation of the Gospel may be refused but the person will appreciate your prayer. This may prove to be a stepping stone for further communication.

h) Try to bring your Jewish friend into contact with Jewish believers in Yeshua (Jesus). This may help to demonstrate that Jesus is the Messiah for the Jews as well as the Gentiles.[2]

i) Be genuine, be yourself and personalize your Gospel presentation by testimonies of what Jesus has done in your life. Also share how God has answered your prayers.

j) Center your witnessing in Jesus and His Messiahship. Plant the seed (Word of God) into your Jewish friend's heart and mind. The only seed that will bring forth fruit is the Word of God. Any other seed (Christian philosophy, opinions ...) is not good seed (Matthew 4:1-20).

5. *Be Aware of Jewish Sensitivities and Objections That can Cause Barriers to Communication*

a) Certain words are offensive to Jewish people. The application of the terms "Jew" or "Jewess" should not be used. Instead refer to them as "Jewish people" or "Jewish man," "Jewish woman" or "Jewish person." The words "cross,' "Christian" and "Christ" have an anti-Semitic influence about them as far as Jewish people are concerned. Instead refer to Jesus as "Yeshua," the Messiah, and to Christians as His followers. A person must also be careful of not telling Jewish jokes to Jewish people, for they will definitely be considered anti-Semitic.

b) Many Christian-related words and terms such as testimony, fellowship, glorious, saved, unsaved, deliverance, conversion, sanctified, redeemed, justified, lay your heart on the altar, confession of sin, etc., will not find a clear understanding on the part of the Jewish people. Use terms that are understandable: Instead of "salvation," use the term "atonement" which means at-one-ment with God. For the term "sin," use Isaiah 53:6, which explains sin to be a turning away from God. The word "repent" can be explained here as a turning back to God. "Conversion" is also a loaded word to Jews implying a changing of religion and background. A Jewish person may feel that once he accepts Messiah and becomes a Christian he "converts" and is no longer Jewish. The term "repent" or "turning back to God" is probably a better term coupled with Old Testament references such as Psalm 51:13.

c) Jewish people assume that Christianity is for the Gentiles and that one cannot be a Jew and be a follower of Yeshua. Jewish people are also taught that they will commit spiritual treason by even listening to or considering the claims of Yeshua and the New Testament. Here the Christian witness must show the Jewishness of the Messiah and point out that a Jew does not have to give up being Jewish in order to be a follower of Yeshua. In a very real sense he becomes a fulfilled and completed Jew when he receives Jesus as Lord and Savior. Emphasize that becoming a follower of the Messiah is not a changing of religion or an abandonment of heritage and tradition, but rather it is a turning back to God. Christianity is not an improvement or a better religion when compared with Judaism. It is rather a completion and fulfillment of Biblical Judaism. It is from this basis that the Christian should approach his Jewish friends.

d) Because of centuries of hatred and persecution from many "Christians," Jewish people are clearly defensive and suspicious in varying degrees of the Christian message. The Christian must understand this problem and be alert to the sensitivity in this area. Genuine love, without qualifications, is a necessary ingredient to overcome this anti-Semitic stigma. The material covered in this work should be helpful in establishing answers to the misconceptions and barriers that have resulted from "Christian" anti-Semitism. Christians should be the very best friends of the Jewish people.

Conclusion

Christians believe and support totally the integrity of the Hebrew Bible and the foundational truths revealed in Biblical Judaism [Old Testament Jewish religion]. The Jewish people are solid evidence of the existence and preserving power of God, and the history and tradition of Israel demands the respect of all genuine Christians. However, the claims of the Messiah, the Lord Jesus Christ, apply to all people, Jews and Gentiles. There is no salvation outside of Christ for anyone (John 8:24; 14:26; Acts 4:2; Hebrews 2:3).

For a Jewish person, receiving Yeshua as Lord and Messiah is not the renouncing of his religious faith, but in reality it is the coming home to the God of Abraham, Isaac and Jacob. Because of the historical rejection of Jesus by Judaism and the sociological problems between the Synagogue and the Church, barriers in receiving Jesus are very real. Moishe Rosen, chairman of "Jews for Jesus," a Jewish evangelistic organization, states regarding this barrier,

> The real and usually unspoken objection to Christ is that the Jewish person is unwilling to face the personal consequences of believing something which will set him apart from the majority of his people and label him as a traitor. He counts the cost and decides that the price is too high. The best way to counter this problem is to voice the unspoken objection with a pointed question: 'If the Bible is true, and Jesus is the Messiah after all, are you willing to learn the truth and believe in Him even though your decision might bring about severe personal consequences?' At this point you can remind your Jewish friend that to follow God was never the easy thing to

do, and that Abraham, Moses, King David and Elijah all suffered because they choose God's way rather than the accepted norm of their day.[3]

Moshe Rosen concludes these thoughts by saying,

> In order to bring a Jewish person to Jesus, you must reach him in his fortress of defensiveness with love and understanding so that he willingly lets down the barriers. It is often a slow process over a period of months and even years, which requires much energy, patience, and love, before a son of Abraham is brought to the point of welcoming Jesus into his life.
>
> In the meantime, the questions and objections must be answered; however it is wise to recognize that many questions regarding Christian beliefs can never be fully explained to the finite mind (for example, the nature of the Trinity). Nevertheless, there is *no* question or problem to which we cannot give a satisfactory answer if the person is seeking to believe. On the other hand, to one who is determined not to believe, no answer will be adequate. In any case, be prepared to answer all your Jewish friend's questions and objections, even though they may not be asked in complete sincerity.[4]

God is not through dealing with the Jewish people, and the future is going to see many Jewish friends turning back to God and His Messiah. Therefore, Christians must not be discouraged but expand their vision and outreach among Jewish people. The answer is *more* evangelism, *more* outreach, *more* prayer.

The key to all, that has been covered here in this section, is to *do it.* Knowing all the answers and methodologies is not the solution. This knowledge must be coupled with the realization of actually seeking opportunities for Jewish evangelism. Being determined and willing are the very qualities that God is looking for, and on this basis He will use the Christian seeking to be an effective witness for Christ. The Christian answer to Judaism is Jesus, His salvation and His promises.

The Jewish community is not an easy mission field to penetrate, but it is a very vital one. The material provided in this thesis is given with the hope that it will prove beneficial to the Christian missionary in overcoming barriers and objections that restrict the reception of the Gospel. The message of the Messiah, the fulfillment of the Hebrew Scriptures and the finalization of God's promises is exactly the message Judaism needs. This challenge rests directly with the Church of Jesus Christ and motivated by His love, and the Spirit of God, this goal can be accomplished.

℘ ℘

ENDNOTES — CHAPTER 15

1. Moishe and Ceil Rosen, *Share the New Life With a Jew* (Chicago: Moody Press, 1976), p. 31.

2. The following is a list of Messianic Jewish Organizations:

American Board of Missions to the Jews
P.O. Box 1331
Englewood Cliffs, New Jersey 07632

Jewish Voice
P.O. Box 6
Phoenix, Arizona 85001

Ariel Ministries
P.O. Box 13266
San Antonio, Texas 78213

Christian Approach to the Jew
1907 Chestnut St.
Philadelphia, Pennsylvania 19103

Jews For Jesus
60 Haight St.
San Francisco, California 94102

International Board of Jewish Missions Inc
P.O. Box 3307
Chattanooga, Tennessee 37404

3. M. and C. Rosen, op. cit., pp. 61-62.
4. *Ibid.*, pp. 62-63.

BIBLIOGRAPHY

Agus, Jacob B. *Judaism and Christianity.* New York: Arno Press, 1973.

_____.*The Jewish Quest.* New York: KTAV Publishing House, Inc. 1911.

Albright, William F. *Archaeology of Palestine.* Revised ed. Harmondsworth, Middlesex: Pelican Books, 1960.

_____.*From the Stone Age to Christianity.* Baltimore: John Hopkins Press, 1946.

_____.*Recent Discoveries in Bible Lands.* New York: Funk and Wagnells, 1955.

Archer, Gleason. *Encyclopedia of Bible Difficulties.* Grand Rapids: Zondervan Publishing House, 1981.

Baeck, Leo. *Judaism and Christianity.* Trans. Walter Kaufman. Philadelphia: The Jewish Publication Society of America, 1958.

Baron, David. *Jews and Jesus.* Middlesex, England: The Hebrew Christian Testimony to Israel, n.d.

_____.*Rays of Messiah's Glory.* Reprint ed. Grand Rapids: Zondervan Pub. House, 1955.

_____.*Types, Psalms and Prophecies.* London: Morgan and Scott Ltd., 1924.

Benson, Ariel. *The Zohar.* London: George Routledge and Sons Ltd., 1932.

Berger, David and Michael Wyschogrod. *Jews and Jewish Christianity.* New York: KTAV Publishing House, 1978.

Bettany, George T. *Judaism and Christianity.* London: Ward, Lock, Bowden and Company, 1891.

Bierderwof, William E. *The Second Coming Bible.* Grand Rapids: Baker Book House, 1977.

Bishop, Claire Huchet. *How Catholics Look at Jews.* New York: Paulist Press, 1974.

Blau, Joseph L. *Modern Varieties of Judaism.* New York Columbia University Press, 1966.

Bokser, Ben Zion. *Judaism and the Christian Predicament.* New York: Alfred A. Knopf Inc., 1967.

Brod, Max. *Paganism—Christianity—Judaism.* University, Alabama: The University of Alabama Press, 1970.

Bruce F.F. *The Books and the Parchments.* Revised ed. Westwood: Fleming H. Revell Co., 1963.

_____.*The Defense of the Gospel in the New Testament.* Grand Rapids: Wm. B. Eerdmans Pub. Co., 1977.

_____.*The New Testament Documents: Are They Reliable?* Downers Grove, Ill. Inter-Varsity Press, 1964.

Burrows, Millar. *What Mean These Stones?* New York: Meridian Books, 1956.

Buswell, Oliver J. *A Systematic Theology of the Christian Religion.* Grand Rapids: Zondervan Publishing House, 1980.

Cairnes, Earle E. *Christianity Through the Centuries.* Grand Rapids: Zondervan Publishing House, 1979.

Cohen, A. *Everyman's Talmud.* New York: E.P. Dutton, 1949.

_____.*The Teachings of Maimonides.* London: George Routledge and Sons Ltd., 1927.

Cooper, David L. *Messiah: His First Coming Scheduled.* Los Angeles: Biblical Research Society, 1953.

Cournos, John. *An Open Letter to Jews and Christians.* New York: Oxford University Press, 1938.

Delitzsch, Franz. *The Prophecies of Isaiah, Vol. I.* Grand Rapids: Wm. B. Eerdmans Pub. Co., 1949.

Edersheim, Alfred. *Old Testament Bible History, Vol. I.* Reprint ed. Grand Rapids: Wm. B. Eerdmans Pub. Co., 1979.

_____.*The Life and Times of Jesus the Messiah.* Reprint ed. Grand Rapids: Wm. B. Eerdmans Pub. Co., 1971.

_____.*The Temple.* Reprint ed. Grand Rapids: Wm. B. Eerdmans Pub. Co., 1971

Eichorn, David Max. *Evangelizing the American Jew.* Middle Village, New York: Jonathan David Pub., 1978.

Ethridge, J. W. *The Targums of Onkelos and Jonathan Ben Ussiel on the Pentateuch, Vol. 1 and 2.* New York: KTAV Pub. House Inc., 1968.

Evans, Robert L. *The Jew in the Plan of God.* New York: Loizeaux Brothers Inc., 1950.

Fackenheim, Emil. L. *Encounters Between Judaism and Modern Philosophy.* New York: Basic Books, Inc., 1973.

Fellows, Ward J. *Religions East and West.* New York: Holt, Rinehart and Winston, 1979.

Fischer, John. *The Olive Tree Connection.* Downers Grove, Ill.: InterVarsity Press, 1983.

Flannery, Edward H. *The Anguish of the Jews.* New York: The Macmillan Co., 1965.

Fleischer, Eva. *Auschwitz: Beginning of a New Era?* New York: KTAV Pub. House Inc., 1977.

Free, Joseph. *Archaeology and Bible History.* Wheaton, Scripture Press Publication, 1969.

Fruchtenbaum, Arnold G. *Hebrew Christianity: Its Theology, History and Philosophy.* Wash. D.C.: Canon Press, 1974.

Frydland, Rachmiel. *When Being Jewish was a Crime.* Nashville: Thomas Nelson Inc., 1978.

Gager, John G. *The Origins of Anti-Semitism.* New York: Oxford University Press, 1983.

Gartenhaus, Jacob. *Can Christians Become Jews?* Atlanta: Cross Road Books, 1981.

_____.*Famous Hebrew Christians.* Chattanooga, Tenn.: International Board of Jewish Missions, Inc., 1979.

Goldberg, Louis. *Our Jewish Friends.* Neptune, N.J.: Loizeaux Brothers, 1977.

Geisler, Norman L. and William E. Nix. *A General Introduction to the Bible.* Chicago: Moody Press, 1968.

Gowan E. *Bridge Between the Testaments.* Pittsburgh: The Pickwick Press, 1980.

Grant, Michael. *The Jews in the Roman World.* New York: Charles Scribner's and Son, 1973.

Graetz, Heinrich. *History of the Jews, 6 Vols.* New York: George Dobsevage, 1927.

Greenleaf, Simon. *The Testimony of the Evangelists.* Newark, N.J.: Soney and Sage, 1903.

Greenlee, Harold J. *Introduction to New Testament Textual Criticism.* Grand Rapids: Wm. B. Eerdmans Pub. Co., 1964.

Greenstein, Howard R. *Judaism—An Eternal Covenant.* Philadelphia: Fortress Press, 1983.

Greenstone, Julius H. *The Messiah Idea in Jewish History.* Reprint ed. Westport, Conn: Greenwood Press Pub., 1973.

Gromacki, R.G. *The Virgin Birth: Doctrine of Deity.* Nashville: Thomas Nelson Inc., 1974.

Gundry, Robert H. *A Survey of the New Testament.* Grand Rapids: Zondervan Pub. House, 1970.

Haley, John W. *Alleged Discrepancies of the Bible.* Grand Rapids: Baker Book House, 1977.

Hamilton, Floyd. *The Basis of Christian Faith.* New York: Harper and Row Pub., 1964.

Hart, Lewis A. *A Jewish Reply to Christian Evangelists.* New York: Bloch Pub. Co., 1906.

Hedenquist, Göte. ed. *The Church and the Jewish People.* London: Edinburgh House Press, 1954.

Heller, Bernard. *Epistle to an Apostate.* New York: The Bookmark's Press, 1951.

Hengstenberg, Ernest W. *Christology of the Old Testament.* Reprint ed. Grand Rapids: Kregel Pub., 1970.

Heydt, Henry J. *A Comparison of World Religions.* Fort Washington, Penn: Christian Literature Crusade, 1967.

_____.*Studies in Jewish Evangelism.* New York: American Board of Missions to the Jews Inc., 1951.

Hoehner, Harold. *Chronological Aspects of the Life of Christ.* Grand Rapids: Zondervan Pub. House, 1977.

Holman, C.H. *A Handbook to Literature.* New York: Odyssey Press, 1936.

Horn, Robert M. *The Book That Speaks For Itself.* Downers Grove, Ill: Inter-Varsity Press, 1970.

Hort, Fenton John Anthony. *Judaistic Christianity*. New York: The Macmillan Co., 1894.

Ironside, H.A. *Isaiah*. Neptune, N.J.: Loizeaux Brothers Inc., 1952.

Jacob, Walter. *Christianity Through Jewish Eyes*. Cincinnati: Hebrew Union College Press, 1974.

Jocz, Jakob. *The Jewish People and Jesus Christ*. Reprint ed. Grand Rapids: Baker Book House.

Jurgens, William A. ed. *The Faith of the Early Fathers, Vol. 1*. Collegeville, Minn: The Liturgical Press, 1970.

Kac, Arthur W. *The Messianic Hope*. Grand Rapids: Baker Book House, 1975.

Katz, Jacob. *From Prejudice to Destruction. Anti-Semitism, 1700-1933*. Cambridge: Harvard University Press, 1980.

Kenyon, Frederick G. *Recent Developments in the Textual Criticism of the Greek Bible*. London: The Macmillan Company, 1933.

Klausner, Joseph. *Jesus of Nazareth*. New York: The Macmillan Co., 1946.

_____.*The Messianic Idea in Israel*. New York: The Macmillan Co., 1955.

Knight, George A.F. *Jews and Christians*. Philadelphia: The Westminster Press, n.d.

Kuiper, B.K. *The Church in History*. Grand Rapids: Wm. B. Eerdmans Pub. Co., 1951.

Laetsch, Theodore. *Bible Commentary: Jeremiah*. St. Louis: Concordia Publishing House, 1970.

Lapide, Pinchas. *Israeli's, Jews and Jesus*. Carden City, N.Y.: Doubleday and Company, 1979.

_____.*Three Popes and the Jews*. New York: Hawthorn Books, Inc., 1967.

Lasker, Daniel J. *Jewish Philosophical Polemics Against Christianity in the Middle Ages*. New York: KTAV Pub. House, 1977.

Leach, Charles. *Our Bible, How We Got It*. Chicago: Moody Press, 1898.

Levine, Samuel. *You Take Jesus, I'll Take God*. Los Angeles: Hamoroh Press, 1980.

Levitt, Zola. *Meshumed!* Chicago: Moody Press, 1979.

Levey, Samson H. *The Messiah: An Aramaic Interpretation; The Messianic Exegesis of the Targum*. Cincinnati: Hebrew Union College Press, 1974.

Lewis, C.S. *Christian Reflections*. Grand Rapids: Wm. B. Eerdmans Pub. Co., 1967.

Lewittes, Mendell. *Religious Foundations of the Jewish State*. New York: KTAV Pub. House Inc., 1977.

Lieberman, Chaim. *The Christianity of Sholem Asch*. New York: Philosophical Library, 1953.

Lipman, Eugene J. trans. *The Mishnah*. New York: Norton, 1970.

Machen, J.G. *The Christian Faith in the World*. Grand Rapids: Wm. B. Eerdmans Pub. Co., 1978.

_____.*The Virgin Birth of Christ*. New York: Harper and Brothers Pub., 1930.

Maimonides, Moses. *The Guide For the Perplexed*. Trans. M. Friedlaender. New York: E.P. Dutton, 1947.

Martyr, Justin. *A Dialogue With Trypho*. Trans. A. Lukyn Williams. New York: The Macmillan Co., 1930.

McDowell, Joshua. *Evidence That Demands a Verdict*. San Bernardino, Ca. Here's Life Pub., 1979.

_____.*The Resurrection Factor*. San Bernardino, Ca.: Here's Life Publishers, 1981.

Mirsky, Norman B. *Unorthodox Judaism*. Columbus, Ohio: Ohio State University Press, 1978.

Montgomery, John Warwick. *Faith Founded on Fact*. Nashville: Thomas Nelson Pub., 1978.

_____.*History and Christianity*. San Bernardino, Ca.: Here's Life Publishers, 1983.

_____.*The Law Above the Law*. Minneapolis: Bethany Fellowship, 1975.

_____.*The Shape of the Past*. 2nd revised ed., Minneapolis: Bethany House Pub., 1975.

Morris, Henry M. *Many Infallible Proofs*. San Diego: Creation Life Publishers, 1974.

Myers, Charles S. *Judaism and the Beginnings of Christianity*. London: George Routledge and Sons Ltd., 1923.

Neusner, Jacob. *Between Time and Eternity—The Essentials of Judaism*. Encino, Ca.: Dickenson Publishing Co., 1975.

_____.*Judaism*. Chicago: The University of Chicago Press, 1981.

_____.*The Life of Torah*. Belmont, Ca.: Wadsworth, 1974.

Parkes, James W. *Judaism and Christianity*. Chicago: University of Chicago Press, 1948.

_____.*The Foundations of Judaism and Christianity*. London: Vallentine Mitchell and Company Ltd., 1960.

Patai, Raphael. *The Messiah Texts*. Detroit: Wayne State University Press, 1979.

Payne, J. Barton. *Encyclopedia of Biblical Prophecy*. Grand Rapids: Baker Book House, 1973.

Peters, S.E. *The Harvest of Hellenism*. New York: Simon and Schuster, 1971.

Phillips, A. *Machzor for Rosh Hashana and Yom Kippur*. Revised ed. New York: Hebrew Publishing Co., 1931.

Prager, Dennis and Joseph Telushkin. *The Nine Questions People Ask About Judaism*. New York: Simon and Schuster Inc., 1975.

Quinley, Harold E. and Charles Y. Glock. *Anti-Semitism in America.* New York: The Macmillan Co., 1979.

Raisin, Jacob S. *Gentile Reactions to Jewish Ideals.* New York: Philosophical Library, 1953.

Ramsay, William M. *St. Paul the Traveller and Roman Citizen.* Grand Rapids: Baker Book House, 1962.

_____.*The Bearing of Recent Discovery on the Trustworthiness of the New Testament.* Grand Rapids: Baker Book House, 1953.

Rankin, Oliver S. *Jewish Religious Polemic.* Edinburgh, Scotland: The University Press, 1956.

Rimmer, Harry. *The Magnificence of Jesus.* Grand Rapids: Wm. B. Eerdmans, Pub. Co., 1947.

Rosen, Ceil and Moishe. *Christ in the Passover.* Chicago: Moody Press, 1978.

_____.*Share the New Life With a Jew.* Chicago: Moody Press, 1978

Rosen, Ceil. *Y'shua.* Chicago: Moody Press, 1982.

Rosenbloom, Joseph R. *Conversion to Judaism From the Biblical Period to the Present.* Cincinnati: Hebrew Union College Press, 1978.

Roth, Cecil. *A History of the Marranos.* 4th ed. New York: Hermon Press, 1974.

Rubenstein, Richard L. *After Auschwitz—Radical Theology and Contemporary Judaism.* Indianapolis: Bobbs-Merrill Company Inc., 1966.

Sandmel, Samuel. *A Jewish Understanding of the New Testament.* New York: KTAV Publishing House Inc., 1974.

_____.*The First Christian Century in Judaism and Christianity.* New York: Oxford University Press, 1969.

_____.*We Jews and Jesus.* New York: Oxford University Press, 1980.

Schaeff, Phillip, ed. *History of the Christian Church, 8 Vols.* Grand Rapids: Wm. B. Eerdmans Pub. Co., 1910.

Schaeffer, Edith. *Christianity is Jewish.* Wheaton: Tyndale House Pub. Inc., 1975.

Schechter, Solomon. *Studies in Judaism, 3 Vols.* Philadelphia: The Jewish Publication Society of America, 1945.

Schneider, Peter. *The Dialogue of Jews and Christians.* New York: The Seabury Press, 1966.

Schonfield, Hugh J. *After the Cross.* London: A.S. Barnes and Co., 1981.

_____.*The Passover Plot.* London: Hutchinson and Company Ltd., 1965.

Sigal, Gerald. *The Jew and the Christian Missionary: The Jewish Response to Missionary Christianity.* New York: KTAV Publishing House Inc., 1981.

Silver, Abba H. *A History of Messianic Speculation in Israel.* New York: The Macmillan Co., 1927.

_____.*Where Judaism Differed.* New York: The Macmillan Co., 1956.

Smith, George Adam. *The Book of Isaiah, Vol. 1.* New York: Harper and Brothers, 1927.

Smith, Wilbur. *Therefore Stand.* Boston: W.A. Wilde Co., 1945.

Stenning, J.F. ed. *The Targum of Isaiah.* London: Clarendon Press, 1949.

Stover, Gerald L. *The Plight of the Jew.* New York: Loizeaux Brothers Inc., n.d.

Talmage, Frank Ephraim, editor. *Disputation and Dialogue.* New York. KTAV Publishing House Inc., 1975.

Thomas, Robert L. and Stanley N. Gundry. Editors. *A Harmony of the Gospels.* Chicago: Moody Press, 1978.

Trachtenberg, Joshua. *The Devil and the Jews.* New Haven, Conn Yale University Press, 1943.

Trepp, Leo. *A History of the Jewish Experience.* New York: Behrman House Inc., 1962.

_____.*Judaism—Development and Life.* Belmont, Ca., Wadsworth Pub. Co., 1982.

Troki, Isaac. *Faith Strengthened.* New York: Hermon Press, 1970.

Umen, Samuel. *Links Between Judaism and Christianity.* New York: Philosophical Library, 1966.

Wagner, Peter. *Look at What God's Doing.* Ventura, Ca. Regal Books, 1983.

Walker, Thomas. *Jewish Views of Jesus.* London: George Allen and Unwin Ltd., 1931.

Webster's New World Dictionary. New York: The World Publishing Company, 1967.

Williams, A. Lukyn. *Christian Evidences For Jewish People, 2 Vols.* Cambridge: W. Heffer and Sons Ltd., 1910.

_____.*The Doctrines of Modern Judaism Considered.* London: Society For Promoting Christian Knowledge, 1939.

Wise, Isaac Mayer. *A Defense of Judaism Versus Proselytizing Christianity.* Cincinnati: The American Israelite, 1889.

Young, Robert. *Young's Analytical Concordance of the Bible.* Revised ed. Grand Rapids: Wm. B. Eerdmans Pub. Co., 1973.

General Index

consummated, 81, 143, 144
consummation, 14, 50, 52
controversy, 1, 24, 159
cornerstone, 72, 96, 157
corrupted, 179
Council of Nicea, 159
court of justice, 183
court of law, 170, 179, 183
crane, 159
credibility, 181, 182, 183
criteria, 44, 50, 58, 64, 74, 81, 90, 169, 182
cross-examination, 125, 180
Crucifixion, 70, 77, 83, 142, 194
Crusaders, 102
Crusades, 2, 102, 104, 109
cubicles, 19
cultural, 48
custody, 179
cutting off, 56, 87
Cyprian, 101

D

dagar, 91
Damascus, 177
Davidic dynasty, 39, 44, 45, 63
Davidic throne, 118
David's throne, 39, 46
debate, 1
Decalogue, 18
decree of Artaxerxes, 51

decree of Cyrus, 51
decree of Darius, 51
deicides, 101, 148
deification, 149
demoniac, 84
demons, 83, 84, 165
demonstrably, 127
denigrate, 3
devastated, 46
Devil, 150, 206
dialogue, 165, 195
Diaspora, 18, 35, 103, 166
dictatorship, 111
dictum, 173
discrepancies, 119, 127, 128, 174, 179, 182
discrepancy, 128, 132, 134, 182
disputation, 1, 2
divine humans, 48
divine spark, 14, 30
dogma, 115

E

echad, 152, 153
egregious, 134
El Gibbor, 63
Eliab, 64
Eliada, 64
Eliezer, 64
Elihu, 64
Elisha, 64
Eloah, 152
Elohenu, 154
emblematical, 84
Emmor, 128, 129, 130
empirical Church, 102
encroachment, 63
entrenched, 155

Ephratah, 58
Ephrath, 61, 95
Ephrathite, 59
Ephron, 129, 131
epi, 132
Epiphanes, 149
errors, 1, 7, 112, 115, 127, 128, 174
etymological, 42
evangelion, 3
excommunicated, 22
exegete, 64
exhaustive, 46
exile, 18, 55, 56, 79, 86, 132
exorcism, 165
expiation, 53
expulsion, 104
extra-biblical, 179
eyewitnesses, 71, 124, 156, 162, 166, 168, 170, 173, 174, 181, 188

F

fables, 162, 174
fallacy, 29, 82, 141, 150, 160, 182
falsifications, 115
fanaticism, 2
finalization, 52, 123, 198
finalization event, 52
folk legends, 184
foreskin, 17
forgery, 179
fracas, 83
fraud, 173
friendship evangelism, 195

L

lamentation, 74, 88
Lateran, 103
Latin, 3, 13, 73, 166
layman, 16
liberal, 11, 12, 15, 161, 165, 194
Liberal Christianity, 12
librarian, 173
lineage, 58, 119, 120
livestock, 130
lugubrious, 112
lunar deities, 42
lutron, 121
Lydda, 22

M

Macedonia, 178
Machpelah, 129, 130, 131
Machzor, 94, 100, 204
magician, 22
Magog, 89, 119
Mahazik ha-Emunah, 2
maiden, 42, 43, 44, 133
Marranos, 103, 205
marred, 75, 82, 87
marriageable, 42, 43, 45
Martin Buber, 4
martyr, 103, 158
martyrdom, 157, 176
mashiach, 53
massacred, 132
math, 168
mathematics, 152
mediator, 15, 16, 30

Meir of Narbonne, 4
Menasseh, 63, 64
meris, 178
Meshiha, 92
Messianic Age, 15, 18, 96
Messianic Judaism, 12
Messianic Kingdom, 118, 121, 122, 124
Messianic Prince, 44
metaphors, 77, 86
metaphysical, 148
methodology, 4, 30, 135, 171, 174
Mibzai Yizhak, 2
Midrashim, 95
min-ha-ketuvim, 3
min-ha-mezi'ut, 3
minyan, 16
misquotations, 127
missionary theology, 57
Mohammedan, 102
Mohammedans, 102
monks, 102
monotheism, 151, 161
mosa, 61
Mosaic Law, 105, 141, 144
Moses Mendelssohn, 4, 11
mourn, 88, 89, 90, 91, 95
MSS, 171
Musaf, 94
mystery, 101, 151, 154
mythological, 125, 156, 161, 162, 164
myths, 47, 48, 149, 162, 184

N

Naphtali Herz Imber, 18
narrators, 182
Nazarene, 119
Nazi Germany, 103
Nazis, 112
Near East, 178
Nehemiah decree, 51
Neo-Orthodoxy, 12
Neurenberg jail, 112
New Hermeneutic, 179
New Testament Canon, 189
Nicene Creed, 149
Nob, 131, 132
nomadic habits, 130
non-believer, 6, 178
norm, 198
Northern Ireland, 109

O

oblation, 50, 52
olam, 60
Old Book of Polemics, 2
Old Jerusalem, 178
on-going existence, 61
oral tradition, 130, 168, 169
orator, 168
Origen, 5, 35, 120, 155, 157, 159, 176
Orthodox Christianity, 12, 101, 170
Orthodox Judaism, 5, 11, 12, 16, 17

P

pagan god, 149
paganism, 149
Palestine, 18, 19, 84, 166, 180, 200
Pallas Athena, 161
Pandira, 22
parthenos, 43
passion, 158
patrol evidence, 179
Pauline letters, 161
pavement, 177
Pekah, 45
pericopes, 165, 166, 184
Phoenicians, 101
phylacteries, 16, 19
pillage, 111
Pinhas, 22
plural nature, 152, 154
Poland, 3, 111
polemical, 2
Polycarp, 157, 158, 164, 175, 176
polytheism, 161
Pontius Pilatus, 22
postmortem, 149
pre-Isaianic, 43
pre-Mosaic, 43
pretenders, 47
primary-source, 180
problem-maker, 137
profanity, 118
progenitor, 10
proliferation, 162
proof-texting, 88, 188
proof-texts, 81, 165
prostrating, 114
Protestant, 9, 20, 32, 110, 149, 193
pseudoChristians, 103

Q

Quirinius, 177

R

rabbi, 16, 21, 28, 29, 137
Raca, 108
range war, 130
rebirth, 85
Reconstructionism, 12
Reform rabbis, 12, 15
Reformation, 5
refutation, 1, 2, 49, 125
rejuvenation, 86
Renaissance, 162, 169
repository, 179
repulsive, 81
revelational, 10
Rezin, 45
riot, 178
Roman baptismal, 155
Roman Catholic Church, 13, 48, 101, 110, 115
Roman Empire, 48, 103, 149

S

sacramental bread, 114
Samaritans, 129
Sarapis, 149
scapegoat, 109
Sefer ha-Berit, 2
Sefer Milhamot Adonai, 2
Semitics, 42
Sennacherib, 63, 64
sexual intercourse, 133

shaddai, 63
shallowness, 57
shavuim, 51
Shechemites, 130
Shechinah, 119, 123
Shema, 10, 11, 16, 19, 152, 158
shiloh, 47, 65, 68
sin offerings, 53, 57
Sir Frederick Kenyon, 173
sired, 48
Sitz im Leben, 179
skepticism, 7, 184, 187
Skull caps, 16
sociological, 10, 197
Solomon Schechter, 12
Sonship, 62
Sopherim, 26
Spain, 2, 103, 104
Spanish Jews, 2
spectrum, 13
startle, 44
stigma, 197
swine, 83, 84, 165
Sychem, 128, 129, 130
synagogue of Satan, 103
Syriac, 72, 73

T

Talmudic, 13, 29, 41, 61, 78, 89
tampering, 179
tantamount, 114
Targumim, 26, 28, 95
tax-collector, 168
teleo, 142
ten Boom family, 111